Leading Edge Marketing

Leading Edge Marketing

Turning Technology into Value

Veronica A. Williams

business**expert**
Press

Leading Edge Marketing: Turning Technology into Value
Copyright © Business Expert Press, LLC, 2014.
Illustrations used with permission from ACT Inc.
Logos included with permission from Federal Express Corporation,
Yahoo! Inc. and ACT Inc.
Permission granted by Merriam-Webster, Inc.
Permission granted by the Harvard Business School Publishing Corporation
Permission granted by the American Marketing Association, Journal of
Marketing Research
Permission granted by the HistoryLearningSite.co.uk
Permission granted by the National Postal Museum of the Smithsonian
Institution.

First published in 2014 by
Business Expert Press, LLC
222 East 46th Street, New York, NY 10017
www.businessexpertpress.com

ISBN-13: 978-1-60649-606-0 (paperback)
ISBN-13: 978-1-60649-607-7 (e-book)

Business Expert Press Marketing Strategy Collection

Collection ISSN: 2150-9654 (print)
Collection ISSN: 2150-9662 (electronic)

Cover and interior design by Exeter Premedia Services Private Ltd.,
Chennai, India

First edition: 2014

10 9 8 7 6 5 4 3 2 1

Printed in the United States of America.

Abstract

Leading Edge Marketing was inspired by the response to several of my articles and speeches, notably The Five Ps of Marketing (www.The5Ps .com). This book is a comprehensive blueprint of the concepts presented in the article. Leading Edge Marketing is intended for anyone who wants to learn how to identify, create, and deliver a hi-tech product or service that will be purchased by a critical mass of people. It presents the techniques and end-to-end process to produce a profit from products and services. The essence of my book is that it takes old principles, updates them to the current environment, adapts them to technology, and, most importantly, explains how they can be put to work to deliver respectable market share and strong profits...*with integrity*. Leading Edge Marketing is a comprehensive guide to deliver a winning solution—*from concept to profit*.

Reprinted with permission from The5Ps.com.

Keywords

product, price, packaging, place, promotion, The 5 Ps, marketing, management, advertising, strategy, principles, techniques, tools, profit, business, information technology, IT, telecommunications, computing, software, computers, phones, cell phone, PDA, systems solution, tablet, channel

Contents

Foreword

Veronica is one of the smartest people I know. I met her many years ago at a private dinner that RAM Mobile Data hosted for leading industry analysts. Veronica was single-handedly jumpstarting the market for wireless data by explaining complex technologies at major events and in trade publications and, more importantly, how they could be used to deliver a strong return for companies across a myriad of industries. She had the attention of top executives, venture capitalists, engineers, marketers, and others.

Over the years, I learned the breadth and depth of Veronica's knowledge and abilities. I have often sought her opinion and advice throughout our 25-year friendship. I have used her as a valuable resource regarding improving operations with technology, building revenue, and the viability of new ventures. *Leading Edge Marketing* reveals Veronica's flair for turning technology into revenue. It also provides a glimpse into her expertise and proficiency in finance, operations, and management. She addresses all aspects of business to maintain control, mitigate risks, and ensure a profit. *Leading Edge Marketing* is an essential artifact and invaluable resource for anyone in business.

—George Pappas
Chief Operating Officer Emeritus
Cingular Wireless (now AT&T)

Acknowledgments

I would like to thank George Pappas who wrote the foreword. George is an accomplished executive who has led the successful development, production, and delivery of high-tech products and services for five global corporations. After serving two tours as an U.S. Airborne Ranger Infantry Officer, this West Point graduate and Maxwell Trophy winner went on to the corporate world providing leadership in executive positions at Martin Marietta, as President and COO of American Minerals, President of Airtech, Inc., President of RAM Paging Company, and COO of both BellSouth Wireless Data (BSWD) and Cingular Interactive. George paved the way for the launch of Research in Motion's Blackberry product in the United States on the trailblazing Ram Mobile Data wireless network, now AT&T. He led the very inception of mobile data when it was done on a palmtop computer, immersed in development and delivery, until Research in Motion achieved critical market share 15 years later. George provided the vision and leadership for hundreds of products and services over his 40-year illustrious career. Currently, he provides advice and direction as a private consultant, speaker, and board member.

I also thank my editors who provided tremendous insight and brilliant ideas, powered by over 60 years of post MBA career successes. They helped me turn my manuscript into a *production ready book*.

Harriett Smiley Barry and Karyn Stewart each hold an MBA from leading universities followed by more than 30 years of professional success in both Global 500 and entrepreneurial firms. Their insight, knowledge, wisdom, and experience were invaluable. Harriett and Karyn helped me fine-tune my assessment of marketing theory and, most importantly, how it does and does not apply to dynamic, operating business environments. Their degrees are concentrated in marketing; they bring editorial experience, as well as marketing and sales experience in the B-to-B and B-to-C marketplaces. Together, they helped me deliver a manuscript that was ready for production. Way to go ladies!

Harriett, who studied under the renowned Philip Kotler, has over 30 years of product and brand management experience in the consumer and business-to-business markets. After gaining a firm foundation at General Mills, Barry moved up through such firms as Kimberly Clark and Soft Sheen Products. Specializing in developing new products for niche markets, she has recently become a successful entrepreneur selling high-end products to consumers and restaurants.

Karyn brings over 15 years of experience in sales and account management in the IT market and over 30 years of stellar results in the consumer and real estate markets. She sold high-end, complex telecommunications systems for AT&T, as well as B-to-C products for her own firm. A skilled manager and investor, she acquired, developed, and managed a real estate portfolio for more than 30 years.

Preface

Leading Edge Marketing is the result of industry demand. The success of strategies and techniques presented in this book was publicly evidenced by results validated at Discover*IT*^{TM} Showcases, leading industry events, publications, and media appearances. My first response to the requests was to write an article; it was published by two trade publications. I still received requests for a book but did not have time to finish writing until the economy and physical challenges slowed me down. It was then that I finished this book.

> Those who once believed in "build it and they will come" have often found that their creations resulted in a pipe dream rather than a field of dreams. Marketing is the main ingredient that determines whether products will succeed or fail.

Marketing is much more than sales and promotion. It is a mindset that allows executives to run a business that delivers the desired products and services to customers in a manner that produces a profit for the company. This feat is not easily achieved. It requires identifying and understanding what people are willing to pay for, and being able to develop, produce, and deliver that product or service at a cost that leaves a respectable margin in a reasonable amount of time. True marketing is an art that few have mastered. Many think sales and marketing are synonymous. Actually, nothing could be further from the truth. Simply, sales are the result of the successful implementation of sound marketing strategies.

This book explains the total scope of marketing. It shows how marketing is the foundation of business and civilization. I highlight the challenges of, and present solutions to, creating and selling technology-based products and services. In doing so, I recast a 50-year old theory to fit today's world. Unlike many books and conventional textbooks, *Leading Edge Marketing* presents updated theories and explains how they can be effectively applied in real-world global and entrepreneurial firms.

Examples of how to effectively execute the recast theories are included throughout the "Putting It Into Action" chapter.

Finally, I have virtually eliminated the obsolescence of printed material by providing references to the site, http://www.the5ps.com/ downloads/LEM_Preview.pdf. This site provides updates for pertinent material.

I welcome you to embrace a new, all-encompassing approach to marketing that espouses ethical and proven strategies as well as techniques for generating revenue and producing profits. My win–win approach will use marketing to make *the world go round* so that everyone can benefit.

CHAPTER 1

Introduction

What is Marketing?

Marketing is *the* process that determines whether a product is or is not successful. For some, it is the excitement and challenge of building a viable business. For others, it is a necessary evil. Regardless of where you stand on the love–hate relationship, the fact remains that products and services are not sold without marketing. Without marketing, no one will pay for what you have created. Period. The better the marketing, the more effective the sales results. Marketing results can be achieved even when those involved may not know what they are doing. Sales, whether measured in units or dollars, is the measure of marketing success. Some achieve sales through luck; others fall into it accidentally. Such sales, referred to as *bluebirds*, are the exception to the rule, however. In virtually every business entity, sales are realized due to effective marketing. It is *the* ingredient that makes a business viable and allows it to prosper.

Marketing Is a Mindset

Marketing is the soul of business. It is the vision, the heart of the resulting process that creates a revenue stream. Marketing drives what is offered, how it is delivered, to whom, and at what price. Business operations, production, and finance support the marketing vision and process to ensure that a profit results. More than a department or function, marketing is a mindset. Marketing is the essence of a business enterprise. Revenue generation and more importantly, profit creation, is the direct result of a carefully developed and executed marketing plan.

Many people think that marketing is simply advertising, promotion, public relations, or sales. These are all part of a solid marketing strategy. *Marketing* is the art of identifying and developing ideas that can be turned into a product or a service that, when sold, delivers a measurable return. The vision of a marketing executive cannot end with the simple generation of revenue. The process of generating revenue must support growth of the product. Most importantly, the marketing process must create a profit. After all, most companies are in business to produce a profit. The astute marketer understands that the initial idea must be converted into a product, and delivered to the customer, so that the customer is satisfied as well as all company stakeholders.

A product begins with an idea. Marketing begins with matching that idea to a group of people who are willing to pay for the solution that it delivers. Ideally, the marketing process should drive the development of ideas by channeling inventors' thoughts into solutions for identifiable challenges. Marketing managers use research, analysis, and intuition to determine what a critical mass of customers is willing to pay for. In the world of information technology (IT), it is essential to understand what functional capabilities are possible and, how they can be configured or combined to create a solution that customers demand.

The marketing process is often not the driving force, however, behind the creation and development of products and services. Often, creative engineers invent new products based on technological innovations and marketers are challenged with finding or creating a market for them. This process can be quite effective and has many proven successes, such as the personal computer (PC) and the Internet. On the other hand, it also can be very costly and has resulted in several failures. Teleconferencing and distributed database technologies were around for many years before products incorporating these technologies generated a respectable profit. Other products, such as the three-button mouse, O/S2, and NET1000 (a precursor to the Internet) simply crashed and burned. In other words, they never found a market with critical mass.

The creation of new products and services should be an iterative process between engineers and marketers. Ideally, customers and anyone who remotely interacts with customers should make some contribution to this process. Salespeople, the hotline staff, and customer service technicians are in ideal positions to learn about what customers want. When companies channel their energy and resources into identifying—and more importantly, validating—what customers are willing to pay for, their efforts in developing and producing products and service are much more likely to bear fruit. Rather than performing proper needs assessment and validation, many companies, particularly in the IT industry, conduct this process in the alpha or beta stage. This is *after* having invested in product design and development. Their resources are focused on creating customer needs and desires rather than identifying them.

Of course, desires or needs do not always exist until a product or service which presents a solution is offered to those who need or want it. That product or service is not commercially viable until one or more of those people are willing to pay for it. In the purest sense, however, people are not willing to pay for anything unless they either desire or need it. Many confuse the collective desire to purchase a specific product or service with being a market. When people buy PCs, we say there is a PC market; when people use the Internet, we say there is an Internet market; and when people buy local area networks (LANs), we say there is a LAN market. When products are purchased in sufficient quantity to attract competition and generate a respectable revenue stream, we say there is a market for that product. But the market is not comprised of the product that has been sold, but by the people who buy the product.

A Market Is a Group of People

A market is a group of people who spend money. It is not the product, nor the geographical region; a market is the people. We often hear the computer market, or the market for General Motors cars, or the northeastern

U.S. market. It is quite common to hear a market described in these terms. But this is not definitive, and can even be misleading, to those who are involved in or attempting to appreciate the art of marketing. It is not the product, nor the company who purchases the product, nor the region where the people who purchase live. The market is the people. It is a group of living, breathing, thinking human beings who make purchase decisions. It is when we begin to define different markets that we lose sight of what a market actually consists of. It is the people; people who either have money or have the authority to spend it. Computers, companies, governments, and associations don't control spending decisions, people do.

So when you hear markets described as the PC market, cell phone market, the luxury car market, to name a few, remember, that product does not define the market at all. Rather, a market is defined by the common characteristics of the group of people who purchase that product. A market is based upon payment for a good or services. And it is *people* who make the decision to spend the money. Understanding the common characteristics, which compel these people to buy, empowers the marketer to generate more sales.

For many years, marketers have relied upon demographic information to define groups of people. This has been quite effective and will continue to prove helpful. The re-gentrification of our world, however, is beginning to blur the traditional demographic lines of market definition. Marketers must not merely learn *what* allows people to buy, but *why* they buy. They do not buy because they have money, or because they are the same age, or race, or sex. People buy because the product or service offers a solution to a need or want that they have. Of course, in some cases those needs or wants are common to people based upon traditional demographic measures. Increasingly, however, purchase groups are not adequately classified by fundamental demographic measures. We must learn to identify the common problems, wants, and desires that compel people to desire certain solutions. This is what will allow a market to be properly characterized, reached, pitched, and ultimately sold.

The Traditional Four Ps of Marketing

A few years after the birth of the computing industry, E. Jerome McCarthy introduced a classification for marketing components, called the four "Ps,"[1] which became widely embraced by marketing educators, students, and professionals. In the 60s and 70s, product, place, promotion, and price became the items that marketers focused on to achieve their objectives. This categorization complemented the growth of the consumer packaged goods (CPG) industry that established the power of branding, coupons, discounted prices, and multiple, large distribution channels. Product managers at CPG companies maintained control of the four Ps as they managed the growth and profitability of their products. The four "Ps" are:

- *Product* is the actual item that is developed and sold.
- *Place* is the collection of distribution channels through which the product is sold.
- *Promotion* is the group of methods used to communicate everything about the product to current and prospective customers.
- *Price* is the amount for which the product is sold.

The Five Ps® of High-Tech Marketing

The proliferation of IT products and services has ushered in the need to view the Ps of marketing differently. The product is no longer a simple item delivered in a fancy box. It is an amalgamation of complex circuits and components, which must be embodied in a functional package that allows the customer to use it with simplicity. The customer does not identify with the core product. The processor, bus, transceivers, and audio components don't really matter if the customer cannot effectively set them in motion. Rather, the customer identifies with the functional interface, which allows them to realize results by using the product.

Technology-based products take on an added dimension. Their use is far beyond watching or listening to traditional electronic products such as the television or radio. Of course, one must turn on a television or radio to use it. Their use is single dimensional and finite. The core product remains relatively the same and the manner in which the customer interacts with the product does not change. This is not the case with today's IT products. Computers, smartphones, and other modern day technology-based products constantly change as customers use them. Screens can be modified, telephone numbers and other stored data change, and functions available to the customer can be added and replaced. Using today's IT products requires dynamic intervention from the user. This dynamic intervention imposes an added dimension to technology-based products and services. This new dimension gives birth to new P: packaging. The 5 Ps of high-tech marketing are product, place, price, promotion, and packaging.

Product

With technology-based offerings, the *product* is the assembly of intelligence that actually makes the item function. The product is the circuitry in computers, the code that comprises software, or the infrastructure equipment that makes up networks. It is the essence of an IT solution, the core that delivers the functional capabilities which combine to deliver performance. The product is the stuff that makes IT work.

Packaging

Packaging is the visual or physical interface that allows the user to operate the product. It is the case, monitor, and keyboard of a PC; the graphical user interface (GUI) of computer software; the phone or software interface which provides access to a network. The packaging of an IT product is what the user relates to when using that product.

Place

Any and all locations, real or virtual, where a user can acquire a product or service are the *place*. The place is the group or entity in control of the location where the product is sold. It is the sales channel. These include retail stores, mail order houses, sales offices, and the Internet. In most cases, the role of distributors is to facilitate delivery of products to small and medium sales channels or places. When distributors are involved in the outbound sale of products directly to end users, they also become a "place".

Promotion

In addition to creating a product or service, there is a need to communicate information about that product to the target market. Prospective customers must understand *why* and *where* they should purchase that product. Advertising, public relations, product collateral, coupons, and trade shows are all tools available to help the marketer promote products.

Due to the need to convey the functional capabilities of complex IT products, *promotion* is more than advertising, demos, coupons, and trade shows. Conferences, seminars, and other forms of education are important tools for promoting technology-based products and services. Education plays a key role in the promotion of IT products and services. It must often be effective before marketers can effectively garnish attention from advertising and other forms of promotion.

Prospective customers need to understand what product solutions can be delivered and how they are achieved. After the *what* and *how* are explained, prospective customers are prepared to receive the reasons *why* they should purchase a product or service. Unlike the conventional productions which are easily and widely understood by most members of the target market, IT products carry the additional need to teach prospective customers what they can do.

Price

Price is the third P of high-tech marketing. The high development cost of IT products coupled with the ongoing cost of delivering and maintaining many products and services, places pressure on the product manager to set an unrealistic price. The price of new products is often much more than an amount at which the offering can be sold in large quantities. The cutting edge of technology is often referred to as the bleeding edge. Vendors are challenged with selling new technology-based products and services at a price that allows them to deliver without incurring substantial losses. Customers buying these new products, also known as early adopters, pay a premium to be the first to own products that are state-of-the-art. Product managers are challenged with setting an initial price that strikes a balance between the two. That is, the price must attract enough early adopters to generate sufficient revenue to deliver the product and support product development.

Setting the amount at which the product will be sold is only one component of pricing. Another factor will determine if the price is marketable. It is the manner in which the payment is structured. The customer's ability to pay can only be met if the level and structure of pricing is affordable. The customer must be willing, and able, to pay. As is the case with magazines, automobiles, real estate, and other forms of capital products, the price of IT services is often presented as a lease or other forms of recurring payment.

This allows the customer to manage payment according to his or her cash flow and, spread their payment over their use of the product. This helps to reduce the *buy-in* price associated with many IT products. A good example of how adjusting the level and structure of price helped to drive sales can be found in cellular telephone service. In the early years of cellular phone service, customers had to purchase a cell phone, pay a service initiation fee as well as monthly usage fees. As more and more people began using cell phones, each component of pricing dropped in individual significance. When cellular carriers began including the price of the phone in the monthly fee, however, the increase in customers, or cellular subscribers, jumped. This was despite the fact that customers had to commit to using the service for a year or more. The level and structure of the price of being a cell phone user changed, making it affordable to many and growing the market precipitously (see Figure 1.1).

People are the Focus—Not a Tool

People are the reason for and focus of marketing, not a tool. I reject the concept that the fifth P is people. Marketing is the process of addressing the needs or wants of people. Our Ps of marketing are the tools that principally allow the marketer to influence people or address their wants. I don't believe that people should be, nor ultimately can they be, controlled. I believe that the humane and honorable way to market is to present your product or service to people that explains what needs or desires it addresses, why they should satisfy that need or desire, and how that would benefit them, much like ancient traders built physical places of exchange and, thus, civilizations and cities (see Demos, Chapter 3).

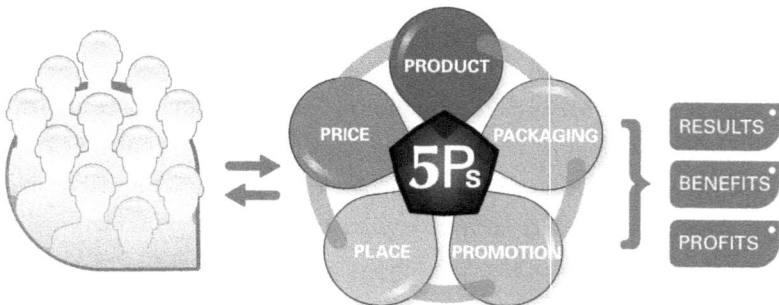

Figure 1.1 *Marketing from concept to profit*

People, then, decide whether or not to purchase a product or service. A win–win exchange can take place. People are the object of marketing or trade. Product, packaging, promotion, place, and pricing are the tools that allow the marketer to address the needs and desires of people to enable the act of marketing. People drive the application of the 5 Ps; they can never be one of the 5 Ps.

GOSPA©[2] and the Five Ps

I learned GOSPA as part of a management training program at Control Data's SBC[3] in 1979. Its principles are consistent with what I had learned from IBM top executives the year before. You see, I was one of about 15 students selected from MBA programs to meet with and learn from the IBM President and his direct reports. It was a red carpet event that lasted about one week. My GOSPA training a year later was reflected in the manner in which the IBM executives approached and managed their well-integrated organizations. GOSPA has guided me ever since.

GOSPA, is an iterative means of defining **G**oal, **O**bjectives, **S**trategies, **P**lan, and **A**ctions. This process starts with the defined goal or mission of the organization. Objectives that support the attainment of the stated goal are developed, whenever possible, with quantified measures and timeframes. Strategies define an environment or tact to be taken to help those objectives evolve. The plan is the blueprint for implementation of the goal and objectives. Finally, the actions are the specific tasks that must be done to turn the ultimate goal into reality.[4]

Throughout this process we keep the customer, stakeholder, and all affected parties in mind. The capabilities of these parties and those of the collective organization are continually assessed to ensure that the overall plan is achievable. Alliances, funding, and other sources of support are taken into account during the planning process. Essentially, GOSPA is the foundation for defining and adjusting a firm's mission, strategies and plan in a manner that establishes the groundwork for targeted and measurable improvements.

GOSPA is optimized by applying the 5 Ps of Marketing. At each step ask if I've addressed **P**roduct, **P**ackaging, **P**lace, **P**rice, and **P**romotion. When building your GOSPA, optimal results can be achieved if the blueprint is defined in support of market demands and profit targets. This allows the marketer and the executives he or she supports to gain a clear vision of the mission as well as define every step and circumstance that will turn that mission into reality. For a sample Chief Marketing Officer's GOSPA visit www.The5Ps.com/LEM/GOSPA_CMO.html

Strategic Versus Tactical Marketing

A strategy is worthless if it cannot be implemented. A brilliant strategy results from identifying the pertinent components, assembling them to achieve a phenomenal result, and then mapping out a blueprint for achieving that result. Strategy is the vision; tactics are the efficiencies of conducting processes which deliver results. Marketing strategies involve assembling the 5 Ps to capture a targeted group of markets. The manner in which the Ps are assembled is the marketing mix. Marketing tactics involve executing each P to optimize its affect on the marketing mix.

It is essential in developing an effective plan not to confuse strategies with tactics. It means not confusing the role of each P in the mix with the measures used to achieve its individual goal. This can be a challenge in marketing since it is such a dynamic process. Exceptional results from promotion, for example, might require changing or increasing the channels or place through which products are sold.

Developing a successful marketing strategy requires assessing the total environment and capabilities of the target markets, and matching them to the resources of the enterprise. The resulting direction taken will optimize that match such that the customer is satisfied and the enterprise achieves maximum profit.

Once the marketing strategy has been defined, and accompanied by an overall business strategy that supports it (see Figure 1.2), the tactics needed to implement that strategy can be developed.

Marketing tactics are best executed by applying the 5 Ps of high-tech marketing (see www.The5Ps.com/LEM/GOSPA_CMO.html). Product

Figure 1.2 Marketing strategy

enhancements, empowered distribution channels, bundled pricing, and focused promotion are some the tactics that may be used to effect marketing strategies for IT products. When developing marketing strategies and the tactics which support them, it is critical to be prepared to make modifications as necessary and recognize the limitations of the market, product, and company resources.

There are several marketing strategies that have proven successful over the years. Oftentimes, strategies mirror trends in our society, achievements in technical innovation, and the resources available for implementation. While many marketing strategies have been successfully implemented, a few stand out as being popular among IT companies:

- Commercial Beta
- Gorilla
- Conquer and Saturate
- Follow the Leader

Commercial Beta

Traditionally, technology companies develop a product and present it to a specific group of people who are narrowly defined. This group could be located in the general geographic vicinity or they could belong to companies in a specific industry. This group of people, often described as *early adopters*, are those who are most likely to purchase the product being introduced. Early adopters want to be the first to have a product. They need to stay abreast of current technology, to beat their competition by delivering enhanced products or services, to be a part of what's new. When prudently introducing new products to a specific target market, that market should be composed of early adopters who have a strong need for the product. Regardless of how this initial, targeted market is defined, it allows the vendor to present, sell, and support their product as their current resource level allows. Since many financiers are reluctant to fully support a new product until it has proven itself, these initial sales by default become part of the validation process. Once the product has received commercial validation with a certain level of booked sales, financiers are more willing to allocate funds necessary to make it a success. This is the turning point in the commercial beta strategy.

Although the product has reached a targeted level of performance and is commercially available, it may not be ready for the total market. In reality, this is commercially testing a product in its Beta phase. Many refinements will take place during this time to prepare the product for delivery to the masses or its complete, potential market.

Gorilla Strategy

Armed with tremendous confidence in their product or service, gorilla marketers blitz their targeted markets with heavy advertising, promotion, and sales. Once their product has achieved a respectable installed base, gorilla marketers seek to expand the size of their market by reaching out to new prospects. Their expansion is generally focused on selling more of the same product line to existing customers or they use marketing muscle to sell their product to new customers. To ensure that their product is deliverable to the rush of new customers, they also establish as many high capacity sales channels as possible. If the Ps of promotion and place don't yield the expected results, gorilla marketers may even aggressively offer discounts or even lower price to achieve their sales objective. The swift and intentional implementation of this marketing strategy has yielded positive results for many companies. It has also proven quite costly for others.

In the mid-1980s when demand began to grow for software suites, Informix software acquired an integrated suite from SMART software. The SMART product was packed with the features and functions in demand. Informix repackaged the product and launched a new product that ran on the UNIX operating system. The promotion surrounding this launch was tremendous. Elaborate trade show exhibits, product announcements, and a focused sales presence were among the tactics employed to establish and grow sales revenue for this new product. It never achieved a substantial installed base nor market share. While the promotion of this product was to be admired by gorilla marketers, the other Ps fell short of what was necessary to win the market. Among other things, the people who sought an integrated software package primarily used MS-DOS- and WINDOWS-based computers.

Also in the 1980s, Sun Microsystems introduced a UNIX-based line of computers that quickly captured the attention of the industry. Sun focused its sales efforts on people who wanted high performance computers and used many custom developed software packages. The Sun strategy also included flexible and aggressive pricing, extensive support to increase the adaptability of its product, and a seasoned, ambitious sales force that sought the benefits of their premium compensation plan. Sun Microsystems made their mark on the computer industry, upending the custom of not harvesting installed base before it had served out its useful life. Rather, Sun wisely chose to introduce next generation computers to its established customers before a competitor could fulfill the customer's evolving computer needs. Some viewed it as self-cannibalization; it was actually good business sense.

Whether the focus of the gorilla strategy is on price, promotion, or one of the other Ps, it is clear that all components of marketing strategy must be considered to ensure the success of highly aggressive marketing.

Conquer and Saturate

The ability to win over a group of people who have a significant propensity and ability to spend money can be quite rewarding. Those companies with products and services that can continually meet the demands of this group usually achieve long-term revenue and profitability. Resellers, distributors, or companies with multiple, related product lines often find success in the **conquer** and **saturate** strategy.

As is the case with any sound marketing plan, the first step is to identify a group of people, or target market, with a need that is not being adequately met. If the company already has a product that they are committed to selling, the target market must obviously have a need for that product or group of products. If the group of people is not easily defined by a specific set of characteristics, it should be broken up into subgroups, which are easily defined. This is one method of market segmentation. The first group to conquer is that group with the most pressing need, the greatest propensity and ability to spend money, and is most penetrable. The company then conquers the selected target market by aggressively advertising, promoting, and ultimately selling their products to this target group.

The next step is important in any sales cycle, particularly in the conquer and saturate strategy. Once the customer's group has been sold, the company or vendor should ensure and confirm that the group is satisfied with their purchase. Customers who are happy, and are *consciously aware* of their happiness, are more likely to purchase again from the same source. Confirmation of purchase satisfaction is an essential element to ensure that a market is saturated in a cost efficient manner. Once the market is predisposed to purchase from the vendor, it is easier to leverage prior sales in advertising, promotion, and sales efforts. Throughout the marketing process the vendor must identify additional products and services which the conquered market needs. The need for these products and services should be validated prior to beginning the next sales and promotion campaign. With a group of products and services that the conquered market needs, coupled with their predisposition to purchase from the vendor, the next step is to sell. To master this strategy, the vendor will continue to sell additional products and services until the needs of this market have been met; that is, until the market is saturated.

Follow the Leader

The IT industry is a cradle of creativity. It is with great honor and pride that vendors work feverishly to be the first to deliver products which incorporate new technologies. Most strive to be the leader. Being first can bring great rewards but, like everything else in life, they come at a price. One of the obvious results of introducing a successful, new product is that it paves the way for competition to flatter the leader by following in their footsteps. Without a clear advantage that cannot be easily duplicated, the benefits of being first to market can be short-lived. As a matter of fact, many companies have achieved tremendous success by introducing copycat products with a clear advantage. The result is that these *follow the leader* companies are able to win market share at a cost which is far less than what was expended by the leader. These companies let others establish the position of their product in a market, and then enter with an alternative product.

Product development of follow the leader companies constitutes identifying high potential products as they are introduced. Their market research entails studying the product, how it's sold, and who buys it. This is far less expensive than trailblazing a new product. Their marketing savvy comes in replicating the product with a clear advantage. The advantage could be a patented feature, lower production price, or another improved feature, which cannot be easily duplicated. With an improved product and a defined, qualified target market, the next step is to prepare to sell the product. The information gained from studying the leader facilitates the process of developing an advertising and promotion campaign. It also makes it easier to identify distributors to carry the product and convince them to add another successful product to their inventory. With distribution and sales channels in place, the last step in mimicking the leader is to sell, sell, sell.

Companies who create and introduce cutting-edge products often find themselves on the bleeding edge of technology. I once had a real affinity for being on the front end and in the mix of new, intriguing products and services employing the latest and up and coming technologies. My enthusiasm was tempered by the extended *time to profitability* that cutting-edge products and services demanded. These products often commanded premium prices from committed, awestruck customers. The aggregate revenue and profits, however, could be limited. Patent protection and being first to market did not always protect the innovator from losing future revenues to copycat companies.

One gem that was passed down through my family over many generations is, "Profit from other people's mistakes." In life, one should observe what others do and avoid falling prey to the same errors as they do. The Follow the Leader strategy, also known as copycatting, is the skill of improving upon the marketing of products and services that have proven to fit the needs of at least one market. This strategy gains its credence from those who demonstrate how to duplicate or excel at marketing existing products. While innovation and pioneering are qualities that have made the United States of America great, astute marketers will implement strategies that minimize the costs and potential losses of products on the bleeding edge.

Three of the early tablet computers are no longer on the market and two of the companies who introduced them are no longer *in the game*. GRiD computer is no longer in business and POQET Computer was acquired by Fujitsu. Apple Inc., on the other hand, learned from their early Newton product and dominated tablet computers with its iPad product. A slew of tablet computers entered the market. Competition intensified as all companies continued to add features and functions to their competitively priced products. Margins narrowed. Apple Inc. relied on its astute marketing strategies and techniques to maintain its industry leader position.

According to a study by Gerard J. Tellis and Peter N. Golder,[5] results show that almost half of the market pioneers fail and their mean market share is much lower than that found in other studies of market share. There are many companies that enter and dominate markets by reverse engineering products and adapting proven marketing and operations tactics. "Indeed, copycats often enjoy larger margins and faster time to market based on what they learned by observing the first to market," according to Oded Shenkar,[6] author of the book, *Copycats: How Smart Companies Use Imitation to Gain a Strategic Edge* by Harvard Business Press Books, 2010. He contends that "the pace and intensity of legal imitation has quickened in recent years".

Patents, copyrights, proprietary technologies, and other techniques are used to protect the market advantage of the products and services of leader companies. The ease and cost of duplication, and cost of infringement, however, often are not a sufficient determent to stop copycat companies. Rather, the speed and effectiveness of claiming and maintaining market position is a far more compelling reason to deter competition. It is for this reason that inventors find it advantageous to team with well-capitalized or well-positioned companies when introducing high potential, new products.

The "Build It and They Will Come" Syndrome

Those who once believed in build it and they will come have often found that their creations resulted in a pipe dream rather than a field of dreams. Marketing is the main ingredient that determines whether a product will succeed or fail.[7]

The IT industry has a habit of creating products in an engineering vacuum. Many innovations are created as a result of the technical challenge rather than an effort to complete a viable and marketable solution. Faster processors, higher capacity disk drives, smaller devices, high functionality software, and computers that weigh less are some of the interim improvements that we have seen over the years. Smaller, faster, lighter, compact functionality—these are the elements of much of the technical innovation that we've seen over the years. This is the essence of electronic innovation. The drive is to improve on existing products or invent a technically elegant alternative to existing functions. The marvels and fascination with technology encourage this. The wondrous results justify the innovations that we now enjoy.

Historically, we have seen many successes from technical creations such as the PC and the Internet. As a young, growing industry, the IT industry does not have the support structure, or organizational restrictions, to focus and direct innovation. Technical creativity abounds and new products continue to emerge which reflect improvements in technology. Phenomenal rates of return attract investors who finance ideas that are neither always understood nor validated. Nevertheless, many successful products emerge from this process, sometimes earning huge returns for developers, investors, and others involved. The lack of an integral support structure to focus and direct innovation can be a double-edged sword.

A technically focused innovative process allows the freedom of creativity by engineers and developers, however, limits the influence of creativity from other functions in the organization. As a result, many products are introduced without the existence of an adequate market to ensure their success. After the investment has been made to develop these products, additional money is spent on advertising, promotion, and sales in an effort to sell them. Too often, this is *good money being spent after bad*.

It can be risky to fund efforts to promote a product that people don't want to buy. Positive results are sometimes achieved, however, when money is spent to help a product without a market. An enhancement can be created which makes the product appealing to a qualified market. Prior to the introduction of GUI software, many functionally robust software packages floundered because customers were unwilling to use them. The GUI did not change the functions that the software was able to perform; it made it easier for the user to perform those functions. Once prospective customers are willing to use a product that meets their needs, they are obviously more likely to purchase it. An enhancement that facilitates ease of use, in some cases, will help a product to sell.

Lacking a market, products can be helped in other ways. For example, they can be bundled with other products that are already being purchased by the target market. As long as the bundle offers incremental benefits to the customer, without harming sales of the successful product, this change in promotion, packaging, and delivery can help the fledgling product succeed.

Companies may also have the good fortune to successfully sell products that lack an identifiable or established market. Circumstances can arise which create a need for the product among a distinct group of people. There could be a change in society, in the lifestyle or landscape of the target market group. A change could always take place in something totally unrelated to the product, which affects the needs of the target market or their proclivity to buy. Yet, there are instances in which a company will sell products without a sound marketing plan.

Despite all the instances when throwing good money after bad may work, it is still a risky and unnecessary step. Market assessment and validation coupled with thorough planning can substantially reduce the risk associated with new product introductions. Yet many who pursue successful new technology products continue to chase their dream without proper preparation. When products don't succeed, lack of preparation can prove to be quite costly. Even when products do succeed, managers can be misled into thinking proper validation is not necessary. They may believe that they can succeed again without proper validation. Regardless of the amount of product validation and assessment that is conducted before the launch, managers must recognize when to abandon unsuccessful products and cut their losses.

Throwing Good Money After Bad

It is often extremely difficult to give up those things about which we feel passionate. This is particularly true for inventors, creators, marketers, and others who have poured their heart and soul into making an idea a business success. There comes a time in every product's life, however, when one must make the decision to *fish or cut bait*. When a product fails to deliver the sales, and profit, which is necessary to make it a viable business proposition, it should be retired. Sometimes this decision must be made early in the product's life. When new products must be retired without achieving a critical mass of customers, it often means that the validation process had errors or was never performed at all.

Developing for the Technical Challenge Rather than Profit

Technical innovation is the cornerstone of the IT industry. The application of creative genius by engineers, programmers, and other developers, has resulted in many of the products which have spurred the growth of our industry. As a matter of fact, discovery and innovation has been the impetus of most new industries. The creation of the automobile, airplane, cotton gin, and penicillin enabled changes, which developed into industries that became bellwethers and major influencers of our economy. The creation of the human genome map has sparked a new phase of growth in the burgeoning genetics industry.

As industries mature, customer demands become more defined and predictable. Products and services, which generate substantial and long-term market share, begin to take on common characteristics. This often makes it easier to identify and develop enhancements, which respond to customer demands. Identifying enhancements to existing products and services is often more straightforward thanks to a customer base to learn from and usage patterns that are often documented. Defining the optimal set of features and functions for new products and services, on the other hand, can be more challenging. Many laboratories and technologists seek to push the boundaries of technology or create technological break-throughs that will change the world. Some of these efforts are funded by groups that want to create a new product or service. Others are funded by groups seeking to improve humanity. Some funding sources just want an environment to keep the creative juices flowing. Regardless of the motive of the funding source, technological development that is not focused on meeting a defined need or want that people are willing to pay for, may not produce a product that delivers an acceptable return.

Whether technical innovation is directed toward creating a totally new product or improving an existing one, that innovation should be directed or influenced so that it results in a product or service, which generates an acceptable return. This just makes good business sense.

It is easy to go down a long, consuming path of development when working with new and innovative technologies. Writing lots of software code, creating multiple prototypes, performing extensive tests, and other product development activities cost time and money. To increase the probability that a saleable product will ultimately be created from development activities, these efforts should be directed by marketing. Marketing direction helps to ensure results that can be used to generate future sales.

Spending Sales and Promotion Money to Sell Ill-Conceived Products to the Wrong People

The product validation process involves matching needs and wants of the target market to a product or service, which delivers a solution to those wants and needs. When a product is developed from an idea that has not been validated, it may not be marketable. Not only does the product run the risk of incorporating the wrong mix of features and functions, the marketer might try to sell the product to a group of people without a justifiable need. Regardless of how effective the promotion efforts might be, they cannot compensate for lack of a justifiable need. An effective promotion campaign might elicit desire from people in the target market. This does not ensure that sufficient revenue can be garnered from products which do not deliver a solution to the needs of the target market. When needs or wants have not been validated, products that deliver upon those needs or wants may not be purchased by the target market. When products are developed from unsubstantiated ideas, they often do not sell. When both occur, it can be a disaster.

A comprehensive and expert marketing approach and management avoids the creation of products and services that have no willing and able buyers, and it avoids sinking resources into an effort that has little or no chance of succeeding. Remember, a key concept of this book is that **marketing is not just promotion**. *It is the application of concepts, strategies, and methodologies that define a product or service from the time it is conceived, through its launch and life cycle, until it is retired.*

The first step of marketing is identifying what customers are willing to pay for. This is the real *raison d'être* of marketing. All new creation by man is driven by a desire to reveal or produce something. That desire could be directly connected to a goal to deliver a saleable product or service. The desire could be fueled by a goal to improve mankind, to push the limits of technology, to be remembered in history, or just to earn a sustainable profit.

Regardless of the reason for the desire which drives people to discover or create something new, many of the resulting creations can be ultimately productized and sold. Selling goods and services is one of the fundamental rights in a capitalist system. Delivering goods and services which improve the health and welfare of man is one of the beauties of capitalism. The ability to productize and sell a creation, of any kind, is one of the beauties of marketing. The ability to influence the creative cycle, without stifling the genius which underlies it, is one of the powers of marketing. Yes, the discovery of penicillin resulted in the creation of a commercial medicine which has saved millions of lives. According to history, that was not Louis Pasteur's intention when he experimented with mold years ago. But penicillin was the result of his experimentation. Technology labs that exist in commercial enterprises and in government organizations share a common purpose—to discover and develop new technologies to help mankind and to grow the industries. All creation is directed and influenced by those who fund it. When marketing plays a role in the direction and influence of new products and services, there is a greater chance of success. When profit is delivered to help and not hurt people, it's a good thing. When marketing is at work in its purest form, it helps to influence and drive the creations which ultimately result in products which can be sold for the good of people and, at a profit.

So how does one initiate the process of defining a new product or service? Is it through research, discovery, or invention? What role does innovation play? In discussions over the years with industry professionals, I have learned that we must first have a common understanding of a few basic terms for a meaningful discussion. Let's start by defining these terms and their meaning in the context of marketing.

Discover

Merriam Webster definition:[8] To obtain sight or knowledge of for the first time.
Marketing role: Discoveries can be directed by defining the outcome or process that is sought.

Invention

Merriam Webster definition:[9] Discovery, finding, or productive imagination.
Marketing role: Invention can be directed by defining the outcome that is sought or the resources to be applied.

Research

Merriam Webster definition:[10] Studious inquiry or examination; *especially*: investigation or experimentation aimed at the discovery and interpretation of facts, revision of accepted theories or laws in the light of new facts, or practical application of such new or revised theories or laws.
Marketing role: Research is directed by defining the thing to be understood or validated. Research can be used to identify and qualify needs and

wants with sufficient tenacity that will move a defined group of people to pay a minimum amount for a solution.

Innovation is fine-tuning or improving upon the outcome of research, discovery, or invention. It is the introduction of the new thing by presenting how it can be used by others.

Innovation

Merriam Webster definition:[11] The introduction of something new; in technology, an improvement to something already existing. Distinguishing an element of novelty in an invention remains a concern of patent law. See www.The5Ps.com/LEM/INNOVATION.html

Marketing role: Innovation is directed by defining the features, benefits, and results desired by a group of people.

Whether the seeker is intentionally in search of a specific outcome, or that outcome is found as a consequence of searching for something else, a new *thing* or *process* is identified through discovery, research, or invention.

Some may question how marketing can play a role in discovery or innovation without hindering the process. Marketing direction depends on who is funding the process and the goal that has been set. A nonprofit or government entity may have a more altruistic goal with a longer timeframe in which to perform the research, invention, or discovery process. Large commercial labs, on the other hand, may have more defined direction or shorter timeframes to produce desired results. Regardless of the source of funding or timeframe provided, the inclusion of marketing in defining the goal helps to direct results that can produce results that contribute to future revenues or enhancing efforts to help others.

The ability to sell depends on **Marketability** and **Marketing Effectiveness.** Marketability is fitting a need at the right price (willingness to pay), communicated clearly to the target market and making the resulting product or service available to the people who want to purchase it. Marketing effectiveness is determined by how well the target market is defined, if it is reached with the compelling message and at the right acquisition place and price.

When compelling needs and wants are matched to the lucrative, ripe target markets, a clearly communicated, poignant message will incent desirous buyers to begin the purchasing decision cycle. When a product's features and functions are not clearly aligned with the needs and wants of the targeted customers, the sales channel often engages in *hard sell* techniques to encourage customers to buy. Such techniques may include repeated messages, highly incented direct salespeople, seminars, time sensitive coupons, bundled specials, or other means of quickly and effectively communicating why the purchase should be made. The more persuasive and intense the effort required to sell the product, the *harder the sell* that's mandated by inadequate marketing.

A strong marketing effort is not pushing the hard sell. A strong effort begins with identifying compelling needs and wants and aligning them with the ripest target markets. The next step is not the hard sell. Rather, it is the application of the optimal marketing mix to maximize sales at the greatest margins. This is achieved through a thorough understanding of the 5 Ps, comprehensive planning, and dynamic implementation.

Accepting and Mastering Reality

Comprehensive Planning

To develop a comprehensive plan to market IT products and services, one must carefully evaluate and provide for the 5 Ps of high-tech marketing —product, packaging, place, promotion, and price. It is necessary to understand how each P contributes to delivering a solution that the target market needs or wants. It is also necessary to understand how the Ps will work together to create a marketing mix which is effective and profitable.

The tactics for carrying out implementation of each P must be carefully thought out. A step-by-step process should be mapped out, showing every task and milestone that must be achieved to successfully implement each tactic. More importantly, the plan should identify what adjustments must be made in the event that changes emerge during the course of implementation. Our business world is ever changing and marketing is a dynamic process. It is critical to prepare, therefore, for anticipated as well as unanticipated events. In doing so, the marketing plan should define and quantify all indicators which will require a change in strategy. This includes indicators which dictate retiring the product.

Dynamic Implementation

Mergers and acquisitions, breakthrough innovations, currency fluctuations, and rampant inflation are but a few of the phenomena that businesses deal with on a regular basis. These and other factors can have a results-altering effect on marketing and business strategies. When embarking upon the implementation of their plan, marketers must remain prepared to change the components of their marketing strategy and tactics as needed. To achieve dynamic implementation one must stay mindful of the interrelationships between each of the 5 Ps and the tactics which enable them. The marketer must often be prepared to *turn on a dime* without losing momentum. To see how dynamic implementation is applied in the marketing cycle, visit www.The5Ps.com/LEM/Dynamic-Implementation.html

To accept and master the reality of marketing IT products and services, one must develop a comprehensive plan which embraces the 5 Ps of high-tech marketing and stay prepared to react to all changes threatening its successful implementation. There are many moving components that comprise a comprehensive marketing plan. To understand all of the components and create a process to effectively manage their interrelationships, I have defined a framework—The 5 Ps—that adapts the components to managing different types of business enterprises. The next section outlines how The 5 Ps is applied to the business of technology.

CHAPTER 2

The Basics: The 5 Ps: Basic Components of the Framework

The 5 Ps

Traditionally marketers have focused on the *4 Ps* of marketing—product, place, price, and promotion. The IT industry has brought a new dimension to the basics of marketing. As technologies have advanced and product usage has become pervasive, IT has given birth to a new P: packaging. The 5 Ps of high-tech marketing are product, place, price, promotion, and packaging.

Product

Technology-based products can be most easily explained by grouping their defining characteristics into one of two categories: feature or function. A *function* is what the product allows you to do. A *feature* defines what you experience as you use the product. The distinction between feature and function is critical to IT products, for the combination of the two is necessary for the product to be successfully marketed. A critical first step in creating the blueprint for a successful product is to identify and prioritize the features and functions that best meet the needs of and appeal to the needs and wants of the target market.

Function of a Product

A function is specific capability that allows a product to perform a defined task. For instance, the ability to add two numbers is one of the functions of spreadsheet software. The ability to process a set of instructions is one of the basic functions of a computer. Transporting information, in the form of electronic signals, from one location to another is the fundamental function of a network. Indeed, it is the function that gives life to IT products and services.

Unlike many consumer packaged goods (CPG) such as laundry detergent, paper towels, or canned soda, technology-based products can be identified by the action they perform in the service of the consumer. Radios, for example, provide the means for you to listen to broadcasts, television provides a visual presentation, telephones make conversation with another possible, and computers allow you to create and analyze documents. These actions are made possible by the product's functions.

In the world of IT, functions are executed in the internal components of products. The circuitry inside a computer, telephone, or network infrastructure equipment (i.e., PBX, router) is where the ultimate functions take place in IT hardware, while processors perform the instructions for functions to take place and power provides the fuel. A function may be triggered by a physical action performed on an external product component. For example, devices are turned on using an ON/OFF switch. A function may also be invoked by the software that directs the processor. For instance, software directs a computer to display certain targeted information, as directed by the user. Software also directs the manner in which that information will be displayed. Functions are not only invoked by physical components nor are they limited to hardware. Software is used to direct these functions through the use of code.

Hardware houses the software that drives the functionality of IT products; however, many functions take place in the software. The hardware is simply a means to display the results of these functions. Software directs functions to take place by using code defined in programs. For example, a search for information is initiated once software defines when, where, and how to locate the defined data. It is the software, resident in a network, which tells the phone to display the name or number of the person calling.

As IT products are inherently complex, it is important to identify the source as well as the outcome of functions. A function often depends on a series of specific and interrelated components. In many cases, the outcome of a group of functions may be viewed as a feature. The ability of a portable device to automatically illuminate in the dark, for example, depends on recognizing the dark, turning itself on, and turning off when in light. The recognition and turning on are functions. Automatic illumination is the feature.

It is the feature–function mix, as we will learn later, which provides the foundation for the product blueprint. Moreover, the requirements to deliver a group of functions also often impact marketing mix components, such as price. When defining the functions to be included in the product's initial "laundry list," remember to identify the source and the results of each function. Thus, identifying the source of and the results gained by a function is crucial.

Creating functions is what drives the creative energies of most engineers. The ability to enable a product to perform a series of complex tasks, with greater speed and efficiency, and within the confines of existing physical limitations is the goal that fuels the ambition of many developers. After all, *it is the function that gives life to IT products*. The technology product has little marketing value, however, if it is not of interest to others. That is, a technically robust product that doesn't sell is merely a set of functions to be used in the blueprint of the next product. To maintain the value of engineering developments and to ensure that a product is meeting the needs of consumers, and to keep the creative energies of engineers flowing, it is critical that engineers and marketers work hand in hand to develop the product blueprint. Both functions and features are an integral part of this blueprint. Technologists continually overvalue the role of functions and undervalue the role of features. They do not understand the dynamics of their interrelationship. Functions are merely one dimension of the product blueprint. Although functions are essential to defining IT products, they do not alone define the product. Features are also a necessary part of the product blueprint.

Feature of a Product

A feature is what drives a person's experience when they use a product or service. It helps to determine what you will feel when you use the product. A feature is the tangible or intangible characteristic that creates tranquility, comfort, euphoria, or other feelings sought by the user. Features provide a framework for managing human interaction with technology-based product.

Easy *accessibility* of function buttons and external drives is a feature of PCs. A slightly elongated form factor with balanced weight is a feature of many handheld devices. A colorful or elegantly styled casing allows many customers to include products in their room décor. Sounds not only notify the computer or cell phone user that he or she is receiving a message, when they are delivered in the form of lively, catchy tunes they also generate excitement or enthusiasm. While the delivery of certain features may not immediately stir enthusiasm in development teams, they are often the defining point in the purchase process and, thus, an integral part of the product blueprint.

As is the case with functions, features may manifest themselves in hardware or software. Hardware features are often incorporated into the casing that surrounds the circuitry. For example, a highly legible screen, with the right size and clarity, is an important feature of IT devices. Software features may be found in the user interface that allow the user to invoke functions. A highly legible screen, with the right fonts, colors, and balance of information, is an important feature of applications software.

The definition and design of features require both artistic and engineering talent. While the definition of features requires an artistic eye and creativity to describe the look and feel of what appeals to the customer, the design *feature delivery* (that is, how each feature is made available to the customer) requires engineering creativity to ensure that the product is efficient and the function is maintained. The feature and function lists should be separate initially. While brainstorming or using some other process to develop functions, features will be identified and vice versa. To maximize the number of features and functions, and create good rankings, these lists should be prepared before the product blueprint is designed. While it is rare for a person to be able to combine these two skills, it is virtually impossible to excel at both. It is essential, then, to select the right team, or reference sources, to define the selection of features and functions to be included in the product's laundry list.

The product blueprint is laid out to identify and define everything necessary to create a product that will be purchased by a critical mass of the target market(s). The laundry list of features and functions will combine to provide the starting point for creating the product blueprint. It is a starting point because it is usually neither possible nor feasible to combine both laundry lists into a product that will sell. Features can compromise or inhibit the performance of functions. Likewise, functions may limit the delivery or expression of features, and in some cases, they could make the cost of production or delivery cost prohibitive. After all, customers do have a limited willingness to pay for a given set of features and functions. The challenge for the marketer is to select the right blend of features and functions to be included in a blueprint for a product that will sell a critical mass of products at a price that delivers a respectable return.

As the functional capabilities of high-tech products mature and technological innovations are not as forthcoming, companies tend to focus on features. Technical functions are easier to replicate, patents expire, and a set of functional capabilities are expected by customers. What will differentiate the mature product are its features as well as other elements of the marketing mix. The selection of features for a mature product becomes an important determinant of both the product's ability to sell and its profitability.

The Right Combination: Identifying Features and Functions that Sell

The process of brainstorming the selection of features and functions for an IT product is very dynamic. When creative ideas flow, a list of features often results. When engineering ideas flow, a list of functions will usually emerge. As the ideas pinnacle into a defined product, both more newly identified features and functions will follow. All of the ideas should be culminated into a laundry list which provides the starting point for creating the product blueprint. Features can compromise or inhibit the performance of functions while functions may limit the delivery or expression of features, and in some cases, they can make the cost of production or delivery prohibitive. The challenge for the marketer is in selecting the right blend of features and functions that will sell the product in sufficient quantity as to make its development and launch worthwhile.

Identifying the best combination of features and functions to employ is a challenge, to say the least. The product may be generally targeted at a group of people with varying needs and wants.

The desired combination of features and functions may be difficult to achieve, from both a technical and cost point of view. The desired combination of features and functions may also impose obstacles in applying the other 4 Ps. After all, sales success is not achieved by simply building a good product.

Defining the right product, nevertheless, is an important step in the marketing process. Achieving the optimal feature–function balance is at the core of defining the product blueprint. To begin, the marketer needs qualified information outlining the needs and wants of the target market. This information can be obtained in a number of ways, but to have credence, it must originate from the target market.

In its purest form, marketing begins with the generation or valida-tion of an idea. That is, one of two things has happened. Either one or more persons have identified an unmet need or want, or someone has pre-sented an idea to a group willing to pay for a resulting solution. In either case, a group of people has communicated their desires as well as their willingness to pay to have their desires fulfilled. Marketing begins before a product is developed; marketing begins with the creation of an idea. Creating ideas that are generated from or validated by future customers is the first step in the marketing process.

In the initial stages of market validation, the group of people who express a desire for a product or who confirm a product idea may be quite small. Expressing a desire says *what* I want. Confirming an idea says *why* I want it and that *I am willing to pay* for it. (I discuss these concepts at length later in this book.) Steps must be taken to determine if a larger group of people, with sufficient need and purchasing power, are willing to purchase the planned product. In other words, are there enough poten-tial buyers to risk developing and bringing this product to market? The answer to this question lies in market research.

Market researchers use a number of techniques to gather information. Questionnaires, focus groups, telephone surveys, promotional discounts, purchase tracking, and solicitational advertisements are a few tools of the trade. A host of information is available in public and private databases, adding to the repository that the marketer can use to define and qualify prospective customers (see Identifying Wants and Needs, Chapter 3).

Market research is an iterative and evaluative process. The researcher gathers information, assesses what has been collected, and based on the results, will usually gather additional information. This process is conducted to help the marketer to better understand the target market and how to apply the 5 Ps to optimize the marketing mix. Once a comprehensive assessment has been made, the marketer is better equipped to act on the results.

The goal of information gathering tools and processes is to reach a representative sample of every type of person who might be inclined to purchase the product. Equally important is defining the type of person, or profile of the future customer. Historically, marketers have used demographic information to profile prospective customers based upon race, age, income, and other demographic information. Trends in our society have made these demarcations less relevant, particularly as they relate to one's proclivity to purchase products. The purchase of products and services often appears to be based on socioeconomic factors. The *reason* that a person makes a buying decision, however, is not necessarily based on socioeconomic factors. The socioeconomic factors may determine their ability and likelihood to purchase a product or service. In other words, these factors help support their purchase decision. For example, a business executive and a construction worker may each choose to purchase a cell phone so that they can be readily accessible or able to make calls without having to locate a wireline telephone. Immediate access is their reason for purchasing the cell phone service. The business executive might select a purchase plan that supports a high volume of steady usage while the construction worker may select a plan that supports a low volume of intermittent usage. While the aggregate spending might be higher for the business executive, the percentage of disposable income spent might be greater for the construction worker. While the financial criteria supporting the purchase decision are different for the business executive and the construction worker, the reason remains the same—immediate access to information. It is the role of advertising and promotion to appeal to the reason that prospective customers want the product as well as inform the customer as to how they can purchase the product. It is the product blueprint that defines the reason for the message.

When conducting market research, the primary purpose is to understand the prospective customers. Pure, unbiased research will not attempt to define the advertising message or sell the product idea. The researcher does not focus on technical function, but rather, on what people want to achieve. The researcher does not focus on features, but rather on how people want to achieve their objectives. The answer to delivering the desired feature or function may not always lie in the product itself, but in how the product is delivered (i.e., training, ancillary products, support). For example, a prospective customer may indicate that they want to add a button to their computer screen or keyboard. Upon further investigation the researcher learns that the reason for the new button is to display prices on demand. Since this can be achieved with functions that are partially available through the existing software and hardware, the researcher will qualify the need further by determining if the customer prefers to learn, build, or buy. That is, the customer can learn to access prices stored on their computer using existing functions in the software; or build an interface to outside systems that provide current prices; or purchase an automated link from a service that provides up-to-the-minute prices. The researchers will gather more meaningful information, if they focus on the customer's objectives rather than on the perceived need for features or functions.

Customers will tell you what combination of features and functions encourages them to purchase a product. That message is delivered based upon information that is gathered during market research, which tells the marketer what the customer wants to achieve. The challenge for engineers and product managers is to determine what functions will help the customer to realize these goals.

Creating a New Product via Market Research

Market research gathered from existing customers is usually easier to interpret. The defined need, and the priority that it carries, is clearer when it is based upon an existing product being used for a particular purpose. Identifying and prioritizing features and functions for products which do not exist can be a bit more challenging. It requires using techniques and processes that educate while eliciting the information that defines what should be produced.

To start, the researcher must select study participants who fit the profile of future customers and gather accurate, truthful, and complete information from these participants. In gathering this information, the researcher should avoid presenting prospective customers with a list of features and functions to choose from and prioritize, as this method may stifle the creative wish list process. Even worse, they risk the customer giving feedback on functions that they don't truly understand. Instead, the researcher may offer a sample feature–function list as a means to checkpoint and feedback the information that they have gathered. The information gathering process should be just that, collecting information. Market research should provide a thorough and carefully defined wish list from representatives of the target market, or prospective customers. This list is translated into a preliminary feature–function list.

It is not enough to simply identify the feature–function list. The researcher must also determine what is necessary to deliver and support the identified functions. After all, features and functions are of no value if the customer is not able to benefit from them. Put yourself in the customer's place. If the customer cannot reasonably acquire everything that's necessary to achieve their desired results, the product fails. Benefits are not realized if customers are not aware of or able to use the features and functions which deliver those benefits. For this to happen, service and support are needed. Feature and function definitions, therefore, identify what is necessary to develop, deliver, and support them. This is the essence of the product blueprint.

The product blueprint details both the *required* features and functions, as well as those *desired* by prospective customers. In addition to the product features, the blueprint should indicate how the customer will achieve the desired results, including any necessary ancillary products and services. The ability to use ancillary products and services will help to determine the design specification. Personal computers, for example, are typically used with printers and telecommunications lines. To accommodate their use, PCs are equipped with easily accessible parallel and serial ports, built-in communications devices and systems software to enable their use. The product blueprint will drive the design specification and, in turn, development of the prototype product.

The Development Process

The development process for an IT product is often an iterative process that moves back and forth between the drawing table and the market. It is often difficult for the market to articulate their needs without understanding existing and emerging technologies. Likewise, it is also difficult for the technologist to describe what a product or service can offer without providing a working prototype. In order to reach common ground of understanding, products are often introduced before the optimum blueprint is identified. This is also due to competitive demands that the development cycle be swift yet qualified.

The product development process can be very involved, complex, and expensive (see Figure 2.1). The interaction and teamwork between developers, engineers, scientists, marketers, manufacturers or production and finance is critical to creating a product that will be commercially successful. While there are many phases in the development process that vary depending upon the nature and complexity of the product, most can be grouped into alpha, beta, and first release. For more information on the development process and how to create a product that can sell, visit www.The5Ps.com/LEM/Development-Cycle.html

The product development cycle should be competitively paced and based on a qualified blueprint of what the target market will purchase.

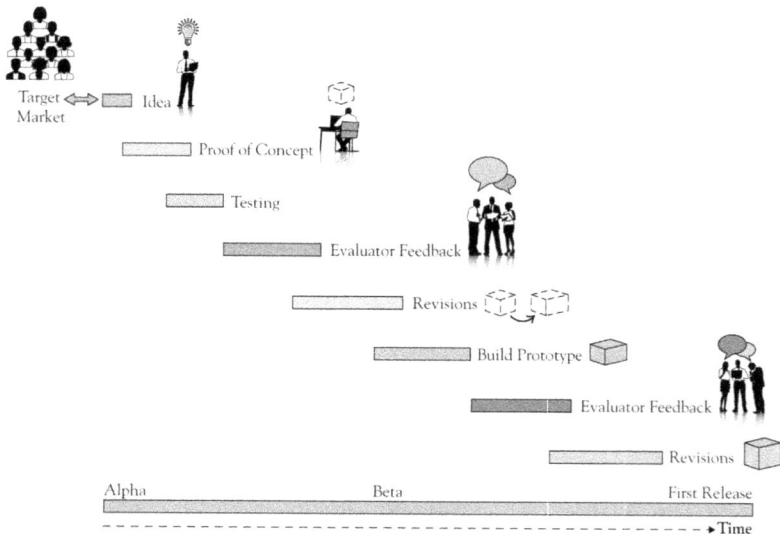

Figure 2.1 *Product development cycle*

This can be quite daunting for the product manager. The challenge is to remain nimble and thorough, while marshaling all of the resources necessary to develop a prototype, and ultimately deliver a product, within a window that allows an acceptable return. The rapid pace of technological development, coupled with the adaptable process of determining the optimal feature–function mix, further elevates the challenge. Once a product blueprint has been determined to satisfy the needs, wants, timing, and price point of target market, the prototype can be built.

The decision to develop the prototype is a validation of the market research and product planning that has taken place thus far. The *acceptance* of the prototype product by selected members of the target market is the final validation to proceed with full production of the product.

To develop a viable plan, marketing must determine which businesses or consumers are likely to purchase the product (target market), how to reach them (promotional), and the most effective means to encourage them to buy. Development must determine how to create a *product* with the desired combination of features and functions (*packaging*), while meeting the cost points necessary to achieve an acceptable rate of return (*price*). Production must determine how to cost effectively manufacture the specified product quantity and make it available to the distribution channels (*place*). Collectively, marketing, development, and production will provide information to help form a baseline product plan. For more information, visit www.The5Ps.com/LEM/Development -Cycle-Plan.html

Since the primary purpose of the prototype product is to validate the product plan, it is essential to gather feedback and evaluate results from everyone involved in its review. Of course, the product manager wants to determine if the prototype product has the right feature–function mix. When the marketer drives the product development process, the product being created must be compared to the product blueprint and the product plan. All modifications necessary to ensure the successful launch and sale of the product must be considered. To ensure that all bases are covered, the product plan and its review should cover each of the 5 Ps of marketing—product, packaging, price, promotion, and place. See Figure 2.2.

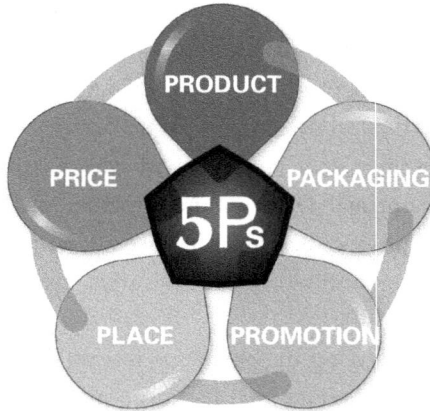

Figure 2.2 5 Ps

After the product blueprint and plan have been re-evaluated, four major questions must be answered:

- What resources are required and how much will it cost to deliver this product?
- How long will it take?
- How much gross profit and net revenue will this product generate?
- When will each of these milestones be met?

The answers to these questions will determine whether to proceed with the final development, manufacture, launch, and delivery of the product.

Maintaining Upward Compatibility

He who sells a product wins the battle.
He who sells the customer wins the war.[1]

Veronica Williams, Inc. CEO Symposium, 2000

The goal of a fully executed sales cycle is to win acceptance from a customer. The goal of a fully executed marketing cycle is to enable the sales cycle, and to *keep* the customer. When customers' needs are properly serviced and maintained, it is unlikely that they will move to the competition. Since needs grow and new solutions are continually available, servicing customers means offering product enhancements and upgrades. See the Lotus 1-2-3 story at www.The5Ps.com/LEM/Lotus -123-Upgrade.html

To keep customers happy, and protect the installed base, the product manager must maintain upward compatibility of the product. This means compatibility with previous versions or models of the product, as well as with other products and services, which are commonly used with the product. To accomplish this, whether the product is software, hardware, or a network, several factors must be considered. These include the basic elements, which affect the customer's ability to migrate to, and use, the next generation product.

The rapid pace of technological development makes it virtually impossible to predict what will become, and more importantly remain, an industry standard. This continuing change makes the term "standard" a misnomer. Since it can take years—or several product generations—for a protocol to become a standard or established, the focus is actually on selecting popular protocols. For example, universal serial bus (USB) is a popular protocol that defines how devices (i.e., thumb drives) communicate with a host device (i.e., notebook computer); Transmission Control Protocol/Internet Protocol (TCP/IP) is a popular protocol that defines how devices on a network communicate with one another. There were many protocols preceding USB and TCP/IP that were used for many years in devices and networks that could not communicate with one another. There are new protocols and there will also be more to come. To cost effectively maintain upward compatibility, it is almost always advisable to adhere to popular protocols.

Modular Design.   In order to meet design complexities while maintaining product elegance, developers are often inclined to integrate subfunctions, which are best kept separate to facilitate compatibility. Although this is not always the case, the challenge remains to encourage creativity in development while providing for current and future compatibility. Designing products in a modular fashion while maintaining optimal performance will help to provide for compatibility in future versions or models.

Conversion of Ancillary Products and Components.   Many IT products are used to store data, develop reports, and communicate with other components and systems. Customers create data and generate reports with IT products when they use them. As the product's value to the customer increases, so does the value of the data, reports, links to peripherals and other systems, and of other products produced by IT products. It is quite understandable, therefore, that customers must be able to continue using data, generating reports, and interfacing with existing peripherals and systems if an upgrade is to be successful.

To accomplish this, software programs must convert files, hardware products must maintain connectors/adapters, and networks must maintain communication interfaces. Essentially, all the fundamental output and interfaces produced by the product must be maintained. Moreover, the customer must be able to do this, and use the upgraded product, expeditiously and cost effectively.

The Role of Packaging.   Product packaging is what the customer interacts with to use the product. It conveys the product's logic; it contains the product's *look and feel*; it is what directs the customer's ability to generate results, and thus value, from the product. It stands to reason, therefore, that the product packaging must maintain as much of the logic and interface as possible in the upgraded version or model. This minimizes the customer's need for training or adaptation, and consequently the need to seek competitive alternatives. It is critical, therefore, that product packaging is maintained or the transitions to modified packaging are simplified for the customer. This will help to eliminate the need to explore competitive solutions.

The Role of Pricing.   The cost of upgrading products can be expensive. Oftentimes, the cost to the customer greatly exceeds the price of the new product. The product manager should be aware of, and prepare for, the total cost that the customer must incur to upgrade to the new product. The price level should be set, and the price should be structured, to make the upgrade affordable to the customer. This may mean offering special support programs, conversion tools, bundled pricing, or other forms of upgrade assistance. When determining the upgrade price, consideration should be given to the revenue from the upgrade as well as future revenues which are likely to be realized from the customer. Pricing affordability to the customer must be balanced against the cost of delivering the complete upgrade package to ensure that profitability is maintained.

The Role of Distribution.   Distribution partners who deliver existing products and services to customers are logical sources to deliver product and service upgrades. Vendors can obviously also deliver upgrades directly. The role of distribution partners is to make the upgrade available to the customer while facilitating their ability to have access to, pay for, and thus, implement the upgrade.

The Role of Promotion.   Facilitating implementation may include providing full support or merely ensuring that the customer receives the information necessary to successfully perform the upgrade. The product manager should understand what is necessary to perform the upgrade and use all means available to make the customer aware of how to successfully perform the upgrade. This should include instructions provided with the upgrade, a properly trained technical support hotline staff, and mailings, advertisements, or Internet site postings that let customers know the forms of support that are available. Whenever possible and financially feasible, field technical support staff should be available from the vendor directly or through distribution partners.

The decision not to maintain upward compatibility in product upgrades or enhancements should be conscious and deliberate. It is a signal that the product may be withdrawn from the market. At the very least, it makes it easier for competitors to win the customer. The marketing costs associated with keeping customers when upward compatibility is *not* maintained may be greater than the cost of winning the customer initially.

Nevertheless, there are situations when it is advisable *not* to maintain upward compatibility. The effort to maintain upward compatibility should be abandoned when the cost of keeping existing customers is greater than the cost of winning new customers. To maintain the company's integrity, this decision must be communicated openly and honestly. *Perceived customer abandonment* occurs when customers believe that the vendor has deserted them by failing to maintain and upgrade the product. Recovering from the effect of *perceived customer abandonment* is difficult, and sometimes impossible to get through. Customers should, therefore, be given notice of the intention to forgo upwardly compatible upgrades or enhancements.

Several situations may arise when the product *should* be abandoned for it is less expensive to win new customers than to keep existing ones. A substantial customer base attracts competitors who may resort to price cuts to win their business. When pricing wars drive margins too low to earn an acceptable return, the marketing strategy must change or the product should be discontinued. When product development costs, or the costs of promoting and delivering upgrades, exceed acceptable levels, efforts to maintain upward compatibility should be discontinued. When the market opportunity to create and deliver a new product is greater than the cost of maintaining the existing product, the new product takes precedence. Regardless of the circumstances, the move to abandon a product is a business decision. When the total cost of keeping existing customers is greater than the cost of winning new ones—with an equal or greater revenue and profit level—the product should be discontinued.

Designing for Maintenance and Support

Effective maintenance and support is critical to short-term revenue and profitability as well as to the company's reputation. A company's reputation plays a critical role in its long-term ability to generate revenue. It makes good business sense, therefore, to design the product or service to facilitate maintenance and support.

There are several methods that may be undertaken to facilitate the maintenance and support. First and foremost, the product should be *designed* and *produced* to minimize the need for maintenance or support. The quality of the product should allow it to be operated at a level which is acceptable to the customer. That is, the average cost and mean frequency of maintenance and repair should be tolerable by the customer. The process of diagnosing and resolving problems should be intuitively easy and logistically simple. To help accomplish this, the product must have an intuitive interface. Hardware might incorporate indicator lights and use a clearly marked casing. Software can display clear error message and logical help procedures that deliver results rather than options. Whenever feasible, IT products and services should incorporate self-correcting functions.

Many technology-based products use communications access to remote systems that provide support. The answers to frequently asked questions (FAQs) and diagnostic tools are available on product websites. Some appliances and automobiles incorporate wireless transmitters that send warnings to the person using them when problems are encountered or pending. In some cases, software patches or instructions are sent to the appliance or automobile to resolve problems immediately after or even before they occur. Products designed to support remote communications and other self-correcting techniques facilitate the delivery of maintenance and support.

In addition to being able to receive fixes to problems, products should be designed so that problems can be reasonably diagnosed. The logical sequence of functional operations, and how well documented they are, will help determine the effectiveness of product support resources. This *logical sequencing* will enhance the efficiency of built-in help functions as well as the ability of product support technicians to diagnose and resolve problems. The complete documentation of the logical sequence of functional operations also aids in the development of product support manuals that are easy to comprehend.

Products designed with maintenance and support in mind will also facilitate product upgrades. Software and hardware designed in a modular fashion will often make upgrades faster and easier. This is particularly true when the replacement components can be swapped for existing components. Whether it is a firmware or one-click software upgrade, or a logical sequence for implementing planned enhancements, a sound product design will help to facilitate upgrades.

Migration

Migration is the process of moving from an old system to a new one. It is a disruptive process for the end user or customer. Business operations and personal routines are slowed down or even halted. Customers must often make adjustments in their use of the IT product or learn how to use new functions. Sometimes peripheral and other related products and services must be modified to accommodate the next generation system. The entire process of preparing for, implementing, and becoming proficient with the next generation system requires considerable adjustments by the customer. It is incumbent upon the product manager, therefore, to take steps to ensure that the migration is worthwhile to the customer.

Preparing the Customer.   The decision to migrate is fueled by a need or desire for features and functions that are not available in the IT system being used. There may be a need for a different set of calculations or a new group of reports. There may be a need to simplify or expedite the process of using the system. Other products that make up the IT system may have been replaced or updated, necessitating upgrades of related products. Many customers upgrade their systems simply to stay abreast of current technology or remain state-of-the-art.

Regardless of the reason for migrating to a new IT system, the decision validates that the customer has an expectation of improvement. The customer's expectation must be shaped with a clear understanding of what is necessary to undergo the migration as well as what can be realistically achieved once it is complete.

The marketer can start by, providing a clear and detailed explanation of how their customer's complete IT system will operate after the migration. This includes, but is not limited to, a review of the new features and functions of the migrated system as well as changes in existing features and functions. Secondly, the customer must understand and confirm his or her financial, operational, educational, and other responsibilities in making the migration a success. After all, a system migration is a two-way street. Finally, the customer must understand how and when each step in the migration process will impact their business operations. Once the migration picture is clear, the customer's expectation will build toward an achievable result. If the customer has a clear and thorough understanding of his or her role and responsibilities in the migration process, and their expectations are fully met, it is likely that the migration will generate lasting goodwill and the increased possibility of future revenue.

A system migration is not sold when the customer buys into the need for new features and functions. The migration is sold when the customer approves everything that is necessary to implement and use the new system. The customer must buy into a *migration plan.*

Selling New Products and Services.   Customers will continue to purchase product related services, and will purchase new products and services, when the product continues to meet their needs. This is made possible with a product migration plan. A well-executed migration plan helps to keep existing customers, and win new customers, during periods when new technologies are being embraced by the market. The tactical migration plan defines and outlines everything that the customer must do to prepare for the changes associated with implementing a new system. This includes products that are being replaced with the next generation product from the same vendor as well as products that are being replaced with products of other vendors. The strategic migration plan defines what must take place to encourage members of the target market to purchase future products. The product manager who understands the customer's decision process and experience during the migration process can best develop a strategy ensuring that his or her product will be included in the customer's migration plan.

The product manager who understands the collective buying criteria and experiences of the market can best develop a product migration plan that compels the customer to structure a systems migration plan around their product solution. As a result of effective planning and support, the value of the product to the customer increases as it is used in practice. To protect that value the customer will usually build a migration plan that includes the product in the new system.

Remember, migration is a disruptive process for the end user or customer. Initially the focus of the product manager is on ensuring that installation of the next generation product goes smoothly. Migration is more than installing the new product, converting files, or moving components. The product life cycle plan should ease the migration for the customer, and also for everyone involved in making the migration successful. The product manager must prepare the customer by identifying everything that must take place to successfully complete the migration to the new system. When the product manager is not forthcoming with what is required in the migration process, they run the risk of spending excessive resources to support the migration or additional funds in damage control to protect the product image. The product migration plan should allow the product to perform in conjunction with other popular products and services. The migration process should be able to be conducted in a timely manner so as to minimize disruption of the customer's operations process or work routine. Developing a problem free migration plan, and implementing it successfully, poses a monumental challenge for many in IT. Strategies that have proven successful are presented in Product Life Cycle Management (Chapter 3).

Pricing.   The entire migration process, end-to-end, must be affordable for the customer. The net purchase price amount must be exceeded by the value that the customer will realize from the features and functions offered by the new product. One common pricing strategy is to offer a discount for earlier versions of the product or for versions of a competitive product. Free or reduced technical support may be provided by the product vendor during a predefined migration period. The product manager may also encourage value-added resellers or systems integrators to provide technical support by offering discount or other plans that make it worth their while.

Affordability can also be achieved through the manner in which the price is structured. Services that are paid for on a recurring basis (i.e., network subscriptions, maintenance packages) lessen the impact of migration costs by spreading them over a period of time. Products can be bundled with these services, or they can be leased, to spread out the cost of migration. Many customers are more prepared to accept the price of migration when it is budgeted for in advance. This is achieved by communicating the costs associated with all phases of the product life cycle to the customer. When a customer is cognizant of the value that they are deriving from a product or service, they are more inclined to protect that value. By understanding migration costs well in advance of the budget process, it is more likely that these costs will be included in the budget.

Delivering New Products and Services.   Once the customer has made the decision to upgrade their products and services, and they have settled payment requirements for the system migration, it is time for the vendor to deliver. Delivery is much more than making sure that the product is on site and installed. Delivery of a migrated system is not complete until the customer is using the system and realizing results that demonstrate its value. Confirmation with the customer that the results are achieved is the final step in the delivery process.

The first step in delivery is to provide the customer with the means to receive and properly install their new products and services. This means that new products must be compatible with other related products in their system, or the customer must be willing to forgo use of incompatible products. Tools that allow integration with other products may be built into the new product or provided by third-party vendors. The selection of products that require integration tools will be based on how adaptable and widely used they are as well as the degree of need for integration with the new product or service. While providing integration tools is not always essential for the purchase of new products and services, the customer's ability to achieve integration will impact their perception of the value of the product. The degree of compatibility with other products, therefore, determines if the installation is successful. Successful installations have a major impact on the current and future revenue stream of a product or service.

Achieving a successful installation requires the right technical support and training. Without these elements, the customer will be unable to use the product or service to achieve their goals. Technical support can be delivered in many forms and will vary from customer to customer. Whether the customer elects to use product manuals, online resources, help functions built into the product, a technical support hotline, or on-site technicians, the choices that meet the needs of most customers must be provided to ensure success. Technical support staff must be equipped with the proper knowledge and resources to efficiently answer questions and resolve customer problems. This will include a means to escalate problems to product engineers when necessary. In order to provide customers with reasonable access to technical support personnel, the product manager may prepare and authorize other companies to provide support. Regardless of the source of technical support, support personnel must be knowledgeable of the possible solutions for resolving problems encountered during migration.

A system migration is not complete until the customer is able to use the system. To achieve this, some degree of training will be required. Many upgraded products maintain the same look and feel as their prior versions, making it easy for customers to quickly learn and use the new product. There are times, however, when new users must learn the product or customers must learn new functions. The product manager should, therefore, always offer some degree of training. Training, as with technical support, also comes in many forms. Some combination of online tutorials, videos, CDs, books, or instructor-led training should be available for customers migrating to new systems.

Technical support and training, as with the product or service, comes at a cost. Whether that cost is bundled into the migration price or delivered separately, it is almost always necessary to complete a successful migration. Technical support and training are, therefore, essential elements of the migration package to protect current and future revenue streams.

Packaging

Packaging, the fifth P, brings a new perspective that can greatly empower the marketer. This is the time to think out of the box. Packaging has a distinctive role in software, hardware, and networks.

Traditionally, packaging is viewed as the box, carton, or other physical item in which a product is delivered. This is particularly true of CPG such as food items, toys, televisions, or shoes. Packaging helps to define and explain products to consumers. It contains information about the product such as what is contained inside the box, where it is manufactured, the model number, and often the suggested retail price (SRP). Packaging protects that product during shipping and protects it from excessive handling before purchasing. It is structured and designed to make it easier to include products in displays so that it is easily recognizable and so that shelves can accommodate many products. Indeed, packaging plays an important role in the promotion, sale, and delivery of CPG.

Packaging takes on a different dimension for IT products. It is the visual or physical interface that allows the user to operate the product. It houses the circuitry, software, or intelligence that constitutes the essence of the product. In the world of IT, packaging is what encompasses the product to make it functional for the user. It is what the user interacts with and relates to when they use an IT product. It is what the customer experiences when they *receive* a product or service. Packaging takes on different forms for software, hardware, and networks.

Software Packaging

Packaging for computer software is the interface that the user interacts with to execute the programs that comprise the software product. Computer software presents characters and images that communicate to the user the results of what has been performed or defines the input that is expected. These characters and images are communicated through the user interface.

In the early days of computing, software presented a string of words or characters, often referred to as command prompts, to request input from users. Command lists sometimes preceded the prompt to show the choices that the user had to choose from. Once the correct command, or sequence of commands, was entered, the program produced results. The results were sometimes delivered in report formats that were often difficult to interpret. The user was not aware of the extent of the functionality available to him or her unless they frequently consulted the documentation or until they became proficient with the software. The experience of using the software and reaching a high level of proficiency left a lot to be desired.

During the 1980s, programmers began to develop graphical user interfaces (see Figure 2.3), also known as GUI, to make it easier for users to operate their software. As computer hardware became more powerful and functionally robust programming tools abounded, GUI-based

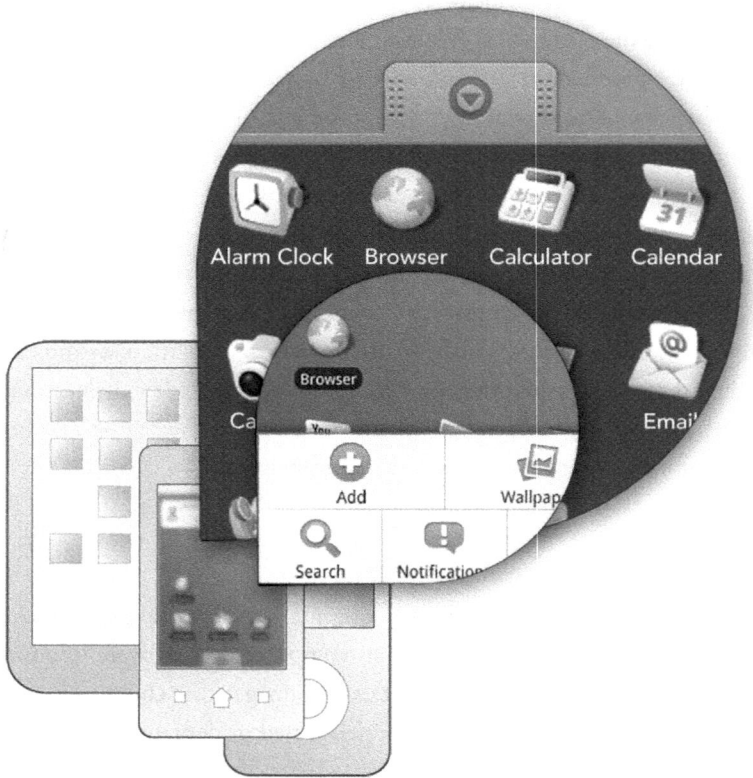

Figure 2.3 GUI—the "look and feel" or packaging

software became more creative and intuitive. Apple computer led the way by creating a graphically intuitive operating environment and recruiting software developers to write programs that conformed to their environment. After a few years, students, noncomputer professionals, and others were using PCs to complete tasks that were formerly done with pen and paper. The explosion of the computer industry was just beginning and the user interface, or software packaging, had played a major role.

The software packaging, or the user interface, plays a major role in how the software is received by the user. Today, biometric devices, icons, navigation bars, and other tools are used to guide the user to explore and use the features and functions available from software or apps. Packaging makes software aesthetically pleasing; it helps to make it easy to use. The placement and flow of commands coupled with the selection and placement of icons, lead the user to produce results from computer software. These elements of the user interface define the *look* of computer software. The look of the user interface is an important part of software packaging.

In addition to defining these qualities for software, the user interface presents the logic that drives the operation of software packages. The presentation of the software logic, or its *feel*, is another important element in determining user comfort with the product. When the flow of commands produces a sequence of results that follow a natural logic, the software feels more comfortable for the user.

The look and feel of a software product is determined by the user interface or packaging. It is the packaging that governs the quality of what the user experiences when using a computer software product.

The experience of using a software product begins with its installation. The ease and speed of installing and implementing a software product is the first thing that the customer remembers about the product. A difficult installation is an early indication that the product may not live up to customer expectations. Even companies with IT departments that install software for their users, will be impacted by software products that are difficult to install and implement. Users will not be able to begin using new software in a timely fashion. When the software technician has a negative experience installing a software product, their poor opinion may be passed on to the user. Worse, the IT department may elect to use a competitive product to avoid future problems.

The packaging of the installation process should vastly simplify this step while giving the customer the flexibility to adapt the product to their environment and needs. Many PC-based software products have done a magnificent job of packaging the installation process. Not only are most popular products installed with few problems, but also the customer has options to modify the implementation of the product. Moreover, customers are often reminded of the product's features and functions during the installation process. This reinforces their purchase decision and prepares them for training and ultimately using the product. Properly packaged installation process, therefore, contributes to solidifying current product sales and opening the door for future sales.

While the user interface is the focus of software packaging, the physical container that houses the software media still plays a role in marketing the product. The software container performs several roles that are important in the marketing process. It visually portrays the product's image. It can define the primary features and functions that are available in the product. It houses the media that the product is delivered on, the documentation, registration cards, and other informative and promotional materials. It carries the universal product code (UPC) that carries the retail price and other information pertinent to the sale of the product. The software container also helps to determine how many products can be displayed on retailer shelves as well as how effectively it draws consumer attention. When software products are sold online, the front of the product container is often displayed, portraying the image and magnetism of the product.

While software packaging includes the container and media that the product is physically delivered in, the most important component of software packaging is the user interface. It is the user interface that drives the customer's experience with the software product, for it is the user interface that the customer interacts with. As more and more software products are delivered online and over the Internet, the physical packaging will be less important. After all, the packaging that matters is what the customer sees when they use the product.

Hardware Packaging

Packaging for computer hardware is the physical casing that houses the electronic circuitry. It is the electronic circuitry that comprises the actual product. It is the physical casing that the user sees; it is the physical casing that the user interacts with. The buttons, keys, switches, displays, and other components that the customer uses to operate the product play a critical role in the user experience. Likewise, the size, weight, shape, color, and design also contribute to the user's experience. Collectively, these elements define and enable the features and functions that are delivered through the packaging of the hardware product.

Packaging for computer hardware products takes on basically two dimensions: functional and visual. That is, hardware packaging allows the

Figure 2.4 Depiction of functional and aesthetic appeal

user to perform the functions that they need. Packaging also allows the user to enjoy having the hardware device. In order for packaging to make its contribution to the marketing process, it must appeal to the customer both functionally and visually (see Figure 2.4).

Functional Appeal.   Computer and communications hardware deliver a host of functions to the user. These functions are normally made possible by using keyboards, switches, buttons, and other manipulative interfaces. As computers, phones, and other devices are in greater demand by consumers, designers have responded to and appealed to their desires by improving hardware functionality. Keyboards have been modified to include keys that are shaped to the finger with positioning markers for easier typing. ON/OFF switches take on different shapes and sizes. They also operate in different manners such as allowing the user to slide a button rather than click it to turn a device on or off. Designers have given more consideration to the shape, protrusion, and location of buttons, ensuring that they are *conveniently functional*; that is, that they easily deliver function to the user when, and only when, they need it. The multifunctional nature of hardware casing and other external components appeals to many users. The functional appeal of hardware packaging plays an important role in establishing users' desire for the product.

Visual Appeal.   Hardware not only has to look good, it must be aesthetically pleasing to the user in all ways. Hardware products, particularly those designed for personal use, come in different colors, shapes, and sizes. Hardware designers can be quite creative in combining shapes and colors into different designs for computers and phones. Visual appeal is not defined simply by the way that a product looks, however. Visual appeal also encompasses what a customer believes he or she will experience when using the product. For example, small, lightweight mobile devices signal several things to frequent travelers including convenience in packing, reduced back pain from carrying heavy bags, or being less conspicuous. A larger console box in a private branch exchange, on the other hand, may signal to the telecommunications manager the ability to expand with minimal disruption. Whether the hardware represents a consumer, business, or industrial product, the message that is sent when the customer looks at it goes far beyond the color, shape, or size. Packaging helps to define a level of expectation for the customer of what he or she will experience when using the product.

As is the case with software packaging, packaging for hardware also includes the physical container that the hardware is showcased and delivered in. The role that hardware containers play in marketing products is analogous to that of software (see p. 49). As is the case with computer software, the physical container used to showcase and deliver hardware products has an important role in marketing; however the casing that houses the product circuitry is critical in determining the product's appeal to customers.

Network Packaging

Packaging for networks is made up of the hardware devices that allow the user to access the network and the software that allows the user to communicate over the network. It is the cell phone, portable computer, desktop computer, or whatever device that is used to access the network. The network access device is what the user interacts with and, thus, is perceived as the enabler of using the network. The device is the packaging that defines the experience of using the network.

Communications or computing access devices provide the user interface to communications networks. The user's perception of network functionality and performance is, therefore, driven by the features and functions of these devices. Network function and performance is delivered via the casing of the device and the software that directs communications. The means of input (keyboard, finger, stylus, and others) and display of the device, or the user interface of the software communicate to the user what the network is doing. The completeness and quality of these communications plays an important role in the user's perception of network value. Whenever feasible, the device and software should let the user know what functions are available as well as the status of network operations. Additionally, this information should be presented to the user in a clear and logical manner.

The logic that underlies IT functions helps the user to understand and anticipate what the product or service can do for them. When product or service functions are presented in a logical fashion, it is much more likely that they will be favorably received and retained by the user. Phones and computers are often designed to strike a balance between optimizing the delivery of disparate networks and maintaining a consistent interface that defines how they are used. This can be quite a challenge indeed, particularly when several methods and protocols are involved.

Data networks that are accessed by Windows-based computers benefit from a common look and feel of the user interface. The logic delivered through the same interface is often fairly easy to follow.

Wireless and other networks that are accessed by cell phones, portable computers, and other devices with interfaces that are not widely used, may be challenged in delivering a consistent logic for the growing number of features and functions that they offer. The continuing emergence of networking standards, however, will help to rectify this.

As networks continue to grow in features and functionality, the product manager should optimize the use of device and software interfaces to deliver network services to users or subscribers. These interfaces are the network packaging. It is the packaging that determines how well the user will receive and retain the functions that are delivered. The packaging also helps to shape the features delivered to the user. Most importantly, the network packaging defines what the user will experience when using the network. This goes a long way in determining the likelihood that existing users and subscribers will continue to access the network. It also helps to elicit favorable feedback and references from customers. Packaging plays an important role in defining the network experience and will play an increasingly greater role as product managers strive to differentiate their product or service.

The Look and Feel

The "look and feel" is a phrase that is often used to describe the packaging of IT products and services. This phrase describes what the user sees and experiences when using hardware, software, and networks. The look and feel of hardware or networks (see Figure 2.5) is determined by the physical casing that encapsulates the product circuitry, and the software that directs the use of functions. While the input mechanisms (keyboard, finger, stylus, and others) and case design drive the look of hardware, it is software that drives the feel. As a matter of fact, it is the software that leads the experience of the user. The look and feel is most often used to describe the software–user interface. It is the visual appeal and the logic delivered through the user interface. The user interface, or packaging, helps to determine the user's desire and ability to use an IT product.

The "Look"   The "Feel"

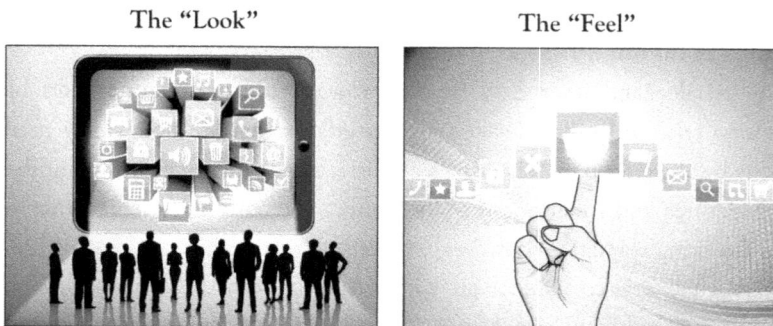

Figure 2.5 *The Look and Feel*

The product packaging helps define much more than ease of use. The *look* of product packaging is the first step in providing it with its identification. The look defines the character and personality of the product or service. The shape, colors, lines, and format of product packaging combine to form a definitive image that is used to identify the product. They provide a recognizable image that conveys the goals and value of the product. The logo is a prominent part of the packaging. It is often the cornerstone of the product's look. The look incorporates a static or dynamic movement that conveys the actions that the product delivers through its functions. When multimedia effects are applied, the product comes to life before it is actually used by the customer. The look of packaging helps prepare users to become actively involved with the product. It carries an aesthetic appeal that softens the process of learning the product or service. It also provides a framework for recognizing future products that are purchased. It not only applies to the user interface, but it also carries over to the physical box that is used to house and deliver the product. The look of packaging helps to ultimately attract and keep customers.

The ease of use that is delivered through the product packaging is not just determined by the look. The *feel* of product packaging plays the leading role in determining the ease of using of an IT product and service. The logic that underlies IT products is delivered through the icons, navigation tools, and visual instructions of the user interface. It is the delivery of this logic that defines the feel of an IT product or service. The flow of commands should follow a sequence that leads to functions available from the product and the results that they deliver. Products that feel comfortable are inherently easy to use.

The logic for an IT product should not be based on the set of commands that the product delivers. Rather, it should be based on the natural, human logic for undergoing a process to achieve the desired results. This process will be impacted, of course, by the functional capabilities of the technologies employed. There are two reasons why logic should follow a natural flow. First, it simplifies the learning process for the user. When the user only has to apply the visual images of functions to a logic that he or she already embraces, it is much easier to embrace the feel of the product. Most GUI-based software products, for example, present **cut**, **paste**, and other editing functions in the **edit** drop down screen from the **file** menu. Secondly, delivering a feel that follows a natural logic makes it easier to incorporate future functionality to enhance the product. When new functions are included in a natural process, they generally respond to a real need. They also meet that need in a manner that allows the user to easily implement that response. New variants of the paste function such as **paste special**, for example, are often presented in the edit drop down screen below the paste function. When the feel of product packaging, or the user interface, conforms to a natural, human logic, it increases the likelihood that customers will embrace that product now and in the future.

The look and feel of IT products and services can help the user to develop a sense of comfort in using the product. The aesthetic and functional appeal of the product is delivered through the packaging. That appeal makes it easier for the user to learn and remember how to use the product. A well-designed user interface improves the quality of the product. It is the packaging that allows the product to demonstrate its value to the customer.

Sexy versus Functional

One of the never-ending challenges of product design is to strike the right balance between what is needed and what is desired. Information technology products and services exist to deliver functionality to the customer. It is function that drives technological development. Buying criteria, however, is based on much more than function. One of the integral components of product design is the set of features that it offers. Both features and functions can be alluring but it is the manner in which they are presented that makes them sexy, that is, attractively exciting to the customer.

Features such as good looks and a sleek design can help to make a product sexy. Functions such as the smooth execution of multiple, inter-related processes can make a product sexy. Many computer users and software developers consider software that connects with a telecom line, utilizes the richest or most advanced methods of data transfer manipulation and security and secures data, and adapts to popular interfaces to be sexy. A sexy product is not merely one which looks or performs with finesse. Sexiness is the allure that features and functions hold for the customer.

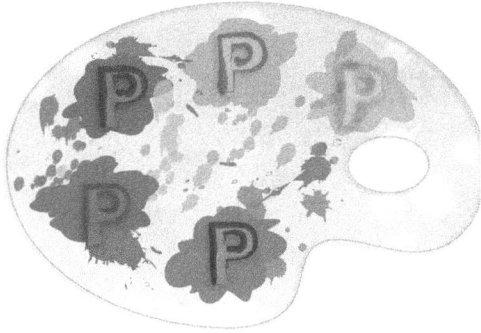

Figure 2.6 An artist's palette

Creating a sexy product means more than incorporating a few bells and whistles. Information technology gives an added dimension to product attractiveness. It allows features to portray more intensity and functions to strive for a higher level of performance. Artistic creativity increases the allure of features. Engineering creativity increases the allure of functions.

Artistic creativity will have an increasing impact on IT products and services (see Figure 2.6). Computers' colors reflect consumer color trends. Their casing has more elegant lines and shapes. Cell phones have cases that flip or slide to cover function keys or touch tone screens that eliminate keys and keyboards completely. Software incorporates multimedia effects and creative images to deliver messages. The skills necessary to instill artistic creativity into the IT products of today and tomorrow require more than those of a graphics designer. Today's products require artistic design and human engineering skills that combine to deliver a physical and visual user interface that is both aesthetically and functionally appealing. After all, good looks and a sleek design do attract the attention of potential customers.

Engineering creativity has been a primary impetus that positioned the IT industry as a leader in today's economy. Computers, phones, and other IT products are well established in the consumer marketplace. In the past, IT products and services were developed largely based upon what technology could do. In the future, IT products and services will be developed based upon what technology can do *for people*. That is, new developments in technology will be largely in response to defined needs of businesses and consumers (Figure 2.7) rather than the functions

Figure 2.7 Deliberate process oriented thought

that developers can create. While this is not a new concept, its continual implementation will become a new reality.

Creative engineers must create performance functions that produce measurable results that are of value to the customer. This means first understanding the customers' needs or requirements. Secondly, it means developing technology that delivers on those needs. Building on the possibilities of technology and creating technologies that respond to defined needs is a chicken and egg process. The possibilities are sometimes not clear until the need is understood; likewise, the needs are not clear until the possibilities are understood. It is the existence of performance functions that often lead to the desire to implement technologies to produce a desired set of results. Nevertheless, once the desired set of results has been identified the engineer must strive to strike the optimal balance between features and functions.

Sexy features can inhibit performance. High performance functions can inhibit the allure of the product or service. Achieving a small, low power device means limiting or eliminating some of the highly engineered function in that device. Building a high performance device that is packed with rich functions means a larger size and greater power requirements. Carrying small devices is sexy. Delivering the power of a desktop computer in a portable device is functional. In the long run, both can be achieved. Although it may take years or even decades, technological development eventually produces what was once thought impossible. In the meantime, however, getting there means delivering devices that provide the necessary amount of allure and function. Creative engineering will strike a balance between what is sexy and what is functional. That balance helps to define the packaging of the product or service.

The Customer Experience

Packaging is what the user relates to when using that product. It is what customers experience when they receive a product or service. The *anticipated experience* is what attracts a customer to a product or service. The *actual experience* is what keeps them using the product or service. The anticipated experience can be quite distinctive from the actual experience, particularly when expectations are not properly set. The power that experience plays in packaging is in setting customer expectations, and being able to meet those expectations. While the goal is for anticipated and actual experiences to be totally congruent, that is seldom achieved in any industry. Nevertheless, experience is the defining component of IT product packaging. It is the experience that drives the existence of IT products and services in the hearts, hands, and budget of the customer.

There are many different ways to describe the experience of acquiring and using an IT product or service. Many customers feel excited when they receive something new. That euphoria is heightened when the new item is an animate object (Figure 2.8). Cars, jet skis, televisions, and appliances can be quite riveting and captivating. That euphoria will be sustained with a well-packaged product that has the proper level of pre- and post-sales support and training. In many cases, the euphoria will subside as the customer learns to use the product. Once the customer has learned to use the product and, most importantly, adapt it to meet

Figure 2.8 Customer experience

their needs, a feeling of comfort emerges. The comfort is underscored by belonging to a group of people who are proficient in using the product or service. It is the feeling of comfort and belonging that helps to solidify the existence of the look and feel of a product or service. The product experience is strengthened and preserved as long as the customer maintains a sense of comfort and belonging. The product packaging, which includes the environment in which it operates, helps to define the customer's experience.

The purchase process is not complete by simply acquiring the product. It is complete once the product has been used and accepted. Product packaging drives the emotions that the customer experiences when acquiring an IT product or service. It is the packaging that the customer sees before purchasing a product; it is the packaging that the customer interacts with to use the product or service. The look and feel of the product packaging plays a primary role in defining the user experience.

Price

Many managers set price by determining the cost to build and deliver a product and adding a margin that delivers an acceptable return to the company. Cost-based pricing is a nice concept but, in reality, the amount that customers will spend is based on their willingness to pay. A price has no value unless it is validated with a critical mass of sales.

Quantifying Benefits

Willingness to pay is determined by the perceived value that the customer will receive from the product or service. The value is assessed based upon the perceived benefits to be received. It is incumbent upon the product manager, therefore, to identify and quantify the benefits that the product will deliver to the target market.

Improved Productivity

Since the advent of computers and communications, productivity has been the primary, and often the only reason, for purchasing IT products and services. The idea of achieving more with a given amount of resources is very persuasive. The idea of doing more with less is even more compelling. The IT industry was built on the concept that the application of IT-based products and services would enable customers to achieve a greater output. Improved productivity (Figure 2.9) is the bastion of benefits delivered by IT products and services.

Figure 2.9 Productivity

While the focus of this book is what it takes to create technology-based products and turn them into profit, the concepts and information presented apply to nontechnology businesses as well. Quantifying benefits is an integral part of establishing the price of any product. The next several pages explain my advocacy of value-based pricing over cost-based pricing.

Of course, technology allows the collection, receipt, analysis, and dissemination of information that would not be available if the systems did not exist to produce it. The alternative is often spending considerable time and resources to compile information. In some cases, the investment of time and resources to produce information is simply not justifiable. Nevertheless, producing information using IT products and services is usually more productive than producing that information using manual systems and methods. Alas, productivity is the underlying reason for using IT to process information that otherwise would not have been available without it.

Productivity gained from IT systems means doing more, faster. It means achieving results without substantial human intervention. Personnel systems track employees and the voluminous information that is maintained for internal and external reporting purposes. Billing systems produce customer invoices, calculating taxes, and other financial details while linking with accounts receivable systems to identify delinquent payments. Manufacturing systems determine and track the materials and labor required to produce products, and identify opportunities to realize greater efficiencies. Truly the productivity gains realized from IT systems have changed the way that businesses, and even households, are run.

Information technology systems have not only produced productivity gains by providing information, but they have also driven the generation of increased results. Development teams are able to focus and streamline their efforts with current information that helps define their process. Salesforces are armed with information allowing them to better target prospective customers and also respond to their needs more expeditiously. The empowerment provided by IT encourages us to perform better. Information that helps to improve performance also helps incent performance.

Productivity gains may be measured in a number of ways. Automating steps along the way can streamline operations processes. Providing information that reduces preparation can reduce the amount of time spent performing certain tasks. To simplify the method of measuring improved productivity, it

$$\frac{\text{Hours Spent Producing Result Before IT} - \text{Hours Spent Producing Result After IT}}{\text{Hours Spent Producing Result Before IT}}$$

Figure 2.10 Formula for labor productivity

is helpful to categorize the improvements. The gains realized from productivity may be grouped into two categories: labor and production.

Labor hours consumed producing a desired result can be determined before and after the implementation of the IT system. The labor productivity gain is easily measured by a simple percentage (see Figure 2.10).

Likewise, the goods produced before and after the implementation of the IT system can also be determined. The improvement in production productivity, or rate of output, is quantified by a similar percentage; see www.The5Ps.com/LEM/Productivity-Production.html

It is important to separate the benefits of productivity and cost savings. Each offers a distinct advantage. Productivity gains are measured by a reduction of time or increase of output. One form of cost savings is the financial benefit attached to the reduction in time or increase of output. That is why productivity gains are generally measured in percentages and cost savings are measured in dollars or hard currency.

Mature products and services maximize the benefit of productivity. As customers become comfortable with using IT systems, they are better able to apply their usage to improve their work processes. Conversely, vendors have had a period of time to collect feedback and deliver improvements that allow their products to make a greater contribution to productivity. As customers become proficient in using products that make a robust contribution to their performance, the productivity benefit is maximized. This benefit, thus, turns into a requirement. Once improved productivity delivered by IT systems becomes a requirement, other benefits must be identified to provide the customer with reasons to purchase the next, more robust offering.

Cost Savings

Along with improved productivity, cost savings (Figure 2.11) has also been a popular benefit of IT since the advent of computers and communications. Productivity is sometimes defined as the ability to do more with

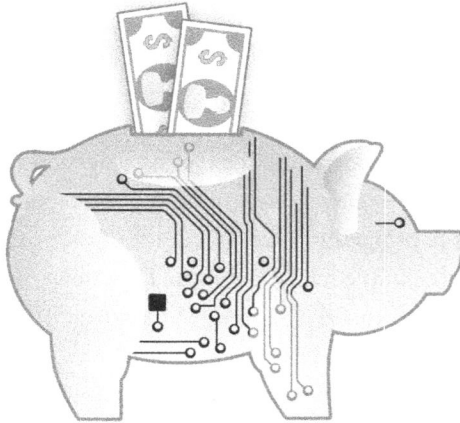

Figure 2.11 Cost savings

less. The ability to reduce the amount of resources required to achieve a given goal is the cost savings component of increased productivity. When headcount is lowered or material needs are reduced as a result of increased productivity, cost savings are realized. Productivity does not always produce cost savings, nor are cost savings always associated with gains in productivity. Cost savings from IT, however, can go far beyond the financial quantification of productivity gains.

There are different types of cost savings that are measured in various ways and delivered in a range of timeframes. Cost savings may take the form of reduced labor or materials. The salary and associated overhead associated with a reduction in headcount is a readily identifiable form of labor savings. The expense reduction from consuming fewer materials in the manufacture or delivery of a product or service is another easily identifiable form of cost savings. Cost savings may be measured in soft dollars or hard dollars. Soft dollar savings is the result of freeing up resources to be deployed elsewhere. Hard dollar savings is realized by reducing labor or production costs. Soft dollar savings is, therefore, a measure of improved efficiencies. The improvement is real; however, there is no impact on the bottom line. Hard dollar savings, on the other hand, is a measure of the direct effect on a company's financial statements. In addition to the type and measure, cost savings are also defined by the period over which they are delivered. Some savings are delivered immediately while other savings are only realized over a period of time. A reduction in material consumption, for example, may be attained as soon as an IT system is implemented. Performance improvements that result in lowering headcount may not be realized until employees become proficient in using the system. The type, measure, and timeframe all combine to quantify the benefit of cost savings from IT systems.

Just as IT systems come in many forms and configurations, so do the cost savings that they deliver. Many office systems eliminate manual processes and ultimately contribute to a reduction in headcount. Many factory automation systems minimize wasted materials. It is impossible, however, to generally attribute certain types of savings to systems. Each different type of system, and the manner in which it is implemented, may deliver a different set of cost savings to the customer. Factory automation systems deliver several cost saving benefits including lower material usage and sometimes reduced power consumption. Telecommunications networks, such as virtual private networks, will often reduce toll costs and may also reduce the cost and quantity of equipment. Automated transport systems used by railroads and trucking companies may reduce food spoilage, lower fuel costs, and lower vehicle repair costs by monitoring operations activity and contributing information to help improve the operations planning process.

Quantifying cost savings is largely an accounting process. Soft dollar savings, of course, can be creatively quantified using various financial formulas and techniques. Many productivity improvements, for example, may be quantified by applying a weighted cost factor to the amount or percentage of productivity savings. Hard dollar savings, on the other hand, are primarily the compilation of statistics that measure individual savings. It is the cost associated with the hard reduction in resources consumed.

Increased Revenue

A primary benefit of salesforce automation systems is that salespeople have more time and improved information. This allows them to call on more customers. More importantly, the improved information allows them to better target high potential prospects and respond to their needs more efficiently. The result is often that their call volume and hit rate, or number of sales closed per calls made, increase. The bottom line is that revenue increases.

The emergence of new technologies has resulted in revenue producing systems that extend far beyond salesforce automation. The marriage of wireless communications and mobile computing has resulted in products and services that allow merchants to accept credit cards and other forms of electronic cash virtually anywhere. Point of sales systems are now found in shopping mall aisles, stadiums, lobbies of hotels hosting conferences, and taxicabs. The ability to accept and process e-cash is clearly an example where IT has enabled an increase in revenue.

Technology has also created new sales channels, providing new opportunities for revenue to be earned. The Internet is a stellar example of a new sales channel made possible by IT. Websites that present and sell products are pervasive. Moreover, these sites are often equipped with the ability to accept checks or credit cards and provide immediate approval without the need for human intervention. Money transfers and other forms of e-cash are also prevalent. The emergence of e-cash is not limited to websites, however. IT-enabled kiosks and automated telecommunications systems also allow customers to scrutinize, pay for, and schedule delivery of products and services. The emergence of IT systems that support the generation of revenue will only be limited by our creativity in developing and implementing technology. Whenever new or additional revenue is earned as a result of the implementation of IT systems, the benefit is crystal clear and easily measured.

Time Value of Information

Information, particularly timely information, provides power. To be sure, there are other forms of power. Money is power—but knowing when and where to invest it, or disinvest it, can make or break the money owner. Nuclear weapons are power—but knowing where they are located, and how to disarm them substantially weakens the position of the owner of nuclear weapons. Presiding over a major country is power—but knowing how to influence and control the people over whom one presides will make or break that position. Knowledge is power. Information is the critical element that fuels the power of knowledge.

Information begets power. The power which can be gained depends on the availability of the information and how effectively one uses it. The effectiveness of using information is dependent upon many factors that are beyond the scope of this book. The availability of information is determined by (a) who receives it first, (b) how many people have access to it, and (c) the amount of time in which it is limited to a single person or small group. Eventually, most information becomes available to the general public. Thus, the timeliness with which information is received is a major determinant of its value. The time value of information is a measure of how long information holds value and the rate of decline of its value. This inherently assumes that all information has some amount of value that declines over time.

In virtually every situation, pertinent information has a declining value. Immediate notification of a movement in the price of a stock will allow a broker to take action to increase or protect the value of client portfolios. Notification of changes in stock prices is of less value if received after losses have been incurred or potential gains are limited. Being able to send a field technician to a client will allow the company to earn additional revenue. If the client is not reached before a competitor responds, that revenue is lost. Receiving late-breaking news reports could contribute to a superior bargaining position during negotiations when all players are present. Responding to the impact of new reports may require more time and effort after the participants have dispersed. The time value of information is largely determined by the means in which that information can be used and what can be achieved from its use.

Information communicated can be written, heard, or seen. The product of communications is the transmission of information. The time value of information depends on its content and the effectiveness with which it is delivered. The combination of written and visual information is a powerful means of communicating an idea. Mobile data is a format for transmitting written and visual content effectively. The power of communications gives information a time value that is fueled by one's ability to gain from the information received. The time value of information is

$$\text{Time - Value} = \frac{\text{(Value of Future Benefits)}}{(1 + C)^N}$$

Figure 2.12 *Simplified formula for the time value of information*

equal to the value of future benefits that can be realized by employing information, discounted by the cost of maintaining those benefits. The formula for the time value of information[2] is provided at www.The5Ps.com/LEM/TimeValueOfInfo.html. The time value of information formula can be simplified as in Figure 2.12.

The major component in calculating the time value of information is the determination of future benefits. The benefits to be gained depend upon how the information is used. Since benefits should be realized as long as the system is used, the value of future benefits is the *sum* of the benefit projections for each year. Keep in mind that competition and other forces may mandate the use of IT systems. In these cases, the benefits will decline as the systems become a requirement of doing business.

Some examples of benefits to be realized from IT are

- market share;
- goodwill;
- efficiency.

Market share is a measure of a company's dominance or relative position against competitors. Businesses can gain additional customers and thus increase their share of the market. Companies can also increase market share by increasing the availability of certain products in the right channels. Data delivered by IT systems can provide the basis for actions that can result in an increase in market share.

To quantify the value of market share, one must identify the profit per share point. Market share can be measured in units, such as the number of products sold. It can also be measured in revenue. To determine the profit per share point, the revenue valuation must go further. The costs of delivering products or services must be determined so that the net profit can be calculated. When assessing costs, be sure to include all costs necessary to maintain or protect the market share.

The net profit per share point is multiplied by the increase in market share (measured in share points) for each year that the benefits are expected to be realized. The value of future benefits (B_F) from market share is the sum of these values.

Goodwill is the result of operating in a manner that makes it easier or less expensive to run the business enterprise. It can result from rendering a higher level of service which increases customer confidence. Physical assets can create goodwill when their use creates a value which is greater than the costs of liquidating the business. The effective use of IT can increase customer goodwill. Customer goodwill can be measured by the lower costs of keeping confident customers happy. The sum of these savings for each year that they are realized is one measure of the value of future benefits (B_F) from goodwill. The revenue from referrals can also measure customer goodwill. Some percentage of customer satisfaction may be achieved as a direct result of using IT products and services. This percentage multiplied by the sum of referral revenue for each year is another measure of B_F.

Efficiency is determined by how effectively an operation is performed with a given amount of resources. Information technology can help companies to perform more efficiently. Resources can be deployed more effectively, sales cycles can be shortened, and steps can be taken to avert or minimize negative effects on the business. For example, dispatchers can select technicians who are closest to the customer, and best equipped to respond, to send on certain service calls. Information in answer to customer questions can be provided right away and trial orders can be immediately initiated. Brokers can sell stock before a decline in price results in substantial losses. Efficiency gains from IT systems are only limited by the company's need for immediate data and their ability to successfully roll out systems. To determine the value of future benefits (B_F) that result from improved efficiency, determine the dollar amount of savings. The B_F is the sum of the savings for each year that they are realized.

Benefits that result from the time value of information will be as widespread as the applications serviced by IT systems. Marketers should give careful thought to the gains that can be made by businesses and consumers from the receipt of more timely information. With a little creativity and objectivity, these gains can be translated into measurable benefits. This is a crucial step in quantifying the time value of information.

The time value of information provides a means of grouping the vast array of benefits that can be realized from IT products and services. Whether IT systems result in a reduction of resources along the flow of information or an increase in market share, the bottom-line benefit to the company or individual is a higher quality of service or increased profitability. These benefits are not fully realized, however, until the system has been successfully implemented and in use for a period of time. The breakeven timeframe will vary with each application. In some cases, the advantages are immediate. In other situations, the advantages may take much longer to materialize. For situations where information has a high time value, the implementation of IT systems carries an attractive and fast return.

Setting the Level

Determining the right price is not a process; it's an art. It means first determining the minimum level that most people in the target market will pay for the product or service. That is the mental hurdle point. Next, the product manager must determine how much is too high and what is too low. Customers have an aversion to the price of some products being raised, especially certain IT-based products and services. So starting too low may make it difficult to raise the price and attain the volume of sales without spending too much in advertising and promotion. Conversely, some customers have an aversion to a price being too low. It signals poor quality to them or a product that is not ready for release. To be sure, determining the level at which a price should be set is the major challenge in pricing.

Covering Product Costs

Many companies use cost-based pricing to determine the amount at which to sell products and services. *The only role that covering product costs should have in pricing is to determine whether or not the product should be marketed and sold.* The only role of the cost to produce a product or service is to determine breakeven. The cost of producing and delivering a product has nothing to do with setting the price level or structure.

While this author is clearly a proponent of value-based pricing rather than cost-based pricing, many companies still use cost-based pricing. This section, therefore, will review how cost-based pricing is performed. One way is to develop product constructs, which is an amalgamation of the different configurations that a product may take. The standard product construct represents the average configuration that a product may take. For a sample product cost construct, visit www.The5Ps.com/LEM/Cost-Construct.html

This standard pricing configuration dictates manufacturing and sales resources required to sell and deliver the product. Once the standard construct is determined, it is relatively easy to determine the costs associated with each element of the construct. A compilation and averaging of costs, applied against the construct, provides the construct product cost or the anticipated cost of producing and delivering the product or service.

Once the cost of the standard product construct is determined, many companies simply mark up the cost by the margins that are being realized by most companies. They now believe that they have a fair, competitive product price level. While this may be true, this method does not take into account product pricing strategies that govern the level and structure of price that the target market is willing and able to pay.

Total Cost of Ownership

The total cost of owning an IT product includes the costs of acquiring, installing, supporting, maintaining, and migrating all products and services necessary to use that product effectively (see Figure 2.13). As is the

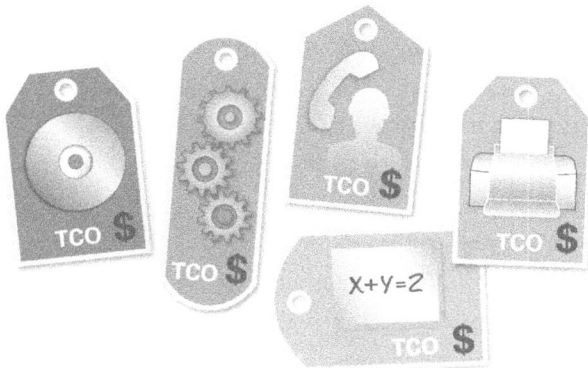

Figure 2.13 Total cost of ownership

case with housing, automobiles, and appliances, businesses and consumers alike must consider everything that is necessary to successfully use and derive value from a product over the period of time that they plan to use it. The need to accurately account for all sources of spending needed to support an IT product is what drives the focus on the total cost of ownership (TCO).

The price for acquiring a product cannot be properly set without taking the TCO into account. If a product is to be purchased repeatedly, over its entire life cycle, the cost of continuing its use must be justified by the value received from it. The amount and manner in which a product's use is paid for over time must be acceptable to the customer. When the cost of using a product becomes excessive it will not be replaced and, more importantly, prospective customers are likely not to buy it.

There are several components of a product's use that must be taken into account to determine the TCO. These include, but are not necessarily limited to, product upgrades, peripheral use, integration, technical support, and training. Additionally, TCO includes the user's time and other resources needed to support these components. In order to accurately valuate the TCO, the cost of carrying all of these components must be determined.

In maintaining upward compatibility (p. 38), I address establishing the *price* of upgrade products and services. This section addresses the *total cost of the upgrade* to the customer.

Upgrades.   The purchase price of a product upgrade is often an incremental percentage of the original purchase price. The price of implementing the upgrade, however, can be substantially more. Although many technology products are backward compatible, maintaining existing links with other products may often require more resources than merely installing the new product.

Names, addresses, and other information in portable devices such as smart phones and handheld computers are usually transferred from these devices to their replacements. Whether the information can be transferred through an automated link, or it must be re-entered, the process of transferring it requires time and effort. If software programs are routinely used with other programs, the links between the programs must often be modified when one or more of the programs are upgraded.

The total cost of a product upgrade includes the purchase price of the upgrade as well as the time and resources required to allow the product to deliver the value received before the upgrade was installed.

Peripheral use.   The process of connecting peripherals to an IT system is often greater than many anticipate. Compatibility is the primary reason for this. In computer systems, software drivers are installed that allow the operating system to direct the operation of the peripheral device. When software drivers are not readily available, or cannot be easily installed, the time and effort of installation will increase because of their addition to the system. Likewise, when answering machines, caller identification, or other peripheral devices are added to telecommunications systems, the time and effort required to attain the desired level of functionality increases the cost of adding them. The addition of peripheral devices increases the value derived from an IT system. The cost of adding peripheral devices also contributes to the TCO.

Integration.   Since most IT systems consist of multiple components from different manufacturers, the need to make everything work together adds to the cost of these systems. Integration costs are not only incurred when installing new components, but they are also incurred to maintain the integrated system. The costs of integration must be taken into account throughout the life of an integrated system to properly value its contribution to the TCO.

Technical support.   Technical support extends beyond the cost of a product support hotline. Technical support includes the purchase of books and manuals, on-site technicians, replacement parts, and other resources needed to keep the system up and running. Regardless of the level of product quality or the degree of compatibility with other products, technical support is necessary to maintain an acceptable level of performance. The cost of maintaining performance throughout the life of an IT system is an important part of the TCO.

Training.   The value derived from an IT product or service is not realized until the customer is able to comfortably use that product or service.
Training helps to speed up the process of building user comfort. Training
can be delivered in a number of different ways. The customer can learn
to use the product with built-in help functions. They can spend time
learning by trying different functions. Customers can learn by purchasing video, CD, online, or instructor-led courses. The cost of purchasing
a course is not the only element of training. One must consider the time
that is required to develop a base level of proficiency with the product
or service. Training is not merely delivering instruction. It is the entire
process of learning to use an IT product proficiently. The TCO includes
the cost of purchasing courses and the cumulative amount of resources
required for a person to use their IT system proficiently.

When setting the level of a product's price, the product manager
should consider the TCO. While the TCO may not always affect initial purchases of the product, it will eventually affect purchases by new
customers and future purchases by existing customers. Customers learn
from many sources including the media, product collateral, other customers, and their own experiences. Their evaluation of the purchase
price will include all costs that they believe are necessary to allow them
to receive value from that product. The costs of training, technical support, integration, and upgrades will be added to the purchase price when
deciding whether or not to buy a product. Informed customers base their
purchase decision on the TCO. Repeat and referral customers base
their purchase decision on the TCO. The total price that the customer
must pay to use a product and derive value from it, or the TCO, should
be established and controlled by the product manager.

Identifying Willingness to Pay

Like marketing, the process of determining what a customer is willing to
pay for a product or service is not a skill, it's an art. One of the common
mistakes made in approaching this process is to focus on how to realize
a price that allows the company to achieve a desired rate of return. The
desire to realize a return has nothing to do with the customer's perceived
value of a product. As a matter of fact, awareness of the cost can confuse

the process. The effort to identify willingness to pay should focus on *what a solution to a given problem is worth* to the customer.

Identifying willingness to pay can be a challenge for a new product or service. The process starts with determining the solutions that are offered by the product or service. Attaching a value to the physical product or service delivered is secondary. The customer first pays for the expectation of receiving a certain result or group of results. Information technology delivers, after all, active products and services. The customer's secondary considerations are the physical characteristics attached to the product or delivery of a service. Once the desire to attain a solution to a problem is quantified, the researcher can then assess the value of physical characteristics associated with delivering that solution.

There are a number of ways to approach this effort. Asking members of the target market can provide direction; however, finding hard numbers always carries more value. Determining the amount of money that has already been spent to solve the problem can provide a solid foundation for this effort. The product manager or researcher can identify the prices paid for other solutions to the problem that deliver comparable results. While these solutions may be provided by products that are in no way similar to the product being priced, it does provide a measure of what a solution is worth to the customer. If the customer paid for multiple products and services to resolve a problem, the cumulative price of acquiring and using these products must be calculated. This is the *comparable price.* The existence of a comparable price does not mean that the customer will be willing to spend that amount of money again, nor does this figure represent the maximum that the customer might be willing to pay. The total amount paid for comparable results provides a starting point for assessing other factors that contribute to willingness to pay.

One of the primary factors that will determine what a customer will pay for a product or service is the *perceived value* that he or she believes that product will deliver. The perceived value may be less than, or greater than, what customers have paid for products that deliver comparable results. The perceived need is directly related to the customer's desire or need for a solution to the problem or set of problems. The perceived need adds dimension to the amount that has been paid for comparable results. It provides an unqualified target price for a product. The amount that has been paid shows that a customer may pay as much as, or as little as, that amount for the product. Together, the comparable price and perceived value give dimension to the target price. Of course, customers are usually not willing to pay more than the price of comparable products and services. Other factors must be considered to determine a realistic target market price.

Informed customers will add TCO to the price of the product when making a purchase decision. Others will have their expectations set by the price of products and services that are advertised to work in conjunction with the product. Regardless of the source of the associated costs believed necessary to use the product, they will have an impact on what the customer is willing to pay. The target price that we have discussed thus far is based on a solution to a problem. The product acceptance price will be its perceived contribution to the total solution. The customer's willingness to pay for the product, therefore, will be that percentage of the target price that they believe the product contributes to the solution.

The target market's willingness to pay is not determined simply by the comparable price, perceived value, and anticipated TCO. The target price must be further qualified to achieve the optimal market position. Several other factors will contribute to the qualification of the target price. The customer's likelihood to buy and willingness to pay will both be augmented by the cost or burden of having no solution to their problem. That is, the strength of their need or desire will drive the target price.

When you are not first to market, determining the target price is easier. The price that competitors charge for a comparable product or service is the starting point for determining the target price. A price performance comparison will allow the product manager to determine how the product stacks up to the competition. For a sample template, visit www.The5Ps.com/LEM/Price-Performance-Comparison.html

Once it is understood how the product compares to its competition, the implications of higher or lower price must be considered in conjunction with how the elements of the marketing mix will be applied. While a higher price for comparable features and functions might indicate a better product to some, it will be a deterrent for those prospective customers who are sensitive to the difference in price. Likewise, a lower price for comparable features and functions might indicate a better value to some; however, it may be a deterrent to those who feel that a higher price indicates a safer choice. The product manager must assess the temperament of the target market and decide on a target price that will win the most customers, given the feature–function mix.

In summary, the art to determining willingness to pay is in evaluating the factors identified previously, and assessing the impact that they will have on the customer's reception to the product or service. There is no magic formula for doing this. It is based upon knowledge of the prospective customers, or target market, and their willingness to receive the product as a solution to their problem(s). The perceived value of the solution and every element of the marketing mix will ultimately determine the market price of a product or service.

Structuring

Determining the amount that the customer is willing to pay is a critical step in the pricing process; however, the pricing *structure* (see Table 2.1) is an equally important step. The structure of the price defines to the customer the amount and the manner in which they will pay for the product. It lets the customer know whether or not they can afford the product. The pricing structure also communicates other elements of the marketing strategy. It defines the desire to sell direct or through third parties. It supports the decision to use heavy promotion to sell a large volume. The structure is an important element of the pricing strategy.

The pricing structure determines the discounts that are given to channel partners. Channel partners are the distributors, resellers, and other companies that sell the product. These companies might include those given in Table 2.2.

Table 2.1 Types of pricing structures

TYPES OF PRICING STRUCTURES	
One Time, Up Front Price	Most popular, easy to understand and administer
Recurring Payments	Common for services, financing
Buy-In Plus Recurring Payments	Commitment driven, financing
Bundled	Hidden discounts or margins
Volume or Incentive Discounts	Drives customer and reseller behavior

Table 2.2 Types of companies

TYPES OF COMPANIES	WHAT THEY SELL
Telecommunications	Telephones, computers, and other network access devices
Systems Integrators	Software, hardware, and network subscriptions for turnkey systems that they deliver
Accounting Firms	Software and hardware for accounting systems that they implement
Commercial Office Developers	Telecommunications systems to their tenants
Airlines	Access to wireless networks to their passengers
Automobile Companies	Subscriptions to wireless networks for vehicle-based systems

Table 2.3 Price discount by channel partner

PRICE DISCOUNT BY CHANNEL PARTNER		
Channel Partners	Value Added for Vendor	Discount Rate[1]
Distributors	Warehousing, Financing, etc.	55%
Retail Stores	Sales, Training, etc.	50%
Value Added Resellers	Sales, Installation, Training, etc.	40%
Systems Integrators	Development, Installation, Sales, etc.	40%
Large Volume Customers		35%
[1]These are sample rates. Actual rates will vary by type of product, company, country, etc.		

As the number and scope of IT applications expands beyond traditional applications, so do the companies who resell IT-based products and services. The willingness to pay determines the amount that the customer will actually dispense for the product. The suggested retail price, or SRP, is the advertised price of the product. The difference is the margin, or the amount that channel partners will earn on the product. The margin must, of course, be large enough to encourage third-party resellers to carry the product.

Discounts that are given to channel partners (Table 2.3) and to direct customers must be managed so as to drive purchase behavior in the right direction and also avoid channel conflict. If the marketing strategy is to move low volume purchases through third-party channels, the largest discounts should be given to those parties that are expected to handle the largest volume of product. Distributors, for example, are often given deep discounts and other incentives to encourage them to sell product to low volume channel partners. Of course, volumes can be managed by setting minimum purchase requirements. The discount structure will also communicate these intentions and reinforce purchase requirements.

The pricing structure should be constructed to complement the value that each type of channel partner delivers in an effort to minimize channel conflict. Discounts are not the only means to give definition to pricing structure. Payment terms and conditions can also be used to drive purchase behavior. Lenient payment schedules and financing assistance will motivate both channel partners and direct customers to purchase. Likewise, re-stocking fees and other post-purchase associated fees will encourage caution and care in purchasing. The different types of pricing structures are only limited by the creativity of those people constructing them. When new elements are added to a pricing structure, thought should be given to the impact that it has on the behavior of customers as well as third-party resellers. This includes, but is not limited to, keeping the pricing structure simple so that it is easy to understand and administer.

One popular way of changing the pricing structure is to bundle it for sale with one or more other products or services. Bundling serves many purposes. It is a means to give an effective discount without amending the discount schedule. It is a means to augment and test the value of products and services offered by third-party resellers. Bundling also provides effective promotion for a new or slow moving product by grouping it with a product that sells well. As is the case with discounts and other changes to the pricing structure, the effect that bundling has on the behavior of direct customers and channel partners must be considered to ensure the integrity of the pricing strategy and business relationships.

Another key role of the pricing structure is to make payment affordable to customers. Oftentimes, the cost of a total system solution is too expensive for an individual or even a business to pay for at one time. Leases, rentals, and other periodic payment plans offer customers options to paying everything up front. These financing plans offer different ownership options and payout schedules that provide the customer with varying tax benefits and cash management alternatives. For example, some leasing companies offer the option of bundling software and services with hardware so that a larger amount can be capitalized and, thus, the customer becomes eligible for tax write-off. The product manager should be aware of the effects that financing options have on price structure so that the product can become more affordable for the customer.

Payout schedules should match the perceived delivery of value to the customer ultimately using the product. For example, when payments extend beyond the useful life of the system, upgrade plans should include pricing options that allow leases, rentals, and other payment plans to be rolled over into the package for the new system. This helps to maintain the customer's confidence in their purchase decision and prepare them for migrating to the next generation product.

The product manager should be aware of and purposefully direct the ability of third-party resellers to offer flexible payment options to customers. The ability to offer financing is one of the value added benefits that vendors should look for in selecting a third-party reseller. Ensuring that this and other benefits are available to customers is the responsibility of the product manager.

It should be noted that although the product manager is responsible for ensuring that customers have what is necessary to purchase and use their product, the vendor need not be the sole source for everything. Providing financing for customers does not mean underwriting those funds. The purpose of banks and leasing companies is to ease the cost of products. Financial institutions make it possible, and sometimes easy, for customers to purchase products. It is the financial institution that determines credit worthiness and payment terms and conditions. The financial institution works with the customer to determine whether they should lease or rent. As the provider of financing to the consumer, the financial institution also assumes the risk of providing credit.

Financing is an important element in structuring the price of a product or service. While a financial institution typically provides credit, the vendor or a third-party reseller can also offer it. The risk of providing credit and the cost of administering it is assumed by the financing source. The product manager influences the structure of pricing by the selection of third-party resellers and the financial institutions it allies with. If the costs of providing credit and need to control price structure warrant it, the product manager may also elect to offer financing directly to customers and third-party resellers. The decision will be based upon who assumes financial exposure, the cost of administering credit, and the need to control pricing to manage its effect on the marketing mix.

While there are numerous ways that pricing can be structured, the majority of pricing models fall into one of four categories:

- *One time, up front price.* This is the most popular and simplest form of pricing. The customer makes one payment and receives the product or system solution that they have purchased. This payment may also include technical support for a defined period of time.

- *Recurring payments.* Many public networks and other IT service based offerings charge in equal periods (i.e., monthly) for their services. These regular, recurring charges may be based on services used or it could be a fixed payment for a defined level of service provided. Financing provided by the vendor, third-party reseller, or a financial institution also allows products and services to be paid for by payments made in equal time periods. Regular, recurring payments are easier to budget and are also more affordable for most customers.

- *Buy-in plus recurring payments.* Many custom system providers and financial options require an initial payment that covers all or part of the cost of acquiring a product or IT system. The initial payment is followed by a series of payments for the product or system. The initial payment is required to buy into the product or system. It is a display of commitment to complete implementation or continue using the product or service. The following, recurring payments ease cash outlay requirements for the customer and help cash flow for the provider.

- *Bundled (sold together with other products).* Bundling is grouping the price of an individual product or service with other, often complementary, products or services. This form of pricing allows the seller to offer discounts by combining low margin and high margin products together. Conversely, it also allows the seller to earn additional revenue by including products and services that may not have otherwise been purchased. Bundling also makes it possible to finance products and services that otherwise would not qualify by including them with other products (i.e., hardware) that can be readily financed.

Discounts, financing, and other factors that dictate the manner in which the product or service is paid for determine the price structure. Price schedules and discount schedules reflect the base pricing structure and drive behavior of customers and third-party resellers. The product manager directs the price structure through the selection of third-party resellers that offer financing and the selection of affiliated financial institutions.

Price structure is not solely a financial decision; it is also a marketing decision. The price structure influences the ability of a customer to purchase a product. Additionally, the price structure helps to facilitate the customer moving to the next generation product.

Promotion

Promotion is the collection of items and methods that communicate the value of a product to prospective customers, and lets them know why they should buy. In its broadest sense, promotion includes advertising, exhibitions, conferences, sponsorships, press releases, giveaway items, and even coupons. The items and methods that constitute promotion are used to attract the attention and raise the desire of prospective customers. To achieve that, the marketer must know how to reach the target market.

Reaching Target Markets

To win the race,
You must first know where you're going.

To develop an effective promotion program you must first know at whom you wish to direct it. Reaching the target market requires knowing who it is. The needs, desires, location, and habits of the target market help to identify the most effective means to communicate with them. In order to reach the target market you must know who they are, where they are, what they want, and why they want it. Understanding these things helps you to determine how to capture their attention.

Ideally, marketing begins by identifying a group of people with an unmet need. Creating a solution to that unmet need drives the development or creation of a product or service. Whether the target market is identified before or after the existence of a product or service, the common characteristics that they share define who they are. The most compelling characteristics that will underlie the promotional strategy are not demographic, but rather, those that surround their reason for buying. Nevertheless, the demographic characteristics do help define the market and should be understood.

Profession, gender, age, race, income, and religion are demographic characteristics that are often used to define a target market. But people who differ in these characteristics often share the same needs, desires, and habits. *Promotion that appeals to these demographic characteristics is not as effective as promotion that appeals to the need and desire for a given solution.*

What members of the target market will purchase is driven by their needs and desires. Understanding their needs and desires, therefore, will help to define the hot buttons that contribute to the promotional plan. Needs are fundamental; desires are opulent. People *need* food, clothing, and shelter; they need the time and money to provide for these things. Managers need to fulfill their basic responsibilities. People *desire* vacations, fancy cars, and big houses. Some desire status symbols such as these to feel a higher level of achievement. Some managers desire to excel in given functions to earn a promotion. It is not enough to understand *what* the target market needs; the marketer must understand *why* they need and desire these things.

Most people strive to earn at least a base level of money. This responds to the need to provide the basics for survival. Some strive to be the first with a new product or using a new service. This fuels the desire for having a status symbol. It is important to understand the distinction between what people want and why they want it. The *what* is the need or desire; the *why* is the motivation for the need or desire. The reasons why people need or desire something may vary. While this may seem obvious, marketers tend to forget this when delving into target markets. Once there is a consistency among one or more reasons why within a group of people, there is a set of common characteristics to define them as a target market. These reasons constitute the motivational criteria that, in turn, inspire the buying criteria. Buying criteria are formulated based upon the features and functions of a product or service that is believed to satisfy a need or want. For example, a mobile professional may want a notebook computer that is less than 3 pounds. A corporate chief technology officer (CTO) may want a telecommunications system with features and functions that are beyond the requirements of the company. The motivational criteria are what compel people to buy. The mobile professional may have a back ailment that is aggravated by carrying heavy bags. The corporate CTO may be preparing the company to handle employees from an impending acquisition. Understanding the common characteristics of the target market that compel them to buy helps to create the foundation for a sound promotional strategy.

People who are members of a target market may live and work in a single geographical area or they may be dispersed across a broad area, even throughout the world. The target market may have a proclivity for attending certain events. They may frequent particular stores, restaurants, or sporting events. It is important to understand as much about the target market as possible, including their location. Knowing the location of the target market tells you where communications should be directed.

Knowing where to direct communications can also be determined by understanding the habits of the target market. Habits indicate where people focus their attention. Reading, writing, watching television, participating in sports and other extracurricular activities are some of the habits that point to communications media. For example, newspapers, magazines, and newsletters are publications that are read regularly by many people. Many people watch television programs regularly. Some people go to health clubs, attend sports games, or visit restaurants regularly. The places and things that people focus their attention on are prime for promotional communications. In conclusion, by identifying the common habits of members of the target market, the marketer can determine the communications media through which most of the target market can be reached.

To develop an effective promotion plan it is necessary to understand the target market. This not only means knowing their needs and desires, but also being aware of their motivational and buying criteria. Once the message has been developed using this information, it can be delivered to the right places by knowing where members of the target market are located and their habits. Thorough understanding of the target market is the first step in developing the promotional plan.

Logos and Branding (Creating a Memory)

A picture is worth a thousand words.

FedEx ®

Reliable. Trustworthy. Efficient. Fast. Move Envelopes, Packages & Freight. Pickup. Dropoff. Delivery. Global. Confirmation. Tracking. Supply Chain. Fulfillment. And more....

Images communicate a wealth of information in a minimal amount of space. Themes provide the stage for delivering a series of messages that

FedEx service mark used by permission.

tell a story. Together, they can be used to attract the attention of prospective customers. A catchy image and theme that portrays a solution to the needs or desires of the target market can provide the *hook* that draws their interest. One of the most widely recognized logos in the world, FedEx[3] has introduced inspiring themes over the years. All of their themes, along with the logo, accentuate the positive image and quality service their customers expect and enjoy. A captivating image alone is not a logo; and a logo is not a brand. To understand the options the marketer has to create a memory in the minds of the target market, let us understand the steps to create a logo, and then a brand, starting with the image.

Types of Images

Images can be people, animals, places, or an object. Those used in a logo should be distinctive and memorable. Images are often accompanied by themes. Themes can be delivered using words or music. Advertisers and promoters will capture the theme with a byline. The method of delivering the theme should complement the image that it accompanies. It gives substance to the image. The strength and lasting memory of the promotional message will usually come from the image. The image is not just the visual item, it is the memory left in one's mind from the picture, words, and sounds that they represent. It is important, therefore, to understand the considerations for choosing the image to represent a product or service.

Using people as a primary image can be a double-edged sword. Many marketers prefer to use a character that represents a specific type of person or profession. The Pillsbury doughboy, for example, denotes someone who loves to eat food made with flour. Recognized personalities bring immediate recognition; however, the product's image becomes tied to the public's acceptance of their personal life. Many companies have spent time and money on damage control after celebrities who represented them were involved in public situations that severely damaged their reputation. History is littered with companies that have had to revamp their advertising campaigns and abandon celebrities as spokespeople when they became embroiled in negative controversy. On the other hand, the popularity of a public figure can initially establish recognition and credibility for the product or service they represent. Several companies have found tremendous success using recognized personalities to represent their products. Bell Atlantic warmed the hearts of consumers with commercials featuring James Earl Jones. The pros and cons of using personalities versus a character, therefore, must be carefully evaluated before making a decision.

As with people, when animals are used as the image they can be real, living animals or characters. Many animals have a special connotation for many people. For example, tigers represent strength and danger; cheetahs represent speed; and eagles represent freedom. Of course, these meanings may change in different cultures or in other areas of the world.

Nevertheless, animals can be used to depict the image that a marketer may seek. They can also be replaced and trained with another virtually identical animal, should the need arise. Places or objects can also represent images. Places can be a specific location or a depiction of a locale that carries a certain meaning. The dome of the United States capitol is used to represent companies offering services that are delivered in Washington, D.C., the capital city, or "capital"-like products or services throughout the entire country. A nonspecific location, such as a lake, may be used to represent products or services that are associated with a body of water. As is the case with personalities, the meaning associated with a specific location can change. While this may not be as likely to occur, or may not happen as often with locations, careful evaluation and thought must be given to the selection of a specific location for a product's image. It is common for an object to represent a product's image. The lines, shape, and design of an object can depict movement, energy, fashion, or meaning that portray the thought, feeling, or emotion that should accompany use of the product or service. The lines and shape of the Motient logo, for example, depict the movement of radio waves that carry the network's transmissions.

These transmissions are the essence of the service that the company provides. The design of the logo allows for multimedia effects to be applied. The movement of multimedia effects helps to give life to the meaning that the object portrays. Whenever possible, the object design should be versatile enough to allow it to be adaptable to all media forms that may be used in promotion.

The colors of an object can represent feelings, physical characteristics, and other traits that the marketer wants to associate with their product. The black, gray, and red colors of the DiscoverIT^{TM4} logo, for example, symbolize power, intelligence, and energy. The purple and orange colors in the FedEx Express logo, on the other hand, symbolize imagination and action to some. Note that various FedEx operating units have a different second color in their version of the logo. The selection of color can be a very strategic step in the logo design.

Elicit a Thought

Whether the marketer chooses to use personalities, animals, places, or an object, a primary purpose of the product's image and theme is to elicit a thought, feeling, or emotion. A thought gives rise to an evaluation process that may ultimately lead to a purchase decision. A feeling is physical. It generally takes place after an action has taken place. An emotion is spiritual. It is incited by the passionate reaction to a thought. Emotion is a powerful force. A person's emotion will help to form their opinions and future actions. Positive emotion will encourage an action to receive that positive feeling again. A picture of the sun and sand or the sound of lively music will often be associated with comfort and happiness, prompting one to take a vacation. A picture of an alcoholic drink and a mangled car might be associated with death, discouraging drunk driving. When fear is elicited, people will by nature take steps to avoid actions that will make the action of the fear become a reality. Emotion will also help them to remember certain things or events associated with that emotion. When someone has a great vacation at a certain hotel, they will likely remember that hotel chain when selecting their next vacation. Contrarily, when someone is hurt in an accident caused by fire, the typical result is to avoid situations where hot objects or unsafe conditions may be encountered.

Many people enjoy the feeling of exhilaration and excitement when they find information or a location on the Internet using the Yahoo! search engine.

YAHOO!

Reproduced with permission of Yahoo! Inc. ©2013
Yahoo! Inc. YAHOO! and the YAHOO! logo are registered trademarks of Yahoo! Inc.

This logo *is not* an interjection, however, but considered an acronym by some for "Yet Another Hierarchical Officious Oracle." The founders of Yahoo! insist the name was selected because of its definition of "rude, unsophisticated, uncouth." Regardless of the initial intention, Yahoo! is one of the most widely recognized brands in the world and carries multiple positive meanings that are nested in the mind of its current and future customers.

The ability to elicit an emotion is a powerful tool in advertising and promotion. As the foundation for promotion, the image and theme should portray a message that allows desired emotions to be evoked. There are many techniques for accomplishing this, such as subliminal advertising. This and other techniques will be addressed later in this book.

The Logo

A company's logo consists of an image, often accompanied by a theme that represents it to the world. The logo should be consistent and memorable so that it will vigorously promote the company's mission for a long period of time. A logo should embody the following characteristics:

- *Message*: The marketer should decide the most important thought about their product the customer should understand. This is likely the most important reason that a customer would purchase the product or service. That thought should be clearly and succinctly communicated in the message.
- *Lasting*: The message and image of the logo should remain in the mind of the prospective customer or influencer as long as possible. Memorization techniques such as association, visualization, LOCI, and others may be incorporated into the

presentation of the logo to increase its staying power. This can be done in milliseconds!
- *Functional*: The logo should be adaptable to all media formats as well as transferable to multiple media. It should be well defined for print, scalable for digital, animated for multimedia, and more.
- *Distinguishable*: There should be no confusion with other logos or brands. The marketer should be able to protect the logo and secure a trademark or service mark. The mark should also be enforceable.

The logos and brands presented meet these standards. The FedEx logo, for example, clearly communicates fast, forward moving, and precise.

The arrow between the "E" and "x" accentuates these concepts, along with other features of the logo. This logo, created in 1994, is one of the most highly recognized logos in the world. It is seen in many media and locations, having proven adaptable with different colors of the "Ex" to represent various FedEx operations. People around the world recognize FedEx. There is no confusion what service and company this logo represents; it is quite distinguishable.

Branding

The purpose of a brand is to create a visual, audible, and emotional image that creates a lasting impression in the conscious and unconscious mind of the prospective customer. A brand is not just a logo, the message communicated in advertising and promotion, or the places where your product or service can be purchased. The essence of a brand is the *purpose, value, and principles* you want to represent. The brand essence is given substance by the manner in which the 5 Ps are created and deployed to convey the principles and value of your product. Is it high end? Is it the most cost

FedEx service mark used by permission.

effective? Is it the lowest price? Does it appeal to the largest cross section of the market? Is there a unique characteristic of your product that no one can match? Once your brand has been clearly defined, every single element of the 5 Ps should be developed and rolled out in support of that brand. This includes the logo and all elements of promotion, product, place, packaging, and price. Most importantly, the marketing mix should be blended to drive home the essence of the brand.

The Discover*IT* brand was first used commercially in 1989 or 1993 (United States Patent and Trademark Office, June 1998), began receiving international exposure in 1998, and the trademark was granted in 2002. The Discover*IT* product line was launched in 1995 using the original logo. Soon the current logo was designed; the Discover*IT* brand was broadened with the addition of seminars, conferences, exhibits, and advisory services. The Discover*IT* Showcases were launched in 1999, making history when President William Jefferson Clinton became the first sitting President to visit a commercial exhibition to see the history making presentation of new and emerging technologies. Within the first 3 years, the Discover*IT* Showcases exploded with over 300% growth as leading companies in wireless and mobile computing participated. The new logo is displayed prominently at major events and in millions of pieces of collateral sent to virtually everyone in the technology marketplace. The Discover*IT* logo was designed to tell a story and instill a thought that remained in the subconscious of all who could benefit from or recommend the brand's products and services. Discover*IT* is a double entendre that has also been used for the education, analysis, development, and delivery of all business and management products and services. It is presented as Discover "I" "T": for Information Technology and Discover "it" as the *thing* that is discovered as a result of our products and services. There are a series of black concentric circles to the left of the word Discover*IT* with a red exclamation point inside the smallest circle. This is symbolic of the journey of entering the unknown (tunnel from concentric circles) to learn about or discovering (the exclamation point) the wonder and value of technology. The gray curve represents that calming effect once the intelligence is gained from understanding new concepts. The red line underneath the wording accentuates the power of discovering something new and powerful. The impact of the colors in the logo was described in the earlier section, Types of Images (p. 87). Finally, the design is highly adaptable to multimedia effects that give life to the meaning of this logo and brand.

Do you need a brand to be successful? No. It depends on what you're selling and to whom you're selling it. There are many products produced on the same manufacturing lines that carry multiple brand names. These are often products that deliver strong profits over an extended period of time with no brand or unknown brands and innocuous names that are price sensitive and appeal to a broad market. Remember, a brand is more than a product and substantial profits can be earned from nonbranded products.

The astute marketer will determine whether to brand and the amount of resources to be invested in branding based on a long list of factors. These include, but are not limited to those given in Table 2.4.

Branding can be an expensive and long-term process that consumes considerable resources. It can box you into a position that may cost considerable resources to get out of (the position). Yet, the power of branding is formidable. The reach of the Internet and influence of social media have leveled the playing field a bit when it comes to building brands. The marketing strategy must give careful thought to the role of the brand to be created and the amount of resources that will be invested in creating and maintaining that brand. Power branding requires the effective use and interaction of all elements of the marketing mix. It is the power of the mix that allows a brand to captivate the customers in the market.

Table 2.4 Resources to be invested in branding*

• The size of the target markets	• The life cycle
• The optimum price point	• Recurring or follow-on revenue
• The margin	• The potential depth and breadth of the brand
• Delivery options	• Role in corporate strategy
• Longevity (TCO for the customer)	

Note: *Presentation version at www.The5Ps.com/LEM/Table_2-4.html

Advertising

Advertising is the communication of a message to a target market to incent the purchase of a product or service. The message is often delivered using a theme or image that portrays a concept that the target market can identify with, understand, and retain. Advertisements should be attention grabbing to establish awareness of the product or service with members of the target market. Advertisements should also be distinctive, clearly understood, and memorable.

A variety of media may be used to communicate the advertising message. As one of the components of promotion and an element of the marketing mix, advertising must support the overall marketing strategy and plan. This is achieved through the meaning of the message that is communicated and the manner in which it is best delivered to members of the target market.

To construct a message with the desired meaning, the marketer must understand the thought process of the prospective customers in the target market. To ensure that the message is received as intended, the marketer must develop and adhere to an effective media plan.

Thought Process

The mind is a powerful and complex entity. It absorbs a myriad of concepts and processes, using methods and experiences that are ever changing. The marketer's quest to understand the mind has given rise to the black box model. The black box model has been espoused by marketers as a tool to predict buyer behavior. Complex black box models built upon multivariate analysis are used to identify the buying responses displayed by consumers as a result of interacting with identified stimuli. Despite the variants to the human thought process, the black box theory of buyer behavior can be described in stages that are fairly constant for most. There are several stages to the human thought process. It is important to understand these stages to understand how prospective customers move from the introduction of a concept to taking action on it. The phases are

- awareness;
- interest;

- comprehension;
- evaluation;
- decision;
- action.

Awareness.   A person is made aware of a concept when it is introduced into their consciousness. While concepts can be introduced using any of the basic senses—sight, feeling, hearing, smell and taste—most advertising uses seeing or hearing to deliver concepts. Astute marketers will employ many of the 20 or more human senses. People often receive advertisements by looking at them or listening to them. These are the methods through which the concepts that underlie ads are introduced into the human consciousness. Awareness from advertising usually starts with the delivery of a message through sight or sound.

Interest.   Once a person has been made aware of a concept, they may have a very high level of interest or none at all. The degree of interest depends on their own needs and wants as well as the extent to which the delivery of the message stimulates their curiosity. When a person has established interest in a concept, they are willing to spend some time and energy to contemplate its real meaning and implications.

Comprehension.   Comprehension involves determining the meaning behind a concept. It means listening to the message that delivers the concept, relating it to your own experiences, and considering the implications to you and those around you. This stage of the thought process entails developing a basic understanding of the concept.

Evaluation.   The next step in the thought process is to evaluate the meaning to determine whether it warrants additional effort. This involves weighing the implications against the pros and cons of the effects on the individual. The evaluation stage involves assembling all of the information necessary to make a decision on whether action is warranted as a result of the person's take on the concept introduced.

Decision.   Making a decision on taking action is the next step in the thought process. The person weighs the pros and cons to determine whether action is warranted. A decision to take action is based on the extent to which the concept and its implications will have an effect on the person's lifestyle or well being.

Action.   After a decision has been made, the final step in the thought process is to take action or refrain from it. The existence or absence of action is one measure of an advertisement's effectiveness.

The human thought process can take place in a split second or it could transpire over an extended period of time. Whether the advertisement addresses all or part of the human thought process, the creator of the ad should take all steps in the process into account.

Media Plan

Developing a creative and influential ad is only the foundation of advertising. In order for the ad to be effective, it must be deployed using an effective media plan. This is what brings ads to life. The media plan consists of five components:

- Reach target markets
- Support marketing strategy
- Media types
- Measurements used
- Implementation

Reach target markets.   The first objective of the media plan is to gain exposure to as many members of the target market as possible. Reaching the target market is the name of the game. The size of the audience is a popular statistic in measuring the reach of advertising. Of more importance, however, is the profile of the audience. It is the audience profile that will help the marketer to determine to what extent the audience being reached matches the target market being sought. The media plan should identify, therefore, the optimal combination of advertising media that will effectively reach the target market.

Support marketing strategy.   The media plan must also support the marketing strategy. The marketing strategy defines how the 5 Ps—product, packaging, promotion, price, and place—will be applied to achieve the desired profit targets. The media plan must effectively convey how the features and functions of the product may be used to deliver the value that members of the target market seek. It must accurately communicate the extent to which the packaging facilitates ease of use. The media plan also complements other forms of promotion while allowing the product to be sold in quantities and at a price that meets profit targets. Finally, media selected should reach an audience that has the means to access the product's sales and distribution channels. A media plan that supports the marketing strategy is necessary if the marketer is to achieve overall success.

Media types.   There are several different types of media including television, newspapers, magazines, the Internet, and others. The effectiveness of each media type is dependent upon several factors such as the size and composition of the audience, the ease of communicating the message, its ability to invoke the thought process, and its role in supporting the marketing strategy. The advertising budget must also be allocated among the media types to maximize the effectiveness of the advertising campaign. The selection of media types is the essence of the media plan. It is the combination of media types that determines the reach and penetration of the advertising message.

Measurements used.   The effectiveness and success of a viable plan is tracked by predefined measurements that are established in the plan itself. Specific measurements for each media type should be determined and goals set for the ads run over each. Although sales revenue is the ultimate measure of advertising success, it is often very difficult to tie specific forms of advertising to the sales achieved. The measurements established to determine the success of the media plan are, therefore, important in reassessing the content, frequency, and combination of media types used in the media plan. For specific examples, see The Raison D'être: Making It Worthwhile (Chapter 3).

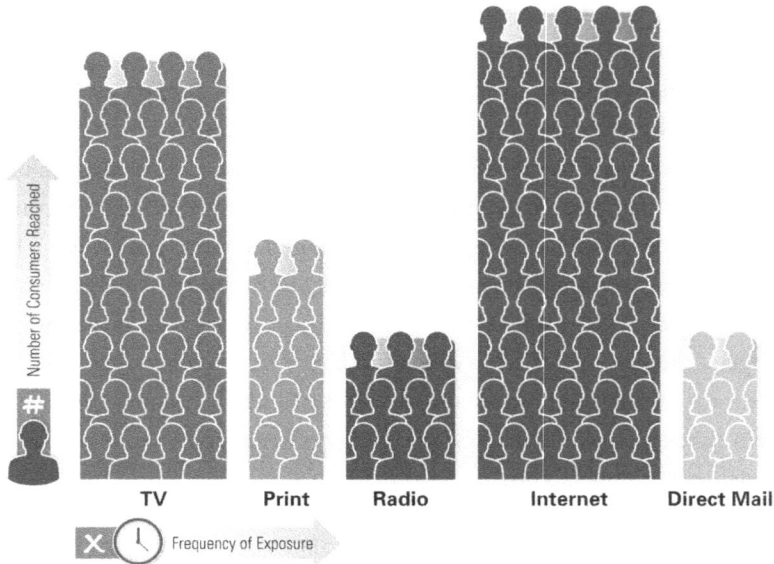

Figure 2.14   Media plan

Implementation.   Frequency is a critical element in the optimal implementation of the media plan. Ads in most media must be run repeatedly,
over a period of time, to be effective. Timing is also important. Product
seasonality, peak rating periods, competitive activity, and other factors all
contribute to the decision of when to run ads. The implementation cycle
of an advertising campaign is demonstrated in a media schedule. When
the media schedule is graphically depicted (as in Figure 2.14), it is easier
to see the pattern of media selection and use over the planning period.
This helps the marketer to visualize the planned effects of the media plan
at a glance.

Other—Marketing Communication (Marcom)

The essence of a sound promotion plan is to attract the attention of the
target market while explaining how your product meets their buying
criteria. Capturing attention of the intended audience is first accomplished by delivering a *hook* that appeals to their interest. The hook could
be an image, sound, words, or combination of these. The hook can elicit
shock value, excitement, sympathy, or another emotion that appeals to

the interest of targeted customers. As the interest is captured, the promotional message moves quickly and smoothly into the reasons why the product or service should be purchased. The reasons need not be stated blatantly; rather they should flow from the tone of the message. These reasons should focus on convincingly demonstrating that the product or service meets the buying criteria of the target market. Once this has been achieved, the promotional message concludes by directing the targeted customer to the location or means to purchase the product or service.

Promotional messages can be delivered through advertisements, collateral, giveaway items, salespeople, or on product packaging. The message can be delivered at one time or through a series of sequential or related messages.

Trade Shows

Trade shows have been a popular means of promotion for many years. In the IT industry, trade events serve as a forum for companies to work together, forming alliances to deliver end-to-end systems and staying abreast of regulatory and other developments. Trade shows can contribute to a company's financial efforts by attracting venture capitalists and validating the company as a real player in the industry. Trade shows can contribute to a company's manufacturing and operations functions by attracting suppliers and service companies who might improve these functions. The primary purpose of trade shows, however, is to contribute to the company's marketing efforts. Specifically, trade shows are used to promote the company's products and services.

Trade shows provide exposure to

- prospective customers who attend the event;
- media attending the event;
- other companies and government entities looking for business partners.

Prospective customers.   Representatives from companies attend trade shows to view products and attend conferences that are often part of the event. These company representatives may control the budget for IT products and services, they may influence the budget, or they may merely serve as an entrée to the company. Collecting contact information from these company representatives, or gathering leads, is a primary goal of participating in trade shows for vendors. Confirming that the majority of these leads are prospective customers, or qualified leads, is one of the key measurements of results from trade shows.

Media.   Gathering leads that qualify as prospective customers is not the only objective of attending trade shows. Gaining exposure to media is another critical objective of trade events. Companies often use trade events to announce products, extend a promotional campaign, and strengthen their image. Journalists, publishers, reporters, analysts, and other members of the media regularly attend trade events to learn about what's new and to stay abreast of technology. Companies not only want to put their best foot forward when these people visit their booths or attend presentations; they also want to attract their attention. While exhibits, advertisements, and other forms of promotion may attract the attention of the media, their rapt attention is best secured before the trade event. Press announcements might solicit a visit from the media to your booth and scheduled press briefings are effective means of getting the media's attention. Trade events are often attended by an array of media representatives and thus provide a cost effective opportunity to extend the reach of your promotional message.

Other companies and Government entities.   In addition to the media, trade events are also attended by businesses and government entities that are looking for companies to invest in or partner with. Venture capitalists and other investors who are seeking to identify or further qualify companies with growth potential sometimes visit trade shows to learn about these companies or their competitors, suppliers, or resellers. Companies and government agencies that are looking for companies to supply products and services, resell their products, or establish an office or manufacturing plant in their locale attend trade shows to identify such companies or meet with their executives. Trade shows provide a time and cost efficient means to learn or conduct several meetings within a short timeframe. Trade shows provide valuable exposure to companies that participate in them.

Whether the goal is to identify prospective customers, gain attention from the media, meet potential investors, identify resellers or other business partners, trade shows can benefit companies that select them carefully and plan their participatory role far in advance.

Sponsorships.   Marketers can grab the attention of a target market by paying for events or activities in exchange for exposing their name, products, and services to people viewing or attending that event. In addition to receiving exposure, sponsoring companies may also receive lead lists or reduced rate advertising and promotion. Sponsorship opportunities might include sporting events, seminars, conferences, or community groups. The type and scope of sponsorship opportunities is only limited by the creativity of the event producer. The value of sponsorships to the marketer is based on the number of prospective customers that will be reached and the extent to which these members of the target market will receive and retain the promotional message.

Promotional Items.   The primary purpose of promotional items is to attract the attention of prospective customers. These items might include cups, t-shirts, clocks, or anything that would draw the interest of members of the target market. Promotional items may include the company name, product name, logo, theme, or any combination of these. The choice of the item is based on the need to attract attention; the message of the promotional item is meant to initiate the buying process.

Promotional items that are lasting, or used over a long period of time, have a prolonged opportunity to communicate the message or buying incentive to the prospective customer as well as to other potential customers. These items are often also informative. They may display a phone number or web address so that the interested party can obtain additional information on the product or service. Product specifications and detailed descriptions may be provided from product literature that is sent to the prospect or displayed on the website. Questions may be answered by information on the website or by hotline representatives. Promotional items that immediately or eventually move a prospect along the buying process by encouraging them to seek additional information have proven themselves as a viable contribution to the marketing mix.

Some promotional items include a preview or portion of the product itself. Videos delivered over the Internet or on digital media show how products are used and how they benefit the customer. Limited or even full-featured versions of software products are offered at no cost to prospective customers who may use it to determine if it meets their needs. Demos help customers to demystify technical products and services by allowing them to experience the value of their use. Offering demo products is akin to an *assumed close*. That is, the marketer takes steps toward post-purchase behavior such as scheduling implementation or making payment arrangements with the assumption that the customer will indeed purchase their product or services. Giving away a full-featured demo product is a calculated promotional risk. The marketer must have tremendous confidence that a high percentage of those who receive a demo product will purchase it.

Coupons.   Coupons are another type of promotional item that offers an increased incentive to purchase the product or service. Coupons usually offer financial incentives in the form of an immediate price reduction, complementary products at no additional cost, or price reductions on products purchased in the future. Not only do coupons attract attention, but they also ease the purchase decision by lowering the cost of acquiring or owning the product.

Place

Even the most compelling product that has captured the interest of the target market will not generate revenue if the customer cannot purchase it. This P of marketing—place—determines where the sales will take place and how the product or service is delivered to the customer. More commonly referred to as the channel, place is the assortment of methods and locations through which customers can finalize their purchase decision or take delivery of the product. In order to choose and manage the optimal selection of sales and delivery channels, the marketer must first understand what they are.

What is a Channel?

A channel is the means through which a product or service is delivered to the customer. A *sales channel* delivers product information and inducement for purchasing. A *distribution channel* delivers the physical product or actual service. Whether the role is to sell a product, warehouse it, or both, a channel is the conduit for providing the customer with a means to purchase and take delivery of a product or service.

It is important to understand the difference between a business partner and a channel partner. Companies might claim to be a channel without actually taking on the role and responsibilities associated with it. Assuming the position of a channel partner might help some companies to strengthen their relationship with the supplier or the customer. In the actual business process, only real channels deliver maximum value of *place* to the marketer.

A real sales channel takes orders and accepts money. A company that makes referrals is not a sales channel. A company that convinces a customer to purchase but does not take an order is not a sales channel. Even a company that takes an order but does not accept payment is not a real sales channel. These companies may be business partners and help to bring business to the producer of the product or service. They do not, however, have a direct or substantial financial stake in the generation of revenue from the products or services sold. A real sales channel depends on and controls the revenue from the products and services that it sells.

A real delivery or distribution channel warehouses and ships products, and also interfaces directly with the reseller or customer. A company that orders shipments but never takes ownership of the product or service is not a distributor. A company that takes ownership of the product or service but not of the relationship with the buyer is not a distributor. The distribution chain is marked by the movement of product. Assuming responsibility for the movement of a product or service means taking ownership of the item as well as the relationships. A real member of the distribution chain takes ownership of both.

The companies that provide an additional conduit for selling and delivering products are commonly known as channel partners. There are different types of sales channel partners just as there are different types of delivery channel partners.

It is important to distinguish between distributors and other delivery or distribution channel partners. The primary difference is the volume of product that they move. Distributors move the greatest amount of product and provide the support services that sustain this process. All distribution channel partners warehouse and ship products or services. In many cases, other distribution channel partners actually purchase the products and services that they sell from distributors.

There are also different types of sales channel partners or resellers. Some sell to different markets and others bundle the products and services into different solutions. For example, a sales channel partner might sell in locations that are not covered by the company that produces the product or service. Sales channel partners might also bundle the product into a customized system that fits the needs of a small market niche. While sales channel partners may operate in untapped markets, they also may compete head on with the producing company and other resellers.

Channel partners can move either products or services. In the world of information, technology products include PCs, telephones, and software on physical media. Services include telecommunications over network carriers or software accessed from the Internet. Product and services are what channel partners deliver or distribute. Support services are part of the added value that channel partners offer.

Channel partners offer value added services to customers who purchase from them. That itself is a benefit to the producing company. After all, happy customers are the source of what companies are in business for—revenue that leads to profit. Keeping customers happy is not the only advantage of channel partners. The benefits of having alternate sales and delivery channels are far greater to the producing company.

Distributors minimize the need for the producer of the product to interface directly with large numbers of customers who purchase smaller quantities of product. They provide a business buffer. As a matter of fact, channel partners assist and complement the producing company in many different ways including reaching new locations, delivering products and services rapidly, offering increased options for financing, and creating new solutions for their product or service. By offering many of the same products and services to the same customers, channel partners also compete with the producing company as well as with each other. In order to maintain the complementary value of channel partners, it is incumbent upon the producing company to maintain healthy competition and sustain a spirit of positive competition where appropriate.

Mastering Channel Management

A real delivery or distribution channel warehouses and ships products and also interfaces directly with the reseller or customer.

A real sales channel takes orders and accepts money; see What is a Channel? (p. 103).

Channel partners offer a clear and distinct advantage to any company that produces IT products and services. The marketer must, therefore, manage the conduct and operations of these partners so that they will continue to contribute to the marketing goals. Sales channel partners should be viewed as the marketer's allies. Delivery channel partners are the marketer's customers. The marketer must take steps to honor and protect the relationships of their allies and customers both within as well as outside of their company.

It should be clearly understood which target markets that each partner will service. When market overlap exists that gives rise to competition, all players should be made aware of the condition of the playing field and the ground rules. That is, all participants involved in the sale or delivery of the product or service should be made aware of the scope of the target market that they are servicing and what tools are available to assist them in their efforts. They should also be made aware of any sanctioned competition that may be faced. Participants include channel partners (i.e., indirect channels) and any groups hired by the producing company to sell and deliver products (i.e., direct channels); see Figure 2.15. These groups may include salespeople, mail order agents, and shipping companies. Participants in the sale and delivery of products and services should also understand the terms and conditions under which they may operate.

Since channel partners are also in business to make a profit, the major terms and conditions include what product or service they are allowed to sell, how much they must pay for it, and when they may take delivery. The marketer needs to structure programs so that these questions can be

DIRECT Channels

- Direct Sales
- Internet
- Television
- Mail Order

INDIRECT Channels

- Producer

- Distributors
- Value Added Resellers
- System Integrators
- Internet-based Companies
- Telemarketing
- Mail Order
- Liquidators

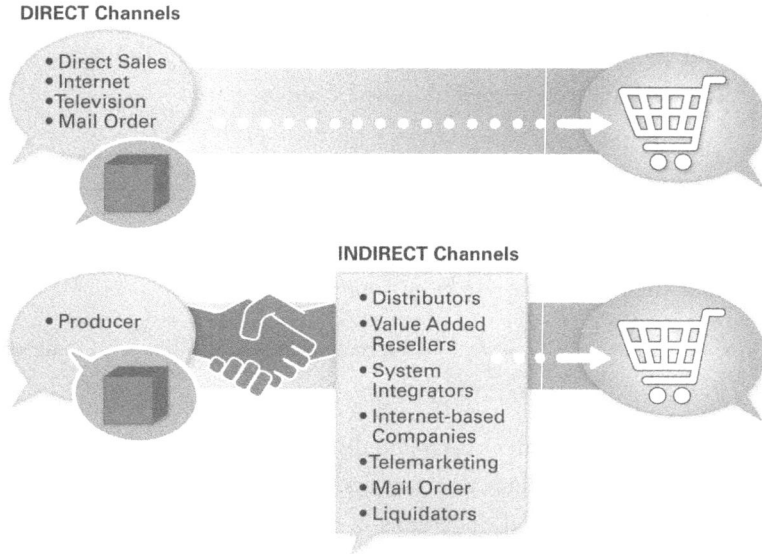

Figure 2.15 Types of channels

responded to fairly while adhering to the company's need to maintain its advantage in using channel partners.

To achieve this, the marketer must structure price schedules that drive large purchases to distributors while allowing all partners to earn a respectable profit. Financing programs should be encouraged, and supported where feasible, to provide end-user customers with purchase options. Channel partners should also be given any sales, administrative, and technical support that can be delivered cost effectively to help them successfully sell and deliver products.

In summary, mastering channel management is much more than providing partners with the tools and services that allow them to sell and deliver products and services for all. Channel management means understanding the strengths and weaknesses of partners and taking the steps to maximize the performance of all. This includes creating an environment for fair competition and encouraging co-opetition when it is mutually beneficial. No matter what, the marketing mix cannot be compromised. The ultimate goal of channel management is to maximize the contribution that the channel, or place, makes to the marketing mix. For the dominant sales and delivery channels for information technology visit www.The5Ps.com/LEM/IT-Channels.html

• Type of product	• Coverage of the target market
• Length of the sales cycle	• Customer access
• Complexity of the systems solution	• Channel conflict
• What's needed to complete solution	• Competition
• Technical support required	• Financing required by customers
• Obsolescence time	• Warehousing requirements

Figure 2.16 Factors for choosing channel partners

There are many factors that have to be considered when choosing channel partners and deciding the pricing, terms, and conditions to offer each one. These include, but are not limited to those in Figure 2.16. For an explanation of how these and other factors impact each of the aforementioned channels, www.The5Ps.com/LEM/Channels.html

Maintaining Product Control

One of the major dilemmas facing marketers is how to maintain product control and also maximize results from multiple channels. The marketer must give channel partners the flexibility to make sales while maintaining the integrity and control over the product. Information technology products and services must almost always be made to work together with other IT products to achieve the desired result for the customer. This opens the door for the product to be altered, or at the minimum, presented differently to the customer or end user. In addition to the product and its packaging, other elements of the marketing mix should be controlled when using multiple channels.

Other elements of the marketing mix can be used to help control the product and packaging. Let's first focus on the tactics and methods that can be used to directly control the product. One way to exert control over product and services sold and delivered through channel partners is to provide them technical support to assist them before, during, and after the sale. Pre-sale technical support for channel partners will help them to sell the products as they were intended to be used. It will also help to sell products in custom configurations that will work. Many hardware manufacturers allow their delivery partners to assemble products for their customers. Some channel partners, especially systems integrators and value-added resellers, regularly modify products or incorporate them into customized systems. Marketers who deliver technical support to channel partners during the development and delivery process have greater assurance that their products will function properly for the end user. Technical support may be delivered in the form of education, detailed documentation, a website, a telephone hotline, or on-site technicians. These technical support resources may also be used by channel partners to support customers who purchase products and services from them. Channel partners should be encouraged to take advantage of all technical support that is available to them. The more likely that channel partners are to use competent technical support resources, the greater control the marketer will have over their product or service.

Marketers can also exert control over their product or service by canceling the warranty on products or services that are modified in ways that do not conform to their technical specifications. Violations of the warranty should be clearly communicated to channel partners so that they will avoid making changes that jeopardize proper operation of the product.

Product control is not only necessary to ensure the quality and proper function of an IT product or service. Controls are also in place to protect the integrity of the channel. This includes ensuring that pricing and margins are protected, that the right level of support is provided, and other types of support to the channel partners are maintained. *Restricted product delivery* to certain channels works best when the marketer understands the channel partner. Certain channels typically sell and deliver to certain types of customers. For example, retail stores and mail order companies usually sell to consumers. Value-added resellers and systems integrators usually sell to businesses. Marketers may restrict the sale and delivery of certain products through certain channel partners. In many instances, low-end technology products are sold through consumer channels while more advanced technology products are sold through channels that service businesses. Although hybrid customers that do not clearly fit the consumer or business profile, such as small businesses, may sometimes not be properly served using this restricted product delivery method, it does work in most cases. When channel partners are informed of the types of customers who should use the products that they sell, and they act in the best interest of their customers, they will direct these customers to the best solution.

In addition to the methods that directly control the product or services, other elements of the marketing mix may be used to influence control over the product. Price is an excellent way to control who sells what. Discount schedules are structured to prevent or dissuade customers from purchasing products from some sources. When consumer oriented sales channels are able to sell products at a price that allows them to earn an acceptable return, their customers will more readily purchase from them than seek alternative sources. Comparable products at competitive prices make it worthwhile to shop locally rather than from high volume distributors (if that is an option). Likewise, purchase discounts encourage channel partners to sell a large volume of certain products.

Product control can also be exercised by restricting channel partners to defined target markets or territories. Products can also be serialized and tracked so that the product manager will know which partners sell products to customers that register their products. These measures are fairly restrictive for the channel partner and add unacceptable expense to the cost of the product.

In summary, channel partners offer considerable advantages for the marketer. The propensity for these partners to modify products or include them in customized systems creates a need for the marketer to take steps to maintain control over their products and services. There are many ways that product control can be exercised including delivering technical support to the channel partner and restricted delivery of certain products through certain channels. The objective of the marketer is to maintain product control without substantially increasing the cost of the product or restricting the ability of the channel partner to sell or deliver the product.

Building a Strong Channel Team

Just as the marketer identifies and defines their targeted customers, so should the targeted channel partners be identified. The selection of channel partners to help achieve the desired level of sales volume and customer satisfaction will depend on several factors:

Table 2.5 Selecting channel partners

FACTOR	CHARACTERISTICS—SUBCATEGORIES		
Type of Customer	Consumer, Small, Medium or Large Business, Resellers		
Average Sales Volume	Low	Med	High
Degree of Technical Complexity	Low	Med	High
Support Required	Financing Available and more		

Table 2.6 *Channel positioning*

Channel Positioning					
Customers	Consumers	Small Business	Medium Business	Large Businesses	Resellers

Particularly with high-tech products, provisions should be made to ensure that the technical skills and ancillary products are available to deliver a complete, functional solution to the customer. The partner should also offer financing options for customers who may require it to purchase the product. To avoid losing customers to competitors, the marketer must bridge the gap in the sales and delivery process so that it is just as easy to close deals with their product. For a full view of this chart (see Table 2.6), visit www.The5Ps.com/LEM/Channel-Positioning.html

The Marketing Mix

The ideal marketing mix combines the 5 Ps to optimize sale and delivery of IT products and services to maximize their long-term profitability.

Identifying the ideal marketing mix is not easy. There are numerous factors that must be taken into consideration; and these factors are ever changing. The ideal marketing mix may also mean the cannibalization of existing products and services. By mastering the marketing mix, the marketer can have control over the entire marketing process and deliver both short-term and long-term profits for the business entity.

Optimizing the Mix

The quintessential marketing plan is one in which the 5 Ps are combined in a manner that maximizes the opportunities presented by the needs and desires of the target markets. To win, the marketer must master the mix. This starts with knowing the market. The lives of consumers and businesses alike involve change. The social, economic, ecological, and political forces that shape our lives are continually changing. Our experiences shape our needs and desires. Our experiences influence our thoughts, moving us to seek things to meet our needs and desires. The introduction of IT stimulates the curiosity and imagination of virtually any group of people. The rate of technological development and new product introduction pushes the mind even further.

The combination of changing life forces and ever changing technological products creates a vibrant environment. This vibrancy drives the buying behavior of people. The result is a dynamic market. The dynamics of today's markets present a challenge for the marketer who seeks to meld the 5 Ps into the ideal mix.

Markets are not only dynamic, they are also elastic. The forces that shape one's thoughts and opinions may have an effect that is temporary. These forces may combine in different ways at different times to create a movement in thoughts and opinions, needs and desires, that impact buying behavior with a similar flow. That is, people may be inclined to adjust their buying habits as the forces that surround and impact them change. In tight economic times, for example, people often cut back on their purchases. When the economy strengthens, the propensity to buy increases. The degree to which purchasing resiliency takes place is a measure of the elasticity of the market. Determining the elasticity of the market is yet another challenge for the marketer.

Markets are enigmatic. There is no clear single answer for the effects that external forces will have. In order to stay in tune with the buying behaviors of any market, the marketer must have a sort of extrasensory relationship with their decision-making process and the forces that shape it. The marketer must understand what forces drive buying behaviors, to what extent it is impacted, and when the change will take place. Knowing the target market is one of the fundamental requirements for being able to determine and apply the right mix of resources to achieve the desired results.

The scope of resources available to the marketer also determines the composition of the mix. When certain elements are not able to make the desired contribution to the mix, other elements could sometimes be modified to accommodate for the shortcoming. For example, if the desired type and level of promotion cannot be achieved, price structure or levels may be modified to draw more attention to the product. It should be noted that price is often not a viable means to manipulate the mix. First, it can reduce product profitability to unacceptable levels. Second, the market may not have the degree of price elasticity to allow the change to make a difference. Regardless of the extent to which elements of the mix can be changed to achieve the desired results, the marketer must first understand the quality and quantity of resources available to implement the marketing plan.

Understanding the buying behavior of the market and the scope of available resources is fundamental to concocting the marketing mix. The initial mix, and the manner in which it changes, should also be driven by market growth. Being able to produce enough *product* and deliver it to *places* where customers can purchase it are two of the challenges faced in meeting the needs of high growth markets. High growth markets can occur when there are more members of the target market than anticipated, or when members of the target market purchase more than expected. Unanticipated market growth can be a double-edged sword. The higher demand signals the opportunity for the marketer to earn more revenue; however, the cost of supporting unanticipated demand can reduce current and future profits. Classic problems often besiege marketers selling to high growth markets. Prospective customers turn to competitors who can supply their needs. The marketer can also incur a profit-threatening surge in support costs in their effort to satisfy the needs of customers. Other problems can also emerge; however, it is best to avoid problems in growth spurts by being prepared. That means to anticipate the growth or to have contingency plans in place, in the event of strong growth in the market.

The elements of the marketing mix—product, packaging, price, promotion, and place—should be combined to meet or exceed targets set for market share and profitability. Market share and profitability are often conflicting goals. One can usually only be maximized at the expense of the other. Selling to more people or a larger market, for example, is often accomplished by spending more in promotion, offering larger margins to channel partners, or lowering the product price. Nevertheless, once the goals are set the marketing plan is gelled by determining the optimal marketing mix. To achieve this, the marketer must not only understand buying behavior, the scope of resources, and future growth of the market, he or she must also understand the dynamics that each P has with one another.

There are key characteristics of each P that drive its role in the marketing mix. For the *product*, the *degree of technical complexity* will dictate how the other Ps will be applied to achieve the ideal mix. In the world of IT, the level of technical complexity helps to define the product or service. For *packaging*, the extent to which it gives *ease of use* will drive its role in the marketing mix. Ease of use will help determine who will use the product or service. For *promotion*, the reach and penetration, or its *intensity*, will drive its role in the marketing mix. The number of people who are aware of the product or service, and their desire to purchase, will help determine the demand. The level and structure, or the *affordability*, of the *price* will drive its role in the marketing mix. The affordability of the price will determine who is willing and able to pay for the product or service. It will also determine the amount of margin that channel partners can earn. Last, but not least, the number and size of channels, *or number of access points*, will drive the role that *place* has in the marketing mix. The number of channels will determine the accessibility of the product or service to the target market. By varying the technical complexity of the product, the ease of use of packaging, the intensity of promotion, the affordability of the price, and the number of access points from channels, the marketer determines the marketing mix. The mix that delivers the sought after market share and profitability will have the right characteristic level of each P.

Determining the right level of each characteristic is not a single dimensional process. The various factors that affect the marketing mix are like prisms that give rise to a multidimensional process. The complexity can be simplified by looking at two primary factors that give a strong ray of light to the prism that engulfs the marketing mix. Interspersed with the characteristics of the Ps is the stage of the product in its life cycle and the dispersion of the market. The product stage and market dispersion determine the degree to which each P is applied to the mix. See the Marketing Mix Matrix at www.The5Ps.com/LEM/Mktg MixMatrix.html

There is no cut and dried answer to striking the right balance of Ps to achieve the ideal mix. There are simply too many variants to consider. The Marketing Mix Matrix provides a guideline for how the Ps can be applied to achieve the ideal mix in general situations. See www.The5Ps.com/LEM/ HowToManageTheMix.html.

In summary, although there may be typical scenarios for which the optimum marketing mix can be defined, there is not a simple, standard recipe for combining the 5 Ps. Markets are dynamic and elastic. Moreover, they are enigmatic. The astute marketer will understand the markets that they target, the role of each of the 5 Ps, the resources available to them, and how they can be combined to reach the goals of market share and profitability.

When Cannibalization Is Profitable

Classical marketing contended that products should be allowed to run their life cycle. Marketers were encouraged to avoid introducing new products that might threaten the sales of their existing products. Cannibalization was avoided so that successful products could realize their full profit potential.

That paradigm has changed. Cannibalization is not only accepted, it is often sought after. Information technology moves at such a dizzying pace that planned obsolescence is the norm. Rather than wait for new products from competitors to hit the market, many companies launch products that succeed their own products that have strong sales. When is self-cannibalization justified?

There are several situations when self-cannibalization is beneficial to the marketer. The most common is when the existing product is nearing the end of its life cycle. To stay competitive or offer an improved product to the target market, the product manager will often introduce a new, next generation product that offers a better price performance. Some customers may elect to accept the inferior features and functions of the older product in exchange for a lower price, while other customers will choose the new product. The result is often a faster demise of the older product.

The marketer should also hasten the demise of successful products when new products can be delivered that better serve the market and offer greater profitability. After all, a primary goal of marketing is to deliver the best solution for the customer while earning a profit for the enterprise. When a new product has completed the development cycle and is ready to be launched, the marketer should consider inventory levels (i.e., in house and in all channels) of the product to be replaced, margins of each product, the level of interoperability, the cost of modified promotion plan, and *all other factors* that will affect the introduction of the product and withdrawal of the current product. When the total costs of realizing revenue from the new product exceed the cumulative hard costs and relationship costs of retiring the current product, cannibalization is justified. Sun Microsystems validated this concept during the 1980s when it shocked the industry by introducing new models of its Sparc computers while existing models were still selling successfully. Sun Microsystems entered the market with force and quickly achieved a commanding market share with its self-cannibalization strategy.

When inventory levels of the manufacturer and the channel partners are moderate to high and inventory velocity, or turn, is low and falling, cannibalization may be warranted. This is often a scenario when new products can be delivered that better serve the market and offer greater profitability. Low inventory turn can signal a weak economy; it can also signal falling market acceptance of the product. Since economic factors should be included in sales projections, profitability scenarios can be developed for two options. The first is to continue selling the current product until an acceptable amount of inventory is sold, and then introduce the new product. The second is to introduce a new product and liquidate the inventory. When the product meets the needs of a market with strong buying power, introducing a new product that cannibalizes sales of an existing product is often the most profitable alternative.

The zenith of the conceptualization, development, and launch of a product or service is the dream of virtually all marketers. The *business* of marketing is to deliver solutions to the target market while earning a maximum profit for the enterprise. An alternative goal is to maximize market share while optimizing profits. The creation of a product or service is, therefore, merely a part of the equation in defining a successful marketer. The effective management of product life cycles is tantamount to success in measuring marketing success. Just as important as knowing how to successfully create a new product or service, is knowing when and how to retreat. In the world of IT, moving at a frenetic pace, cannibalization is not only accepted but for many it has become the norm. Marketing plans should be constructed with this in mind, so that overall profits can be maintained even when new products are introduced.

Once the components of the 5 Ps of marketing have been laid out and the marketer has developed strategies to deploy them in a mix that can yield success, it is time to make it happen. The next chapter will present tools and techniques to actually implement and deliver a successful technology-based business.

CHAPTER 3

The Marketing Process—
Putting It into Action

Table 3.1 The TUMAC principle

T	Identify and qualify prospective customers of the **T**arget market
U	**U**nderstand what they need and desire
M	Deliver the **M**essage: Communicate the features, functions and benefits of your product or service. Excellent technique is the FBR – feature, benefit, response.
A	Remain **A**vailable and in the minds of prospective customers.
C	**C**lose, close, close. seek the response to whether the prospect will buy or the reasons that they will not buy.

The TUMAC Principle[©1]

The TUMAC principle is the essence of marketing. It is how all the strategies and techniques are put into action to turn ideas into booked revenue. Whether you are a salesperson, product manager, public relations agent, customer service representative, or a general-purpose marketer, TUMAC defines the basic steps (see Table 3.1) necessary to sell a product or service.

Throughout this book, the elements of the TUMAC principle are explained as they relate to each phase of the marketing cycle and each components of the marketing mix. See www.The5Ps.com/LEM/TUMAC-Principle.html

Potential Markets Versus Potential Products:
The High-Tech Chicken 'n Egg

The decision of whether to create products that people are asking for, or to create products based on the next phase of technological progression, (or what technology can perform) can be quite a dilemma. On one hand, creating products that deliver what people are demanding can be very expensive and time consuming. It may require inventing new technology. On the other hand, creating a product (from new technologies) that is a natural progression of technology can create or uncover a need or desire that was previously unknown. That is the essence of the high-tech chicken 'n egg problem. What comes first, the technology or the need? The answer lies in having an intimate relationship with the markets served as well as a solid understanding of the technologies underlying the products and services offered.

The market will let you know the functions and features that they want. In most cases, they will even describe their ideal product. The challenge for the product manager is learning to listen to what the market is asking for, and producing a mutually profitable solution that responds to their need. Listening to the market means having the proper two-way channels of communication between the product manager and the primary sources that interact with the members of the target market, including the prospective customers themselves. Listening requires being able to receive every type of communication that is delivered. Listening also means being able to discern the real meaning behind the communication. Once the meaning is understood, it must be translated into a viable product or service. The product manager must then determine if he or she can produce and deliver the product or service at an acceptable profit.

In its purest form, marketing starts with the creation of an idea that responds to a market need. Many products, however, are created as a result of technical innovation rather than a market need. Technical innovations may be the result of intellectual challenges to push the limits of technology or a change to the approach to doing something. In an effort to improve the performance of computer chips, many researchers shifted their focus from silicon to gallium arsenide. The properties of gallium arsenide allow faster processing, lower heat dissipation, and other inherent advantages over silicon. The move from copper to fiber as a communications conduit is the result of improved properties that fiber has over copper. Faster speed, improved durability, and greater capacity are a few of the advantages that fiber offers for telecommunications.

Sequential programming techniques invoked processes, as they are required to perform tasks in the order that they are needed. Object oriented programming, on the other hand, placed functions in memory and left them there until their tasks are no longer needed. When the resources needed to perform object oriented programming are less than those to perform sequential programming for the same group of processes, object oriented programming is more efficient. The design of programs coupled with the resources available in the computing environment dictates when object oriented programming is more efficient than sequential programming. Many technical developers strive to make current technology faster, more reliable, more efficient, in short, better. Sometimes products are created that are not a logical progression of existing products, but rather, an entirely different approach to a given problem. The PC was such a product.

The sales volume of mainframe computers was holding its own as the minicomputer was just beginning to gain acceptance. Some customers were purchasing intelligent terminals that stored only a few very basic functions.

Computer buyers were largely businesses that purchased mainframes, minicomputers, or timesharing (i.e., purchased computer time delivered through telecom networks). There was little indication that a PC would be accepted, much less was there any demand for such a product. Nevertheless, it was a fascinating innovation. With the help of software products developed to give it a purpose, like VisiCalc, the PC found a market among corporate financial groups. As a result, the PC improved, the number of software application packages grew, and the market expanded. The rest is history. The technical innovation without a market had found a home. The PC was a market maker.

So what is the best course of action? Does the product manager respond to the demands of the market or try to create a market maker? What comes first—the technology or the need? The first step in answering these high-tech chicken 'n egg questions is to determine the cost, time, and risks associated with each option.

What Comes First—The Chicken or the Egg?

When a new product is developed that responds to a market need, the first step is to define and validate that need. The cost of conducting a market validation study in a time efficient manner is one of the first major cost components. The next major cost component is the design and development of a product or service that fits the defined need. If the need pushes the envelope of technology, product development could be cost prohibitive, could require too much time, or both. If the need exceeds the current limits of technology, product development would be impossible without a major technological breakthrough.

The market validation study will provide the fundamental information that will help the product manager determine whether or not the product can become successful. If a product can be developed within the technical, financial, and time constraints necessary to achieve commercial success, the remainder of the marketing process should be put into action. The product should be developed, sales and distribution channels established, pricing set and structured, and the promotion plan is initiated.

When a new product is developed solely from technical innovation, on the other hand, the marketing process can be much more resource intensive as well as risky. Essentially the product manager is charged with finding a target market or home for the product and mixing the marketing elements to achieve a minimum sales volume.

Table 3.2 summarizes the steps to marketing a new product created expressly in response to market demand, and marketing a product that is purely the result of technical innovation.

In order to properly assess the profit potential of each approach, one must determine the cost of identifying, developing, and selling a product that responds to market demand as well as the cost of advertising, promoting, and selling a product that has been created primarily by technical innovation. In some cases, the cost of developing a product

Table 3.2 *Steps to marketing a new product*

IN RESPONSE TO MARKET DEMAND	FROM TECHNICAL INNOVATION
• Define and validate market need • Develop product • Advertise and promote • Sell	• Create product or service • Identify target market(s) • Promote to generate focused interest • Sell to early adopters • Broaden market • Promote to generate interest • Sell to total market

Table 3.3 Cost categories of bringing product to viable market position

COST CATEGORIES	RESPONSE TO MARKET DEMAND	TECHNICAL INNOVATION
Replace these numbers with those from your projects.		
Identifying Product	50,000	0
Developing Product	100,000	250,000
Advertising	30,000	500,000
Promoting	100,000	300,000
Selling	100,000	150,000
TOTAL		
All figures are relative and dependent upon market factors.		

to a specific set of criteria can be quite expensive. Development of the product may not be possible if the baseline criteria exceed the realm of possibilities. If the development costs exceed the levels to allow an acceptable margin, profitability from the product may not be possible. Sample cost categories of bringing products to a viable market position are outlined in Table 3.3. Fill in numbers for your projects to quantify your comparison.

In most cases, the entire marketing process is much more resource efficient when it is conducted in response to market demand than from technical innovation. Opportunity is a collection of the value that a product holds for all members of the target market. The market opportunity of a product developed in response to demand is far more clear and compelling than the market opportunity of a technical innovation product. The value of a product produced by technical innovation is, therefore, a hard sell. While the functionality may be awesome and cool, a reason to spend money on that functionality may not be easily discerned. The value of a market demand product is an easy sell, since it has already been identified and quantified by the market.

When marketing direction is engaged at the point of product conceptualization, it can drive the entire process from concept to profit. A product or service solution that is created or discovered as a direct result of a defined market need can be more easily moved through the business process so as to produce a profit for the enterprise. The foundation for building such success is constructed from a comprehensive target market assessment.

Target Market Assessment

The first step in deciding whether to bring a product to market is to determine if the target market has a desire and ability to purchase the product or service. The most important qualifying factor is whether or not the product can earn enough money to warrant its development, production, and sale. The answer lies in the collective revenue that can be earned from members of the target market (see Chapter 1—A Market is a Group of People and Chapter 2—Pricing, Identifying Willingness to Pay). To determine potential revenue, the product manager needs to know individual prospects' *willingness* to pay, their *ability* to pay, and the *collective* amount of money that everyone can pay.

Willingness to Pay

This concept, introduced earlier, is now explained in depth. One of the most difficult, and critical, factors to assess in qualifying prospective customers is the value that a product or service holds for them. The perception of what the product will deliver will drive its value to the customer. Most importantly, the priorities of the individual consumer or the criteria that drive the company's performance help to define and drive the value system. Whether the objective is to identify the willingness to pay for a consumer or business target market, the best place to start is with the prospective customers themselves.

People will often reveal what they are willing to pay for a product or service, either directly or indirectly. The key is in posing the question so as to elicit an amount that the prospective customer is willing to pay. This does not mean presenting a product or an idea and asking *how much is that worth to you?* It is, rather, presenting the *results* of using the product or service and determining what having those results is worth to the prospective customer. The results can be presented in a tangible or intangible form and apply to products that exist or might be considered for development. For example, a market research might ask a prospective customer "what would it mean to you if you could write your bills in 1/3 the time that you spend now?" The prospective customer might answer "I would be able to spend that time with my children" or "I would eliminate a lot of aggravation." When asked "what is that worth to you" the customer could probably put a dollar amount on the time spent with their children or the aggravation that is gone. Even if a single question cannot be immediately provided, the value has been established in their mind making it easier for the market researcher to use a series of questions or other tactics to place a number on that value. Questions posed to businesses that identify their willingness to pay are also designed to find out what a solution would be worth to the decision maker. Since businesses are generally more responsive to IT products that contribute to mission critical or strategic applications, let's consider an example that is both strategic and mission critical. The market researcher might ask "what would you be able to achieve if you could process orders 40% faster?" The business decision maker might answer, "I would gain a significant competitive advantage" or "I could lower operations costs." It would be fairly straightforward to place a value, tangible or intangible, on those benefits.

Asking prospective customers to place a value on a result rather than an object makes it easier to quantify the willingness to pay for an existing product as well as a conceptual product. If the market researcher does not have the opportunity to ask prospective customers directly using interviews, questionnaires, or focus groups, they can use a host of other techniques to elicit information including conducting comparative analyses, gathering point of sale statistics, and more. Pricing for competitive products can easily be gathered from sales information, point of sale statistics, and research studies. To adequately assess prices of competitive products, more than price should be considered. Marketing criteria such as the product's features and functions; its ability to adapt to the environment of the target market (i.e., packaging); the number and reach of distribution channels; and the effectiveness of its promotion should define the comparison. For a table that may be used to prepare a product pricing comparison, visit www.The5Ps.com/LEM/ProductPricingComparison.html

The criteria selected for inclusion in the product pricing comparison chart depends on the type of product, nature of the target market, and the business environment. The criteria in the aforementioned chart are representative but not absolute. Likewise, the assessment of the comparison is not an absolute process. A qualitative assessment must be made, much like that described in the Marketing Mix Matrix in Chapter 2, p. 114.

The degree to which each of the criteria affects the target market's propensity to pay, and the interrelationships they have with each other, will collectively determine the price.

A qualitative assessment is satisfactory in most cases since the factors that shape it are highly qualitative themselves. Many focus on price elasticity; however, price is not the only element that affects a product's elasticity. The elasticity of a product is a measure of the degree to which a change in the element being measured has on the product manager's ability to sell the product. The cumulative effect of an element's elasticity defines the probability that someone will purchase the product. For a sample price elasticity chart, visit www.The5Ps.com/LEM/PriceElasticity.html

Models that incorporate the elasticity of product elements must also include the independencies that the changes in elements have on each other. A reduction in price, for example, might reduce the elasticity in the number of stores that the product is sold in. (see Marketing Mix Matrix, Chapter 2, p. 114). The dynamics of the interrelationships between product elements can be captured quantitatively in the method of aggregating the effects that each element has on the probability of purchasing the product. An understanding of the impact of product element elasticity is essential in setting the optimal price for the product. Once the optimal combination is found, the price is validated by the prospective customer's willingness to pay.

The market researcher must use solutions-based comparisons or "imagine if" studies to determine the willingness to pay for a product that does not yet exist. To develop a solutions-based comparison, the researcher can determine the amount that prospective customers pay to achieve a result similar to what they will achieve with the new product. For an example, see www.The5Ps.com/LEM/ImagineIf.html

The Imagine If Solution process delivers more than one result. The market researcher could prepare a statistical evaluation of the results using one or more of several routines including multivariate analysis, weighted average, and others to determine the price that prospective customers would be willing to pay based upon the representative sample.

The best way to qualify a product's price is to sell it. Before the product has been launched and sometimes before the prototype has been developed, the product can be sold. To avoid selling *vaporware*—products that don't exist and never come to fruition—the customer should be made fully aware of the status of the product and protected by a sales order or contract that provides full reimbursement if the product is not delivered. After all, maintaining honorable business ethics is not only the right thing to do, it also helps to protect the product and the company. Skeptics may fear that full disclosure prevents the sale of nonexistent products; however, such sales have been made for many years including several by this author.

Selling products or systems is the best way to qualify a customer. These qualifying sales also make a strong contribution to the determination of price. Very early adopters are often willing to pay much more for a product before the launch or at the very beginning of it's life cycle than customers who purchase later.   While the pre-launch sales price does not necessarily mean that all members of the target market will pay that amount, it is nevertheless an indication of the value that the product holds. A product's price can be tested by selling it as a

- prototype product in a complete system;
- pre-release product.

When prototype products are sold as part of a complete system, the prices of other products in the system, and price of services included in the delivery of the system, collectively comprise the system price.

The value, and effective price, of each system component can, therefore, be discerned by mapping the prices of each component against the system price. For example, the relative percentage of each component's value is calculated and multiplied by the total system price to determine the implied component prices. For a chart showing component price estimate for system sold, see www.The5Ps.com/LEM/SystemPriceEstimate.html

The price of a pre-release product sold separately, on the other hand, is straightforward. It is simply the amount that was paid for the product. The pre-release price is more of an indication of that customer's willingness to pay, than an indication of what the suggested retail price (SRP) of that product should be.

In determining the willingness to pay, the product manager must take several other factors into consideration. The amount identified should be representative of what the vast majority of the target market is willing to pay. It should not be too high or too low, so that price increases and discounts can be applied without exceeding what the market considers reasonable. Unreasonable price movements invalidate the price and, thus, the worth of the product or service. The willingness to pay is not the price. Rather, it provides a foundation for the determination of price (see Setting the Level, p. 72). The astute marketer will learn to listen to the market and understand their needs and desires, including their willingness to pay.

Ability to Pay

A prospective customer's willingness to pay is worth nothing if they are unable to pay for the product or service that they want. The marketer must, therefore, determine the target market's ability to pay for the product. For consumers, this means quantifying the target market's disposable income; for businesses, this means quantifying their available budget or borrowing power.

There are a number of means of estimating consumer income or corporate borrowing power. Both government agencies and private research firms offer statistics on disposable income that is often delineated by category of spending or geographical area (see www.The5Ps.com/LEM/Statistics.html). Since both earnings and disposable income are often provided as a measure of spending power, it is important to use disposable income or calculate it from the earning figure provided. The marketer must determine what percentage of that disposable income represents the amount owned by their target market, and what percentage of that income is likely to be spent on their type of products.

A consumer oriented bill payment service, for example, might offer their customers the ability make payments using computers that communicate via the Internet or a private network. Customers could use their own PC, portable computer, smartphone, or a computer or device provided by the service. The target market for such a service might be technical savvy, busy people who value flexibility in managing their finances. It is likely that the core target market would consist of Internet subscribers and those who own desktop or portable computing devices. While many more descriptions should be used to define the target market, the aforementioned description shall be used to explain how to quantify the market's ability to pay.

The description of the target market is applied against available statistical information to estimate the number of people who comprise the target market. A sampling study can be conducted, for example, to estimate the number of people who conform to the description within defined groups. The groups would be defined, in turn, based on descriptors used to delineate databases that are available. If the available database categorizes people based on geographic location, age, and race, the samples may be taken among people who belong to those groups. Once the samples yield a statistically significant percentage of people in each group that meets the defined criteria of the target market, that percentage can be applied against the total population of the available database to determine the size of the target market. The sample can also be applied against databases that provide disposable income statistics to estimate the amount of available money for purchasing. As an alternative to using the top-down approach that incorporates disposable income statistics, a bottom-up estimate can be developed. The sales effectiveness of each channel can be determined, to use in sales projections, both units, and revenue. When these projections are aggregated, the results should be adjusted downward to account for overlapping sales projections.

The next step is to set boundaries for the target market. The boundaries may be based on sales channels, geography, or other factors. In the case of the consumer oriented bill payment service, the market boundary would likely be the continental United States, if the bill payment systems were set up for U.S. financial institutions and U.S.-based companies rendering bills. The boundaries are used to aggregate members of the target market and their buying potential.

Once the target market has been defined, including set boundaries, criteria must be identified that allows the marketer to map the market against information sources that provide disposable income. Since many databases and other information sources use demographic data to demarcate, age, race, gender, and other demographics, these offer the best means to glean disposable income. The mean demographics of the consumer target market are mapped against available information to estimate their disposable income. When the target market consists of businesses, however, other criteria are appropriate. Industry categorizations, company locations, number of employees, and net income, for example, help to measure a company's ability to purchase many goods and services. In some cases, budget size and past spending patterns are available, providing an indicator of that amount of money that businesses are likely to spend. Finally, when the budget is not large enough the marketer can also consider the capital spending power of the group of companies or consumers in the target market. In order to invoke a change in spending patterns, however, a product or service must be quite compelling or exceed the buying criteria of the target market. The budget, spending patterns, or capital spending capacity of businesses in the target market must be evaluated and compiled to estimate the market's ability to pay. Of course the strength of the economy must be factored into all financial projections, including revenue and expense. For an example of assessing ability to pay, visit www.The5Ps.com/LEM/AbilityToPay.html

Collective Revenue Potential

While willingness to pay and ability to pay are often applied against aggregate numbers to determine the total revenue potential of a target market, it is not always the case. When revenue potential is calculated based on information from individual prospective customers or market segments, the amount of money that the collective target market will likely spend must reflect the differences of each segment. The aggregate revenue potential is not always calculated by simply adding the potential of individuals or market segments. There are other considerations that may affect the aggregation of potential revenue. Is the ability to pay consistent throughout the target market? Is there consistency in spending patterns among members of the target market? When the factors used to calculate revenue potential of individual consumers or market segments do not reflect the *relative* factors that influence their propensity to buy, then these factors must be included in the aggregation of the overall revenue potential.

Let's consider, for example, a hypothetical service—mobile assistant—that would appeal to a broad group of people whose needs may be substantially different. Mobile assistant would offer a selection of products and services designed to provide extended administrative help to people on the go. The products and services might include

- wireless phone service with companion paging option;
- forwarding all phone lines wherever you want;
- telephone answering service;
- purchase or rental of all popular portable devices;
- choice of handheld computer and cell phone;
- peripheral products for popular notebook computers, cell phones, and other portable devices;
- instructor-led, video, CD, or Internet-based training courses;
- 24 hour, 7 days a week toll-free support hotline;
- equipment maintenance and repair option;
- scheduling appointments;
- printing and mailing documents.

Indeed, such an extensive and varied selection of products and services would appeal to a wide variety of people. The price for each customer would vary greatly based on the products and services selected. Likewise, the prospective customers' ability to pay would also vary a great deal. In addition to their ability to pay, there are other relative factors that would affect prospective customer's propensity to buy. They include, but are not limited to

- information technology proficiency;
- amount of support available elsewhere (i.e., like at work);
- products and services already owned or provided elsewhere;
- number of useful applications that deliver value from immediacy.

The determination of revenue potential is an iterative process. Price elasticity, for example, can affect the amount of revenue that can be earned from a product. When price is lowered, a larger number of prospective customers may purchase the product. When the scope of the target market is widened without adequately increasing promotion and channels, the revenue potential may also be reduced. The method of calculating collective revenue potential for a product or service must take these and other factors into account.

The collective revenue potential is used in the calculation of product profit and loss projections to determine whether to engage in developing a new product, and also whether to retire existing products. Its calculation and elasticity, therefore, must be carefully thought out. Since every situation is different, there is no cut and dry formula.

Identifying Wants and Needs

The first step in identifying needs and wants is to understand the difference between them. Each plays a distinct role in defining a product and, more importantly, what the customer is willing to pay for it. The concept of need and wants varies between consumers and businesses but the principle remains the same. A need is something that is absolutely necessary to maintain a fundamental lifestyle[2] or level of operations. A want, on the other hand, may offer an improvement or hold intrinsic value but is not essential to maintaining lifestyle or operations.

The Definition: Want Versus Need

Many consumers, for example, may consider a phone or video (i.e., blu-ray) player to be an essential household item. While these items, unlike food, shelter, and clothing, are not necessary to sustain life, many consider them a requirement to sustain a certain lifestyle. Conversely, a high-end telephone system with voicemail and music on hold is a luxury item for most consumers. The importance that a product or service has to a consumer helps to define their value system. Items essential to life sustenance are at the top and items essential to lifestyle maintenance come next. Increasingly, consumers are placing PCs high in their value system.

Businesses define the high end of their value system by what is necessary to maintain a base level of operations. Mission critical applications such as telephone systems, payroll, and production management systems are essential to keep most companies in operation. There are a host of other products and services, however, that offer desired improvements such as added convenience, increased productivity, increased time value of information, or cost savings. Energy conservation systems, call management systems, more powerful computers, and high-speed networks are desired improvements for many businesses. The ranking that a product or service has in a business value system depends on the perceived contribution that it will make to the company's goals and objective and, ultimately, the bottom line.

Perception is reality. The perceived value that a product or service offers a consumer or business buyer defines the place that it will hold in their value system. Identifying needs and wants means much more than simply asking a prospective customer what he or she would like to achieve. The identification process includes defining needs and wants, prioritizing them in the prospective customer's value system, and confirming that the customer is willing to pay for the product that satisfies the needs and wants. The marketer must be able to discern between an expressed desire and a confirmed idea. An expressed desire indicates *what* the prospective customer wants. A confirmed idea indicates *why* he or she wants it and that *he or she is willing to pay* for it. It is the *confirmed idea* that the marketer uses to define future products and services.

Information Gathering Tools—Direct

Information can be collected from prospective customers in a number of ways. One of the more effective methods of discerning information from prospective customers is the *umbrella* technique. This technique starts with giving the prospect a broad, open-ended question designed to elicit the array of results that he or she desires. The answers that define the customer's overall goals form the crown of the open umbrella. For example, an executive might identify her company's goals as increasing revenue by 10% maintaining a 16% profit margin, expanding the customer base, and improving operations by 20%.

An understanding of what is required to achieve each of these goals is the next step in the process of revealing the resources needed to meet these requirements. The products, services, and other subgoals and objectives, and other requirements that are necessary to achieve each goal make up the spokes of the umbrella.

In order to increase revenue by 10%, for example, a sales and marketing executive might launch a new product or expand advertising and promotion, increase the number of sales calls, cut prices, improve sales collateral, or any combination of these. While it may be fairly easy for executives and managers to identify the goals and objectives of their organization, the supporting tasks and resources that will be used to achieve those goals may not be as forthcoming. In some cases this is because their plans are confidential. In many cases the plans are not complete or are not set in stone. To glean additional information from executives, invoke creativity, and keep the ideas flowing, the "imagine if" questioning technique is often quite effective.

An *imagine if* question creates a scenario in the executive's mind of achieving a goal with the help of results from a product or service; for example, "imagine if your sales and marketing staff could access a database with twice as many qualified prospects as your current database." Increasing the number of qualified leads is one of the ways in which sales activities will lead to the 10% increase in revenue. The executive will invariably think about the effect that the increase in leads might have on achieving the overall goal. By asking the question "what would that allow you to do?" the executive and the marketer will affirm the value that the leads will offer. This helps to round out the umbrella (see Figure 3.1) by

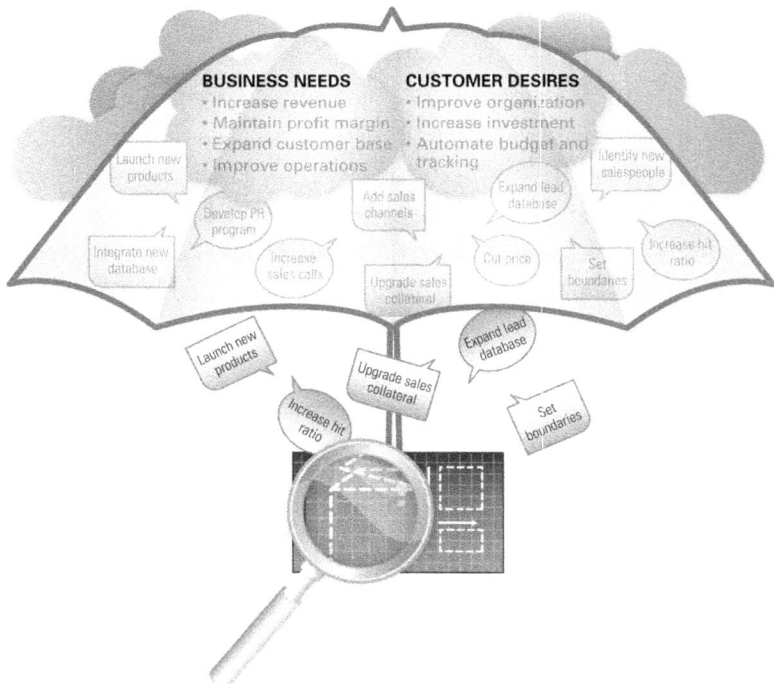

Figure 3.1 Imagine if umbrella

creating closure at the end of the spoke by validating the need for the product. The spokes in the umbrella represent the tools that support the canopy of the business. To understand this technique better, visit www .The5Ps.com/LEM/ImagineIfUmbrella.html

Questions and other information gathering techniques need not be delivered face to face. Once the concept and flow of questions and statements that will be used to elicit information have been determined, they can be delivered in the form of verbal or written questions, pictures, video, sound, or any combination of these. Earlier in this Chapter (p. 123), we identified questionnaires, focus groups, telephone surveys, promotional discounts, purchase tracking, and solicitation advertisements as a few tools of the trade. When an individual is leading the questionnaire, focus group, or other information gathering processes, he or she can redirect the questions as necessary to identify and quantify the prospective customer's needs and wants expeditiously. When the interviewer is not present during the information gathering process, however, other techniques must be used to lead the prospective customer to reveal goals, objectives, needs, and wants. The development of a "self-propelled" information gathering process requires making certain assumptions and decisions about the requirements, and needs and wants of the respondent. The questions and other information gathering tools should elicit responses that follow a natural flow. The flow should follow the interviewee's thought process and lead to the identification of needs and wants that support each goal of the objective.

Other Information Gathering Tools

There are many different types of information gathering tools. They can be grouped into two categories based on the type of interaction with the prospective customer—direct and indirect. Direct information gathering tools might include surveys, focus groups, and questionnaires. Indirect tools include purchase-tracking analysis, research studies, and gathering information from databases.

Direct information gathering tools may be administered by an individual or simply provided to the customer to respond. Surveys are usually administered, for example, by asking prospective customers questions in person or by telephone.

Indirect information gathering tools are often enhanced with information provided by direct tools such as surveys and questionnaires. Questionnaires, for example, may reveal areas or items of interest that are further qualified by reviewing spending patterns of the target market. Surveys or focus groups may reveal demographic trends and population growth that can be validated. Trend charts, dispersion graphs, and other reports produced from statistical analyses can provide information that helps to identify an individual or group's needs and wants.

Techniques used to gather information may be applied to both direct and indirect information gathering tools. The umbrella technique, for example, can be used in interviewer-led questionnaires such as focus groups and telephone surveys, and it can also be used to design indirect tools such as questionnaires. The structure and flow of questions is based on responses provided or anticipated responses from the interviewee (i.e., prospective customer).

As an alternative or complement to gathering information, marketers can also use information that exists in public and private databases. Numerous databases exist with a vast amount of information collected by private companies, government agencies, and associations. Financial, housing, demographics, and a host of other criteria may be used to identify and define target markets. When putting these databases to use, the marketer must consider the source of the data; the manner in which the data was collected; the age of the data and how often it is replenished, as well as the accuracy and degree to which the data is categorized, and more. Some companies are very methodical and meticulous in their collection of information for databases. The criteria and source for inclusion are carefully selected and data is verified before it is accepted. This is often true of companies that collect information that is used for financial approval and ratings. Other companies, on the other hand, may collect extensive statistics that are not verified but are refreshed on a quarterly or annual basis. People are encouraged to respond in detail and truthfully so that they may receive information or offers that are of interest to them. This is often the case with magazines and other publications, particularly when subscription revenue is small or nonexistent (i.e., most or all revenue is from ad sales). Some databases contain information that covers a very extensive area or a large number of people which, in some cases, can be validated by the power or influence that they have. For example, spending patterns can be gleaned from the number and type of licenses that have been purchased, taxes reported, or census surveys. Databases containing such information are often maintained by government agencies or trade associations. For information on our data base providers, visit www.The5Ps.com/LEM/DatabaseProviders.html

Putting Information Gathering Tools to Use

Information gathering tools are given value when they are used effectively to garner and compile data to assist in the marketing process. Once the tool has been designed and developed to elicit desired information, it must be delivered to encourage a response from the targeted audience. Salespeople, resellers, market researchers, the Internet, regular mail, and other sources that have access to members of the target market, for example, may distribute questionnaires. Salespeople, resellers, and market researchers can deliver questionnaires in person, often with a personalized request for its completion. In many cases, they may wait for the questionnaire to be completed and submit it to the product marketer. Questionnaires delivered through the Internet, regular mail, or another source are usually accompanied by an attention grabber that encourages the targeted interviewee to read, and hopefully, complete, and return it. Questionnaires may be delivered with promotion items (i.e., coupons, giveaways) that may be redeemed by the person delivering the questionnaire, the person completing the questionnaire, or by each. The key to questionnaires or data collectors is to have prospective customers complete it truthfully, completely, and return it in a timely manner.

Data collected from information gathering tools can be used to further refine future data collection efforts. The content of questionnaires can be changed, targeted audiences can be more precisely defined, and research studies can be selected with more narrowly defined criteria. Data collected may also be used to more precisely define the elements of the marketing mix such as promotional discounts, distribution channels, or price. For example, if data collected indicates that members of the target market are more sensitive to price than previously believed, future questionnaires could discern the reason for and degree of the price sensitivity. A special promotion or sale could be run to determine the increase in sales volume due to lower price or revised price structure.

Summary

To identify the wants and needs of a target market it is important to discern between a need and a want. Understanding the difference will help to determine the combined features and functions that are desired in a product or service, as well as the prospective customer's determination to buy. Several information gathering tools may be used to help identify and define a qualified target market. The ways that these tools are developed and used are important in determining their success in the marketing process. As the marketer becomes proficient in using tools and techniques, he or she will become aware of how the market communicates through what it buys, does, or how it exists; that is, actions and characteristics that uniquely define the market. Spending patterns, earnings levels, living locations, and changes in other market characteristics are means of communicating needs and wants. The astute marketer will learn how to "listen" to the market. To listen to a market one must

- observe trends;
- listen to the latest buzz;
- ask "why";
- analyze buying patterns;
- understand the reasons behind objections.

The marketer must watch, listen, and then qualify what they have learned by thinking through all scenarios and information and, most importantly, by asking questions. Qualify information is received by verifying it from multiple, independent sources and by identifying supporting trends. The marketer should review economic trends and the results of questionnaires to discern what the market needs versus what it wants. They should remain aware of new and emerging trends. In the early 80s having a PC in the office was a trend; however, by the early 90s that trend became a requirement.

Observations are validated, or often created, by using information gathering tools to identify needs, wants, and trends. Ideally, market research should collect information from the target market, research studies, engineering, and all relevant sources to define the specific features and functions of products that customers are willing to pay for.

Identifying Potential Products and Services

For many outside of the marketing discipline, there is a magical quality to identifying products and services that are destined to sell. Magic to one person, however, is a known process to another. The key is to keep an open mind to the possibilities rather than trying to match requirements to existing technologies or products. The objective is to define a solution to market requirements; then match existing products and services to that solution or design a new product that fits.

The core process of developing products and services from identified customer needs is the "i." This process is initiated from basic marketing processes discussed in Chapter 2 (The Right Combination: Identifying Features and Functions that Sell), and you have just read Chapter 3 (Identifying Wants and Needs). Customers' needs and wants define the desired outcome of a product or service. It is the prioritized outcomes that determine the features and functions that underlie the product design. When operating in the creative solution mode, the marketer moves from the identification of customer needs and wants to a preliminary product design. See Figure 3.2.

The first step in understanding customers' needs and wants is to ask them what they intend to achieve and, most importantly, why they need to achieve the stated result. The answer not only provides the value that the solution will hold for the customer, it also helps the marketer define an appropriate solution. For example, a publishing company may want to add

IDENTIFY the customer's needs

DEFINE the project scope

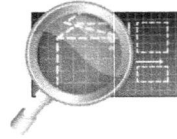

CREATIVE SOLUTION MODE

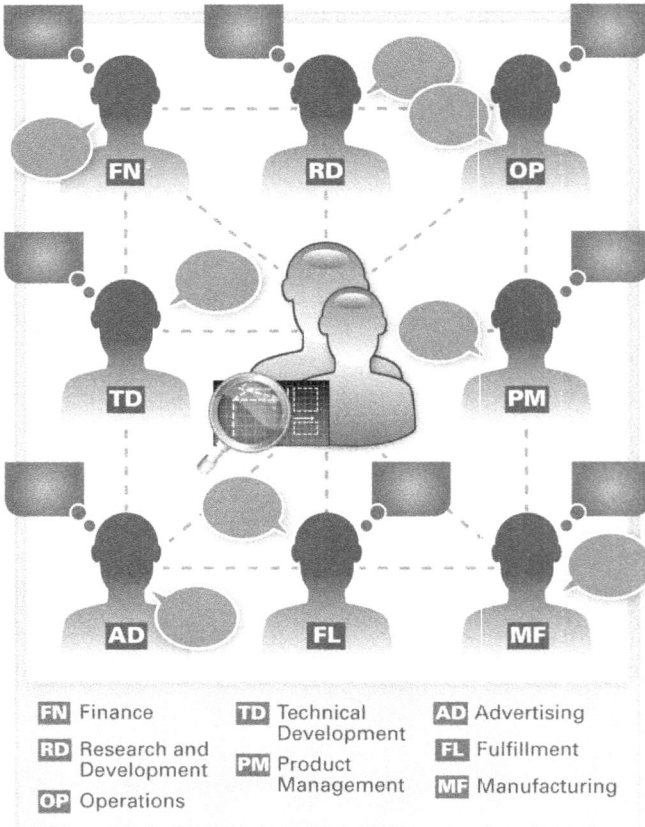

FN
RD
OP
TD
PM
AD
FL
MF

FN Finance	**TD** Technical Development	**AD** Advertising
RD Research and Development	**PM** Product Management	**FL** Fulfillment
OP Operations		**MF** Manufacturing

CONFIRM proof of concept ✓

budget ✓

CLOSE purchase plan

Figure 3.2 *The creative solution mode*

e-commerce functions and descriptions of all products to their website. The company's ultimate goal is to increase sales and improve cash flow. (In this case the prospective customer is the publisher, not the publisher's prospective customers. The "product" is what the marketer will deliver to increase sales and improve cash flow.) The marketer will determine the amount of additional revenue that is expected as well as the reduction in days receivable (i.e., a measure of improvement in cash flow). The astute marketer will realize that simply adding product descriptions and e-commerce functions to the site is likely not sufficient to sell more products. The company must ensure that customers who visit the site are willing and able to purchase products. In addition to understanding the intended result and the reason for seeking it, the marketer must understand what the customer is expecting to experience and willing to endure to achieve the result.

Once the expected result and process for achieving it has been clearly identified, the marketer must identify parameters around the process that will define the scope of the solution. The parameters can be defined by identifying the functions required; an acceptable form factor; a comfortable manner for executing functions; the level of performance expected; and how and when the solution will be used. The marketer armed with this information can engage in the creative solution mode prepared to create a picture of a solution that will meet the customer's requirements. Visualization is an important initial step toward achieving a defined objective. The marketer engages in the creative solution mode by creating a picture of the prospective customer's defined goal. In Figure 3.2, the person is looking at the publisher's goal of increasing sales and improving cash flow. Not only does the person, the marketer in this instance, see the goal, he or she also sees the product and service components that allow that goal to be attained. **Understanding what these components are, and how they can be combined and implemented to attain the desired goal, is the essence of identifying potential products and services**. This requires the ability to intuitively discern what the prospective customer actually wants, which is often different from what they say they want; and, more importantly, to creatively apply that knowledge to the available and soon-to-be-available technologies that can turn that vision into a reality. When it comes to IT, this is usually a combination of software, hardware, telecommunications, and other services.

We have learned that (in Chapter 2) the marketer creating products and services doesn't have to deliver all of the components necessary
to achieve the result. To achieve success, however, the marketer should
understand what the prospective customer requires to use the product or
services and how they will acquire and use these components. When visu-
alizing the solution that will turn the vision into a reality, the marketer
must see the total solution. Information technology solutions generally
consist of seven components: software, hardware, telecommunications,
maintenance, support, implementation and training. The marketer must
understand how much of each component is necessary to deliver the
intended result. For an explanation using our publisher as an example,
visit www.The5Ps.com/LEM/IdentifyingProducts-Publisher.html

In many cases, the list of needs and wants is more difficult to satisfy
than in the example of the publisher. The creative solution mode is
more challenging and involved when the list of needs and wants is more
extensive and the technologies that satisfy those needs and wants are not
obvious. In Chapter 3 (Identifying Wants and Needs), we learn several
techniques for defining confirmed ideas. In Chapter 2 (The Right Combination: Identifying Features and Functions that Sell), we learned the
importance of identifying a complete list of customers' needs and wants.
This list would be used to create a product blueprint. The next step in
the creative solution mode is what takes place between identifying needs
and wants, and beginning the product blueprint. The innovative marketer
gives life to a product or service by tying the needs and wants of prospective customers to features and functions made possible by current and
emerging technologies. This is where art and science converge. The art of
turning ideas into features and functions; and the science of matching current and developing technologies to a stated set of features and functions.

The art and science of technology marketing is better understood
with an example. To understand how an appliance company created a
solution that dramatically improved customer service, visit www.The5Ps
.com/LEM/IdentifyingProducts-ApplianceCo.html. The quintessential
solution ultimately depends on the circumstances of the customer. The
specific circumstances of the companies implementing these systems varied as well as the value they derived and the profit realized by the vendor
delivering the systems solution.

Matching the needs of the prospective customer to the features and functions of the solution provides the content for the product blueprint. This is the step that gives life to the product. It is the point of conception. While this is the lion's share of the effort, the process is not complete. It is the creative solution mode that determines what will sell. Engaging in this mode gives the astute marketer success. Once the product solution has been identified it must be confirmed. The marketer will conduct feasibility studies, run focus groups, and produce trials to redefine the target market and determine how much they are willing to pay.

If the marketer can skillfully create an environment or scenario that mimics the result desired with the impending product, the trials can be run without a prototype. Once the trial has been completed, the next step is to determine the cost, time, risks, and feasibility of producing the product or service. The creative solution mode will, consequently, determine where resources will be deployed. This process will determine whether the product can be produced, promoted, and sold at a price that will allow an acceptable profit to be earned. (see The Right Combination: Identifying Features and Functions that Sell, Chapter 2).

The process of identifying potential products and services is critical in being first to market with a winning product or service. The astute marketer who is on target with identifying products or services that respond to the specific requirements of a defined target market is said to be in the creative solution mode. This process cannot be adapted to a static formula for it is dynamic. It is both a science and an art. There is no guarantee that following this model will produce results; however, it has proven itself repeatedly in the past. Using the process presented here will surely increase the odds of success.

Identifying User Interdependencies

There are numerous factors that contribute to the dynamism of the process of identifying potential products and services. Price, competition, distribution, and other elements of the marketing mix affect each other in different ways and to varying degrees. In other words, they are cross elastic. There is a cross elasticity between and among features and functions. Adding more features to a software product, for example, may result in functions taking longer to perform. Likewise, there is a cross elasticity between and among the needs and wants of customers.

A customer's willingness to pay may be dependent upon when the product or service is received. The cross elasticity between customer needs and wants is also known as user interdependencies.

The ability to recognize and measure user interdependencies is a powerful skill in the design of any product or service. This is particularly true when these interdependencies affect the features, functions, and cost of the product. To review some classic user interdependencies that typically confront IT product managers, visit www.The5Ps.com/LEM/UserInterdependencies.html

Indeed, having a grasp of user interdependencies will help the product manager determine the optimal mix of features, functions, and costs. Understanding user interdependencies also helps the product manager recognize when complementary products or services will serve the customer well. For example, a customer's need for instant gratification may be balanced by their need to maintain simplicity and style. They may be willing to carry devices that support messaging, receive stock prices, and directions as long as the device is easy to use on the go and does not interfere with what they are wearing or carrying. So in addition to a cell phone, the wireless network subscriber may also need to subscribe to a stock and news alert service. This presumes, of course, that the device and function of its accompanying software and services allow the subscriber to carry and use it with ease throughout the time period the software and services are required. Recognizing and accommodating customer interdependencies can create tremendous growth opportunities.

The product manufacturer, distributor, or anyone in the value chain can take advantage of growth opportunities made possible by user interdependencies. A company may expand vertically or horizontally to accommodate the wants and needs of customers. A computer manufacturer, for example, might expand vertically by adding software, training and other services in response to the customer's requirements. The manufacturer could expand horizontally by offering a larger selection of computer models that appeal to a broader customer set.

The product manager who understands user interdependencies may also recognize tangential and divergent needs that give rise to additional products and services that can benefit the customer. For example, after installing and implementing a new accounting and operations system, a major financial services company needed to revamp their organizational structure and create new job descriptions. After using a new contact management system for a year, a professional services firm chose to reorganize the office and filing system in response to the decrease in paper required to track critical information. A professional organizer was hired to facilitate this process. In each case, the implementation of technology gave rise to the purchase of additional products and services. The product manager who recognizes the needs, and takes steps in advance to accommodate them, will increase customer satisfaction and loyalty while opening the door for new sources of revenue.

Understanding user interdependencies also helps the marketer to modify the marketing mix to optimize the return from the target market. That means not only understanding the response to the features and functions of the product, but also understanding the response to the manner in which the product is made available and used.

The ability to identify and respond to the needs and wants of customers is a valuable skill for the product manager. Being able to prepare for the cross elasticity between customer needs and wants, or user interdependencies, vastly increases the value of that skill. The astute marketer will recognize many opportunities to increase customer satisfaction.

New products, new partnerships to deliver broader solutions, a referral or recommendation list for customers, and improved service due to better understanding of current and future needs are just a few of the things that have resulted from responding to user interdependencies. This is yet another marketing skill and opportunity that should not be ignored.

Creating Products That Sell

One of the primary objectives of marketing is to create and deliver products that people pay for. This is easier said than done. In Chapter 2 (The Right Combination: Identifying Features and Functions that Sell), we explored the process of using research to define a feature–function set that is turned into a product blueprint. A prototype is created, the 5 Ps of marketing are applied, and a product is created. In this chapter (Identifying Potential Products and Services), we learn how to translate customer needs and wants into a set of features and functions that define a product. Once engaged in the creative solution mode, the marketer can determine whether the product can be produced, promoted, and sold at a price that will allow an acceptable profit to be earned. In the real world, the marketer does not always have the luxury of creating a product blueprint or assembling all of the components necessary to turn the concept from the creative solution mode into reality.

The marketer must always stay tuned to the market. He or she must listen to what the market is saying. Listening is much more than merely hearing what is said; it is actively understanding the message being delivered. Listening means hearing and comprehending verbal messages; interpreting and discerning the unspoken meaning behind the words; observing trends and understanding what motivates people to follow them; defining and quantifying values that are placed on needs and wants. In short, listening means understanding what people are willing to pay for, how much they will pay, and when they will make their purchases.

While the marketer should be armed with the techniques presented, he or she usually has three choices to create a product that sells. The marketer can create a new product, redirect an existing product to a new target market, or modify an existing product to meet what the market wants.

Create a New Product

Creative engineers must craft performance functions that produce measurable results that are of value to the customer. This means first understanding the customers' needs or requirements. Secondly, it means developing technology that delivers on those needs. Building on the possibilities of technology and creating technologies that respond to defined needs is a chicken and egg process. The possibilities are sometimes not clear until the need is understood; likewise, the needs are not clear until the possibilities are understood. It is the existence of performance functions that often leads to the desire to implement technologies to produce a desired set of results. Nevertheless, once the desired set of results has been identified, the marketer and the engineer must strive to strike the optimal balance between features and functions.

Find a New Target Market

The product may be a great idea and willing to be purchased, but by a different group of people than those who are currently targeted. The world of IT is flush with products looking for a home. In some cases, the product is an interesting idea without a market; in other cases, the product is a good idea that has been presented to a group of people who have no need or desire to purchase it. The marketer who is in tune with their overall market will recognize a product that fits a need or want of one or more segments in the market they follow. He or she will also understand how to apply pricing, promotion, distribution, and packaging to spur sale of the product.

Modify an Existing Product

In many cases, products are created that dazzle the wonders of technology but evade the needs and desires of potential customers. The feature–function mix may be off; the functions could have been implemented in opposition to the market's desire; or the packaging could lack appeal. If the product has one or more of the features and functions that fit the needs or wants of a market, and more importantly, if additional features and functions can be added, a product that might sell could be created. As with any newly modified product, there are several factors that determine whether its launch will be successful. The intensity of the needs and wants of the market that this product responds to; the amount and strength of the competition; and the success of its launch and promotion are a few of the factors that can determine a product's success. Whether the product being modified is new and didn't sell, or has been around for a while, revamping can be a more cost effective and timely means of bringing a "new" product to market that fulfills new demand.

When a product is first to market and its presence attracts copycat products, it is often called a *market maker*. In this case the products that are sold, not the people who buy them, define the "market." This is a misnomer according to the definition of a market that we embrace (see A Market is a Group of People, Chapter 1). Theoretically, the predisposition of a group of people to purchase a new product already exists. The introduction of a new product simply unveils the predisposition to buy. There is no market maker —only people who know how to recognize and deliver what the market is willing to pay for. The market may or may not be consciously aware of the need or desire that gives rise to a market maker product or service. It is the astute marketer who is, in reality, the market maker.

There are several techniques and tools for identifying and developing products that will sell. In most companies, however, the marketer will ultimately have three choices. To create a product that sells, he or she must (1) understand what the market wants, produce it, and deliver; (2) find the right market for an existing product; or (3) modify his or her product to fit the profile of what the market is willing to purchase. Whether the decision is **create a new product**, **find a new target market**, or **modify an existing product**, the marketer has options for adapting existing and new technologies to the needs and wants of defined markets.

Funding Development Versus Product Acceptance: The Cat and Mouse Game

I'm from Missouri, show me.

Research and development funding by IT companies is often directed toward new technologies rather than new products. Scientists and engineers focus on turning a new concept into reality. Projects might include using new materials to create energy, or new processes to achieve an end result. Information technology research and development projects are also based on reaching the next stage of existing technologies. An example is accomplishing one or more functions more efficiently, that is, faster, less expensive, or by using fewer resources. Computer chips are designed to run faster, process more data, and use less energy. Storage devices are designed to hold a larger capacity. The cost of research and development can vary immensely from project to project. Moreover, it is quite difficult to accurately estimate the cost of developing new technologies.

The research and development budgets of companies tend to amount to a given percentage of annual revenue. Projects are evaluated, ranked, and funded as the budget allows. Funding can be provided from sources other than the company's budget, however. Government grants, nonprofit associations, trade associations, and other private entities provide funds for research and development. Many companies, like those in the pharmaceutical industry, for example, work with colleges and universities to develop new technologies and processes. Regardless of the source of research and development, the funding must be justified. The group that is funded for research and development must meet the requirements of the funding source. The justification may be provided in the form of proposals, presentations, or both. In many cases, additional justification must be provided so that funding can be provided over an extended period, from year to year, for example.

The focus of product development can be the result of new or emerging technologies created in research and development, the result of opportunities identified by sales and marketing, or an idea from another source. Funding can come from a number of sources including venture capitalists,[3] customers, or the company itself. In entrepreneurial companies, product development is conducted, and thus funded, by the entrepreneurs themselves.

Confirmation of engagement in product development is a continuing process. Entrepreneurs and pioneers often fund prototype development. Their money and time is a leap of faith that demonstrates their belief that the product will sell. Their confirmation is fueled by their belief in the product and continues until they run out of time, money, or until revenues and profits are realized. In the case of established companies, marketing research and customer feedback must be compelling to gain funding for new products. Some companies expect customers to fully or partially fund prototype development as a demonstration of their intent to purchase. One or more letters of intent is the minimal show of faith that's expected. Companies with a well-rounded, solid marketing process will rely upon market research and develop product prototypes. Once prototypes have been developed, there must be approval by funding or other prospective customers to purchase the product. In many cases, additional development or revisions to the prototype are required before the purchase can be made. This is where the cat and mouse game turns into full gear. Prospective customers who want the product, particularly those who have paid for development, strive to get a set of features and functions that expressly meet their needs. The product manager, however, strives to produce a set of features and functions that will universally appeal to the entire target market. **The goal is to strike the right balance**.

The process of confirming development of a new product can become much like a cat and mouse game. It starts with the belief in an idea. Once belief in the product's success is accepted by a funding source, and funds are deployed to development, development begins. If the funds are not sufficient to cover development until completion, the confirmation and funding process must continue. In most cases, the confirmation process is not complete until development has been completed, the product has been promoted and sold, and revenue has been collected.

Funding New Products and Services

Budgeting

Most corporations operate using a defined financial planning and budgeting process. While this process varies from company to company, understanding how it works is essential to get funding for product development. Budgeting is normally done bottom up or top down. In bottom-up budgeting, the product manager estimates the cost of everything that's needed to develop the new product and bring it to market. All the items in the estimate are added together to determine the required budget amount. In top-down budgeting, the product manager starts with the amount they are likely to be allocated and determine what they are able to achieve with that level of funding. Several other budgeting techniques exist (i.e., zero-based budgeting) to estimate the cost of resources required to develop and deliver products. All, when implemented properly, can be effective in arriving at a credible estimate.

In addition to ensuring that the budget is sufficient to meet the requirements of the product life cycle, the objective of the product manager in the budgeting process is to win approval for funding their product. This means building a business case that demonstrates the product's compliance with the company's strategic direction, adhering to an acceptable level of risk and achieving the objective with a realistic amount of resources. Of course, internal company politics will always play a role in the approval of the budget. Comprehensive estimates and a sound business case are nonetheless required as a baseline preparation for winning budget approval. To prepare for unpredictable development and other costs, the business plan should include contingency actions. The contingencies might allow for a different feature–function mix, a higher price, or even a new mix of distribution channels. The purpose of the business plan described herein is to gain budget approval to fund the development and launch of a new product or service. Once the funding has been granted, the product manager may have to adjust the plan to fit the amount provided.

Financing

It is the treasury department of many large corporations that handles financing requirements. Entrepreneurs, small and medium sized businesses, however, consider the costs and consequences of financing in new product and service decisions. Since financing a product can extend beyond the scope of the treasury department or financial institutions, this section shall address financing from the perspective of the product manager.

Financing can be provided by financial institutions, business partners, or through the structure of the product's pricing. Conventional business financing includes taking out loans, opening or increasing lines of credit, selling stock or bonds, or other marketable securities to raise cash. Generally, the interest rate, terms, and conditions dictate the cost of financing. If and when the cost of financing is an integral part of the product development decision, it is factored into the financial projections (by discounting future cash flows by this cost or reducing revenue by this cost to accurately present profits).

Financing can also be provided, usually at little or no hard cost, by business partners or product pricing. Business partners can include any company involved in helping the company attain its goals. Financial partners can provide virtual financing by facilitating the customer's ability to buy products. Retailers team with consumer credit companies, for example, to offer special promotions that include low interest or delayed payments. Channel partners, such as distributors, team with manufacturers to share in discounted promotions that encourage consumers to purchase in greater quantity more immediately (i.e., bundled pricing). In each case, the company is able to increase the flow of revenue, reduce costs associated with moving (i.e., promoting and selling) the product, or both. These gains serve to reduce or eliminate the need for financing and are, thus, considered virtual financing. The financing deals that are provided by business partners are only limited by the creativity and determination of the company and its partner.

Finally, financing can be provided through the structure of a product's pricing. (see Structuring, Chapter 2 p. 79). The pricing structure can provide financing by increasing the cash available from product purchases and making it available earlier. In Table 2.1, five types of pricing structures were presented including recurring payments and buy-in plus recurring payments. In each of these examples, effective financing can be provided by accelerating the amount of money received from recurring payments. When a buy-in is included in the pricing structure, the amount of that buy-in can be increased.

Of course, there are costs to be borne from using marketing tools to finance products. Changing the structure of a product's price can result in repositioning the product in the eye of the customer. A more accelerated payment structure, for example, could be interpreted as the product having a shorter life. A higher buy-in could be interpreted as lower quality, particularly if the return policy is stringent. Increases in advertising and promotion or realignment of sales and distribution might be necessary to compensate for reduction in revenue from restructured pricing. All changes in product revenue and associated marketing costs must be taken into account through adjustments in the business plan.

Whether financing is provided by restructured pricing, business partners, financial institutions, venture capitalists, or other sources, there are fundamental issues that should be considered in evaluating its viability. The availability of total resources, given the selection of a source; the hard and soft, direct and indirect costs; and the risks associated with the choice and source of financing are among the major considerations. Even when financing doesn't have a direct affect on the marketability of a product, it does have a direct effect on the product's profitability. To the extent necessary, the product manager should consider financing in the product planning process.

Bringing Products to Market

The marketing, development, and production departments should, therefore, have a primary plan (plan A) and an alternate plan (plan B) that allows for the cost effective production and delivery of the product to a target market. The primary plan is the baseline product life cycle plan.

To develop a viable plan, marketing must determine which businesses or consumers are likely to purchase the product (target market), how to reach them (promotional), and the most effective means to encourage them to buy. Development must determine how to create a *product* with the desired combination of features and functions (*packaging*), while meeting the cost points necessary to achieve an acceptable rate of return (*price*). Production must determine how to cost effectively manufacture the specified product quantity and make it available to the distribution channels (*place*). Collectively, marketing, development, and production will provide information to help form a baseline product plan.

The next step is to determine when and how to go forward with development of the prototype. The real question is "Are you in a race to be first in the market?" A cost-benefit analysis is warranted to answer this question. Being first to market often means setting criteria and meeting expectations of the target market. It means establishing position and gaining an edge by capturing market share. This comes with a certain cost and risks, however. There is the cost of educating the market on your product, particularly if it incorporates new technologies. There could be the cost of establishing new sales and distribution channels, and new support resources. The risks include educating your competition and helping them enter the market, getting into a promotional battle, or missing the mark on the feature–function mix or price point for the product.

Copycat companies have proven time and time again the financial rewards of being second, third, or even later to market. Nevertheless, being first to market with an effective marketing plan will guarantee success virtually every time.

The Beta Phase

A good marketing plan requires an understanding of what is required for the target market to purchase and receive your product. An effective means of qualifying and refining this understanding is through the beta process. Beta, the second letter in the Greek alphabet (i.e., β), has come to be known as *a* measure of the deviation from what has been defined as the norm. Beta is a step above the lowest level; a precursor to the next thing. In molecular biology, a beta sheet is a regular structure in an extended polypeptide change that has been stabilized in the form of a sheet. In science, beta-carotene is the precursor to vitamin A. In finance, beta is a measure of financial risk; it is the monthly change in the price of a stock in relation to the monthly price change of a specified index (i.e., Standard & Poor's 500). The beta version of a software product is the second phase of testing in which a subset of the target market uses the product. Regardless of the industry or discipline, the purpose of the *beta test is to determine if the product is ready to be released to the general target market.* This means more than determining whether the product functions properly; the beta phase offers an opportunity to confirm how the customer will use the product, the benefits and value that will be gained, how much they are willing to pay, where and how the customer prefers to purchase the product, and more.

The first step in the beta phase is to define clear, measurable objectives. The primary objective should be to confirm and uncover all information necessary for a successful product launch. It is important to recruit evaluators from the target market who will devote the time and energy needed to provide critical and informative feedback. This means that the recruiting criteria and methods must be carefully planned and prepared. Beta facilitators can search in sales teams, retail stores, and other sales channels. They can also search among customer focus groups, advertising contacts, website visitors, or from selected databases. The search should be broad enough to get a good sampling of the target market. Some companies offer databases of people who are ready to beta test products.

A profile should be developed to guide interviewers through the screening and selection process. Consider the time that they will be able to invest in reviewing the product, their interest in the product, their skills and ability to deliver a candid evaluation, and other criteria necessary to provide information for a successful launch. The potential evaluators should be thoroughly screened and qualified. They should be re-qualified before the evaluators are selected. The facilitators should not turn away a lot of candidates to avoid damaging the target audience. Also, do not give away too big of a prize or award so that evaluators are not motivated by money, but by the *product.*

The beta facilitator will advise the evaluators of their selection and equip them with everything necessary to do a thorough job. The facilitator should map out, at the beginning of the process, what the evaluator needs to do to provide the feedback that is expected.

It is essential to establish a clear and timely communications process between the facilitator group and the evaluators. This is particularly helpful to the process since marketers find that many evaluators do not give feedback in typical beta programs. The evaluators should be instructed on their responsibilities in the evaluation process and provided with a schedule that includes items and dates of delivery. The testing phase needs structure. *People need to be told how to evaluate a product.* Evaluators should be given detailed instructions so that they know what to expect and how to use the product. Remember, beta facilitators need quantitative and qualitative information from evaluators. Fulfillment is an important part of the process. The evaluators should also have sufficient support to use the product effectively. Handholding and efficient organization are essential. After all, it is easy to lose focus in a beta project when you don't have what you need—the evaluator simply refocuses on their real job or more pressing responsibilities. Finally, timing is critical to managing the beta project. Everything should flow smoothly so that the evaluators can focus on the activities that allow them to provide the necessary feedback on the product, purchase process, support required, and other criteria defined in the beta phase.

After the initial testing phase has been completed, a mid-term review is conducted. The results of this review will help the product manager to determine if any of the objectives must be changed. For example, feedback might determine that there should be more product configurations or models to choose from or if a feature or function should be changed. After the mid-term review, the appropriate adjustments and changes are made and testing resumes. The same rules and processes apply to the second phase of testing as were implemented in the first phase. The second phase of testing is concluded with a final review.

The data is accumulated and then reviewed by the product manager and designated key people. The results are used to add or remove features and functions to the product, as well as make other changes to the marketing process before the product launch.

There are several factors that can impede the beta process. The impediments depend on the circumstances of each individual beta project and are too numerous to be covered in their entirety; however, a few will be highlighted here. In many cases, there is no closure in the communications between the facilitator and evaluators. Evaluators send feedback that is not considered nor is any response given. That is more than a waste of time and money conducting the beta process; it also runs the risk of damaging the reputation of the product and company. This is sometimes due to the communications process and, in other cases, due to a lack of resources allocated to the beta phase. Inadequate resources are the second popular impediment to the beta process. In other cases, the beta phase is used solely as an extended quality assurance process rather than a means to gather comprehensive marketing feedback. This results in lost opportunities and the evaluators being misled. To make the most of the beta phase, it should be conducted properly and in its entirety. When the beta phase is conducted as intended, that is, to determine if the product is ready to be released to the general target market, the likelihood of the product's success is increased.

Using Fear, Uncertainty, and Doubt (FUD)

"Are you sure you're willing to risk your system's security to the anti-virus software alone?"

"Do you feel comfortable with the quality of service that your telecommunications system delivers? Even given the fact that your company's growth has put you at 96% of capacity?"

Fear, uncertainty, and doubt, otherwise known as FUD, has been a sales and marketing technique for a long time. While it is not always delivered in a noble manner[4] and is illegal in many countries when used deceptively, it is often effective. FUD has been used for basically two reasons: to allay the product introductions of competition, and to make the customer feel compelled to buy the product.

Being first to market offers tremendous advantages. The product can gain recognition as having superior expertise; the manufacturer can establish or strengthen its position with distributors; establish promotional messages in the minds of prospective customers; and more. It is no wonder that some people try to slow down sales of a competitor's new product when they cannot offer an alternative. FUD can be used to question the readiness of the new product. It can also be used to convince the customer to wait for a product that has not been released or may be not even announced yet. FUD has been used to help customers think through the implications of installing a new product that is not compatible or does not provide a level of integration that allows it to be implemented cost effectively.

In other cases, the customer needs to consider the consequences of not installing a new product or an upgrade that is necessary to ensure the smooth operation of their system. New products can offer a level of service that is necessary to maintain a competitive advantage. New products can also offer functionality that reduces operations expenses. The purchase and installation of an upgrade can reduce maintenance expenses. In some instances, the customer needs to be reminded of the advantages or costs of not purchasing new products. Fear, uncertainty, and doubt can be used to help customers realize those advantages or avoid the costs by purchasing a new product now.

Premature Introductions

Products can be introduced prematurely for a number of reasons, some are intentional and others are not. Premature introductions take place when the beta phase or other parts of the due diligence process are skipped. They also take place when companies try too hard to keep up with competition. Some software companies have had the dubious distinction of having one or more of their products called *vaporware* when they failed to perform as promoted or, worse, never existed at all. When a product can deliver a baseline of functionality, and market circumstances warrant, an early introduction can be quite advantageous. When the rewards outweigh the risks, the product should be introduced early. On the other hand, a little restraint and patience can prove to be extremely valuable. In order to make the call, the product manager must understand the pros and cons of introducing a product early.

Pros. Products are sometimes introduced before they're ready to ship. This is to encourage new *customers to wait* for the product. It is also a means to convince existing customers to wait rather than converting to a competing product. A product can also be introduced before it is complete so that the customers can *become accustomed to the user interface* or simply get into the habit of using the features and functions that do work. This works well for software or services that can absorb feature and function enhancements fairly easily. The full product functionality can be added in an interim release after the customer has completed the purchase and installation. The early introduction of products and services also helps to *unearth high potential customers.* Early adopters often represent high revenue sales, particularly when they represent large corporations. They will keep an eye out for new products and services that fit their needs and aggressively take steps to purchase them.

Cons. The premature introduction of products and services also has associated costs. There are likely to be problems with the early introduction of products and services. Product shipments may not arrive on time, the product may not perform as expected, support resources may not be capable of providing needed assistance, spare parts and related peripherals may not be available, and more. Such challenges will try the patience of customers and the business partners who service them. Some *customers may even turn to competitors* as a result of the experience. It takes time and resources to make amends for problems that plague customers. Generally, it is more expensive to win customers back than it is to provide the quality of service necessary to keep them. When problems arise, it is not uncommon for related problems to become exposed. With a little extra time and preparation, some of these problems may have been resolved without being exposed. A company *can damage its reputation by exposing problems that could have been conquered.* Premature introduction of products increases the likelihood of this happening. Finally, extra expense will be incurred from the *increase in sales and support effort and resources* needed for the accelerated introduction.

There are numerous pros and cons to introducing a product or service early. They will vary with the product and the circumstances that surround its market. To be sure, there are costs and risks associated with early introduction that must be assessed.

Likewise, there are benefits to early introduction that sometimes make it well worth the effort. The product manager should carefully weigh the pros and cons and make a decision whether or not to introduce early.

Getting Ready for Production

One of the most important steps in bringing products to market is actually preparing for them to be produced. Much of the information that is collected during the product qualification process can be used to prepare for production. Engineering creates prototypes to validate design and manufacturing processes that become a part of the product plan. This feeds into the financial and operational requirements for producing the product. To prepare for production, the product manager needs to map out roles and responsibilities in four primary areas. The product manager must do the following:

- Establish Schedules and Project Flow
- Prepare Production Components
- Schedule Production
- Engage Delivery and Fulfillment Process

Establish Schedules and Project Flow.   Regardless of whether you are producing a software or hardware product or telecommunications service, schedules have to be put into place. Everyone in the production process should know when his or her contribution is due and, if necessary, how it affects the entire process. One of the pivotal dates is when development is completed. This date is easier to project after a prototype has been created and the needed refinements have been defined.

Whether the schedule is for a new software or hardware product, or a new telecommunications service, the date that development will be completed must be confirmed and scheduled. The production lead time should also be determined so that the next phases in the production process can be scheduled. Since advertising and promotion should take place in tandem with the production process, these schedules (media, launch, and others) should be set in connection with the production schedule.

Prepare Production Components.   It is necessary to identify and prepare for everything that is needed to create the product or deliver the service. Responsibility for all phases of production, including ordering parts and components, may rest with manufacturing, engineering, operations, product management, or another group. Regardless of the point of responsibility, parts must be ordered to manufacture hardware products; the golden master must be created to replicate software products; and hardware and software must be ordered to get networks up and running. The timing and process of ordering parts and components is dependent upon the schedules and project flow that have been established as well as the planned production process.

Schedule Production.   Producing the hardware device, software package, or network service is, obviously, a critical phase in bringing products to market. Timing is essential. All parts, equipment, and labor must be in place for manufactured products. Information from pre-production runs, parts ordering, schedules, and other sources should have been compiled and reviewed by production management to allow for potential obstacles and protect the process to ensure timely delivery of product. In the case of software, the replication of media and packaging drives production.

All packaging components, graphics copy, media parts, replication equipment, and labor must be in place and ready. Production for network services focuses on ensuring that the network is configured and set up properly. This ensures that fulfillment will result in the delivery of services. That is, when the new subscriber is equipped with the hardware and software necessary to access the network, and their subscription is activated, everything runs smoothly. Whether it is a software or hardware product, or network service, a well-planned production schedule and process is critical to a successful launch.

Engage Delivery and Fulfillment Process.   The final step to ensure that a product is in full production is making sure that it can reach the customer. Initial orders to distributors, resellers, first run customers, the media, warehouse facilities, and others must take place accurately and expeditiously. The process to handle subsequent orders whether to warehousing or one of the locations in the sales channel, must be in place and running efficiently. This is particularly important when just-in-time inventory methods are in use. Product shipping schedules and processes should be clear to all players; the order and fulfillment process should be easy for all; finally, other financial processes such as payment receipt, invoicing, collection, and reporting should have been modified to incorporate the new product or service.

The product manager should have production in mind from the beginning of the marketing process, that is, conceiving of the product or service. Production considerations are taken into account when determining whether to pursue evaluation of a prospective product or service. Keep in mind that engineering creates prototypes to validate design and manufacturing processes that become a part of the product plan.

This feeds into the financial and operational requirements for producing the product. That, in turn, helps to determine the profit potential of the product. Any and all information gathered in the early stages of evaluating products can be used to prepare for the production process. To bring a product to market successfully, all phases of the production process must be put in place.

Establishing Price

The willingness and ability of the target market to pay for a product or service provides the basis for price. If the willingness to pay is within the ability to pay, then the willingness to pay provides the foundation for the determination of the price. If the willingness to pay exceeds the ability to pay, the foundation for the determination of price will be lower if conditions permit. For example, the price can be structured to facilitate payment by stretching out payments. If the use of indirect channels is part of the marketing strategy, the willingness to pay must allow room for reseller margins and discounts.

The last consideration is whether the price is sufficient to provide an acceptable return on the product. Pricing is a marketing process, not an accounting or financial process. Once it has been determined the price at which the desired market share can be achieved, the product manager must determine whether that price will deliver an acceptable return on the launch, sale, and delivery of the product. If the product will meet minimum levels of profitability, its launch should proceed. Otherwise, it should be abandoned.

Setting the Level

Market research and validation testing can help determine the amount that the target market is willing to pay. Determining the willingness to pay is more of an art than a science (see Identifying Willingness to pay, Chapter 2).

Based on techniques presented in Chapter 3, the market research and testing may focus on determining the price that, in the eyes of the target market, is comparable to the product being priced; or what the target market perceives the solution being delivered by the product is worth. Once a target price level has been determined, it is qualified by comparing it to what competitors are charging for like or comparable products; determining its elasticity; and confirming its ability to deliver a profit.

Competitive products or comparable solutions offered by other companies are excellent sources to qualify the price that has been set. The amount that customers have actually paid for a comparable product is virtual proof of willingness to pay for your product. The factors that affect price elasticity must be understood so that the price at launch can be modified, if necessary, to reflect the market condition at the time of the launch. The degree to which the price might be increased or decreased should be understood so that the level set at launch leaves enough room for change without negatively affecting future marketability.

Finally, once a price level has been determined, the product manager should re-confirm that an adequate gross margin could be attained. All direct and indirect costs associated with the product must be covered. In other words, product profitability must be achieved (see Covering Product Costs, Chapter 2).

Defining the Structure

The product price should be structured to allow a critical mass of targeted customers to purchase the product. Remember, *the structure of the price defines to the customer the amount and the manner in which they will pay for the product. It lets the customer know whether or not they can afford the product* (see Structuring, Chapter 2). There are several objectives that should be kept in mind when designing the pricing structure. These objectives may be used individually, collectively, or not at all. The product strategy will determine which, if any, of these objectives will be pursued.

One objective may be to reduce the burden of cash disbursements on the customer. In other words, the vendor is offering an alternative means of financing by agreeing to accept payments over a period of time. Another objective may be to tie in the value of the product with the value of other products. In actuality this is piggybacking on the customer appeal of other successful products; or it is demonstrating the increased value that both products have when used together. Still a third objective may be to ensure a profit or value to channel partners for selling the product. This is particularly important to the product manager when the channel partner is instrumental in the sales process. Another objective, that often complicates and slows down the purchase process, is to ensure that all cost components are covered. Ongoing product related fees, for example, are measured by ongoing expenses incurred in conjunction with delivering the product or delivering the service that accompanies the product. A common example is when a customer bases their purchase of wireless communications services on the price of the cell phone itself rather than the pricing of the subscription service that they sign up for. In this case, a pricing structure that is difficult and expensive to administer but simple for the customer to understand, may be just the answer to increase and maintain revenue streams and, ultimately, long-term profitability.

When developing pricing structure, the product manager should take into account all factors that affect the target market's ability to purchase the product as well as the company's ability to deliver it and earn a profit. The *relative importance of the want or need met by the product*, coupled with the strength of the promotional campaign, will drive the extent to which the structure should encourage the purchase decision. If the product is a necessity, for example, and the promotional campaign is strong, it may not be necessary to structure the price to incent the purchase. Once the objective of the pricing structure is clear, the basic rules of its design and implementation should be kept in mind. The pricing structure should be simple. It should be easy for the customer to understand. It should also be easy to implement. The pricing structure should also take into account the *timing of when the product's value is delivered*. If value is delivered over an extended period of time, as in many software packages, the structure might allow for additional revenue to be earned through future charges. High profit upgrades, maintenance services, or bundled services might be included in the pricing structure to bring additional revenue. If the value is delivered in a relatively short period of time, on the other hand, it might be wise to structure the price so that payment is received up front or in a short period of time. Finally, the pricing structure should consider the financial circumstances of the vendor and customer. This, of course, includes the economic conditions of the target market. The structure should accommodate the customer's ability to disburse the funds needed for the product. This can be achieved by teaming with financial partners to provide third-party financing.

If the business entity offering the product is financially healthy, financing may provide an opportunity to identify or present new sales opportunities. The product manager should strive for simplicity when designing the pricing structure. The structure is one means to implement a product strategy. It is also a means to reveal the competitor's strategy. While the level and structure of the product's price will help determine its profitability, the objective of price is to increase the product's *marketability*. A low price does not necessarily increase a product's marketability; it can often make the product less attractive to the prospective customer. Rather, the manner in which the price is structured and communicated will drive its effect on product sales.

THE MARKETING PROCESS—PUTTING IT INTO ACTION   163

Exercising Market Control

Exercising market control means having a handle on the 5 Ps of marketing. The product manager who achieves profitability throughout the life cycle never loses control of product pricing. One of the first steps is to decide whether to establish and publicize an SRP. There are several pros and cons that must be evaluated; however, let's focus on the major considerations.

An SRP positions the product with the market. A high price suggests a higher level of quality to many people while a lower price may suggest less quality. The SRP is also a measure against which to rank a product against the competition. It can sometimes help the product manager to prevent the channel from undercutting the intended price by raising the market's expectation of what it should pay for the product.

When the SRP is not set as high as many members of the target market are willing to pay, however, it can serve to limit the price that the channel can realize from selling the product. This is particularly true with new products. A lower price also means less profitability. Striving for a higher volume with an SRP that is not as high as the market will bear might discourage sales outlets patronized by early adopters from carrying the product or other new products from the same family.

An SRP also gives the market a frame of reference to measure changes in the price of the product. Many customers expect prices to decline after the product has been on the market for a while. In some cases, the amount and anticipated timing of a drop in price can stall sales. This is known as the *post introduction price decline syndrome*. The ongoing quest for improvements in price performance reinforces this expectation by the market. It also conditions customers to resist purchasing products whose price has increased. The prospective customer, whose expectations about a product are not colored by an SRP, must learn the *street price* by researching the product. The street price is the amount that has been set by retail outlets, value added resellers (VARs), and other channel partners. An SRP, when implemented properly, helps the product manager strongly influence, and sometimes control, the street price.

The SRP is a powerful marketing tool. Setting the level and structure of the SRP is a critical step in the marketing process. This is not only the case when the product is introduced; it is important throughout the product life cycle. The manner in which the price is set (i.e., level and structure) and the effectiveness with which it is communicated, together define the way that the market receives the product. The timing, direction, and strength of changes in SRP can provide the product manager with control over the street price.

A moderate decrease in price, for example, coupled with more attractive bundling options, may serve to maintain the product's perceived value. This could help to maintain profitability and prolong the product life until a suitable replacement can be introduced. A reduction in price in advance of competitors, on the other hand, might *change the flow* of market share to prepare prospective customers to receive a soon-to-be-released product. The strength of a change in SRP is measured by the amount of the change; the effectiveness of the promotion about the change; and the percentage of the target market that responds to the change. To maintain control over the product throughout its life cycle, the product manager will maneuver SRP to influence the actions of the market.

Using an SRP is not the only means of exercising market control. When taking a baseline approach to establishing price, the product manager will set the level at which resellers can purchase the product. The difference between the reseller's purchase price and the expected street price of the product should allow the reseller to realize an adequate margin from the product. Of course that margin can be pumped up by offering additional benefits to the reseller, such as cooperative advertising and promotion, shorter lead times, and other benefits that improve the reseller's position.

The product manager can use other types of manufacturer's pricing incentives to control the market. Rebates on product purchases, discounts on future products and consignment are a few of the tools of the trade. With a little creativity, the same pricing strategies that are used to exercise market control using SRP can be achieved using manufacturer's incentives. For example, a manufacturer's rebate can be used to lower the price to the customer.

Couple this with a discount coupon on a companion product, and the product's value may be strengthened in the eyes of the market. Sound familiar? "This could help to maintain profitability and prolong the product life until a suitable replacement can be introduced."

Manufacturers can also influence control over the market by offering financing incentives. One means of providing financing is by extending payment terms to the channel. Another is to offer financing to customers through the channel. The manufacturer would either team with a financial institution or underwrite the costs of financing itself. Again, the same pricing strategies employed using SRP or manufacturer's pricing incentives can be implemented by using financing creatively.

While price alone is often not an effective, long-term product strategy, it can be an effective tool in controlling the market. The level and structure of the price communicates a message to the market participants; both to prospective customers as well as resellers and all channel partners. Changes in the suggested retail market can influence market behavior by managing their timing, direction, and strength. Manufacturer's pricing and financing incentives can also influence behavior. Pricing strategies can be implemented using all of these tools. The effectiveness of these strategies is only limited by the creativity of the product manager and his or her understanding of the market.

Establishing Support

An important step in bringing products to market is establishing the processes and resources needed to help customers derive value from that product. We have learned that, ideally, support is taken into account during the product design process (Designing for Maintenance and Support, Chapter 2). The customer often needs technical support to make the purchase decision.

Preparing preliminary systems design, delivering demonstrations, or simply just answering questions are a few of the responsibilities of pre-sales support. Since the product manager needs virtually the same set of processes and resources to establish pre-sales support as ongoing support, we shall start by focusing on what he or she needs to get prepared.

Delivering support is a very labor-intensive process. Careful planning is essential to deliver meaningful results to customers cost effectively. To prepare, one must consider labor requirements, product fixes (i.e., corrections and improvements), and resource deployment.

Labor Requirements

The labor requirements encompass product documentation, training materials, and technical support staff. The skill set necessary to develop and produce useful manuals and training materials must be identified and engaged. Creating manuals is much more than describing features and functions in words. The manner in which the product information is conveyed must allow the reader to readily comprehend the features and functions. That is, the explanation should *leap off the page* to the reader. More importantly, the sequence in which the information is presented should follow a logical learning process. Documentation and training manuals that accentuate the customer's learning experience have the optimal mix of words, sequenced thoughts, and pictures to convey usage concepts to customers. The team that produces these documents needs a combination of technical, writing, teaching, graphical development, and layout skills. Other training materials, such as presentations for instructor-led courses and self-paced tutorials, also require similar skills from the production team. The technical support staff also needs a skill set that goes far beyond understanding how to use the product. This staff needs strong *interpretive, assessment,* and *interpersonal* skills.

Technicians in the field, and those manning support hotlines, should be able to listen attentively. The first step for the technician is to understand what the problem is. The problem may not be a lack of understanding how to execute a particular function. It may have nothing to do with the product at all. Attentive listening requires hearing what is said as well as what is not said; it requires asking the right questions to clarify or affirm the request; it requires making sure that the customer and the technician feel comfortable that each one understands the problem. Once the technician has interpreted the problem, he or she must determine how to resolve it. The technician's analytical skills must extend beyond the scope of the product itself. The source of the problem may lie with incorrect input or interference from another product or service. Technicians who resolve customer problems effectively are able to quickly and accurately assess the cause of the problem and present a viable solution. Finally, technicians who service customers should be able to leave customers with a feeling of satisfaction after the service has been delivered—even if the problem has not been resolved. This requires a high level of interpersonal skills. Of course, as the old adage goes "you can't satisfy everyone all the time." The technician who is customer savvy, however, is in a position to reiterate to the customer that the company *appreciates their business* and *will make every effort to find an amicable and fair resolution* to their problem. Most importantly, the technician will follow up to achieve acceptable resolution. To equip technicians with the resources to provide that follow-up, second and sometimes third tier support groups are established. The technicians who staff these support groups need a higher level of product knowledge and analytical skills than the technicians who provide front line customer support. They also need ready access to development teams, administrative support, and customer service groups to get the information or approvals necessary to deliver a satisfactory response for the first line customer technician.

Indeed, the skills that technicians require depend on the amount of interaction they have with the customer, and the complexity and speed of response that is expected of them. While some of the skills that customer technicians require can be taught, others cannot. Moreover, there may not be sufficient time to provide comprehensive training before the product launch. The product manager must prepare to deliver support after the launch by ensuring that there is adequate staff and they are equipped with adequate resources.

Product Fixes

Most problems with IT products and services are revealed through customer support. Hardware components may break, network performance may falter, and software functions may not execute properly. By establishing a procedure and process for tracking problems before the product is launched, the product manager is better able to identify and resolve them. Product flaws and shortcomings are exposed early on as recurring problems. A sound tracking process, particularly backed by an automated system, makes it much easier to identify product flaws. When this process and system are populated with information that helps customer technicians to resolve problems, it improves customer support. This information may be available from the beta process and other pre-launch activity. The process and system that tracks problems can also provide an early indication of the amount of spare parts inventory that is needed and how often it must be replenished.

Performance monitoring of networks and other systems also provides information that can contribute to delivering a high level of support. All procedures, processes, and systems should be set up and tested before the product is brought to market. This not only helps the support staff to do their job more efficiently, it also helps the product manager to identify the next set of improvements that should be put in place.

Deployment

Once the support team has been hired and support materials have been produced, they must be deployed so that customers may be serviced. There are several factors that should be considered in mapping out the deployment of support resources. The *location of the target market* is one determinant of where and how support resources should be deployed. Location for deployment purposes is characterized by where customers are physically as well as how they can be reached. After all, support resources can be provided on site by a technician, through telephone hotlines or the Internet using live technicians, with manuals and other documentation, or through self-paced learning tools. As a matter of fact, the type of support is only limited by the creativity of the support team and the willingness of the customer to receive it, which brings us to the next factor that should be considered in deploying support resources—*the manner in which customers are accustomed to receiving direction.* Some people are comfortable receiving instructions over the phone, yet others prefer face-to-face discussion. Still other people are at ease reading manuals or pamphlets. Whether an image is delivered through an oral description or on a piece of paper, most people experience increased comprehension and retention when information is delivered through pictures. Multimedia software and the Internet and other technologies have created opportunities to deliver animated explanations to millions of people. Support organizations are increasingly in a position to build repositories of mini explanations that can be dynamically assembled on the fly to answer customer questions. Until these repositories reach a sufficient size and can be delivered through an assortment of communication channels, customers will benefit most from support delivered in a manner that is most comfortable for them.

Support that is delivered in a manner that customers are accustomed means they can absorb it easily. The combination of services used may be different for each product. One reason is because of the nature of the product. Another reason is that the characteristics of each target market will vary. The *effectiveness* of training, hotlines, on-site technicians, and other support methods will vary from market to market. The deployment of support resources will, therefore, also depend on the combination in which they are most effective. Since support comes at a price, and all customers are not willing to pay, the choice of support will also depend on the cost to deliver it and *what customers are willing to pay*. This includes the money they are willing to spend as well as the time and effort that they are willing to invest. Sometimes customers will pay more to receive an answer faster or with less effort. In other cases, they will seek an alternative to the product or service they are using.

Once the labor requirements have been defined, a process of defining and tracking product fixes has been established, and the resources have been deployed, the support resources are employed by delivering answers to customers. After the product or service has been purchased, some customers may need help completing the installation. The next phase is helping customers learn to use products efficiently. Customers should be aware of, and have access to, training tools that help them learn to use the product effectively; product upgrades that improve performance or increase functionality; and sources to repair damages and fix breakage. In short, to bring products to market the product manager must identify, develop, assemble, and deploy the right combination of support resources to help the customer make their purchase decision, get started using the product, and also develop a base level of proficiency. Effective support helps keep the customer in the fold until they upgrade or convert to the next generation product.

Administrative Requirements

One of the less glamorous but extremely important phases in getting products ready for market is completing the administrative requirements.

Manufacturing and production systems need to have the right components in sufficient quantity and labor in place, to produce products and services to market demand. Likewise, there should be an adequate supply of spare parts in the right locations to meet customer requirements for replacement and repair.

The entire fulfillment process should be equipped with the information necessary to process orders and deliver the product or service. This includes product numbers, prices, special bundles, associated fees, shipping weights and instructions, refund policies, and other pertinent information. If products are to be serialized, the process must be in place to assign and track numbers. Checks should be in place to signal the need to order new parts or produce new products. All channel partners should be prepared with information necessary to distribute and sell products and services.

All management information systems should be set up to deliver the information necessary to track and manage the product. This includes inventory tracking, sales unit and revenue reporting, and profit and loss reports delineated by product, channel, and other relevant categories. It is generally easier and more reliable to implement tracking and reporting systems before the product is introduced than after it has been launched and brought to market.

Administrative and technical support is essential to bring products to market. This is particularly true in the field. Thorough planning and preparation is necessary long before the product is brought to market. This will help to avoid impediments to the sales process. Adequate administrative and technical support will also provide the product manager with the information necessary to manage the product effectively through its life cycle.

The Product Introduction

The product launch is one of the most important events during its life cycle. The launch sets the stage for how the product is defined to its target market, as well as to markets that it may not have anticipated. The euphoria created during the product launch focuses attention on the product. The prospective customers in the target market are being prepared to purchase—right away. While it was once quite common for IT companies to introduce products long before they were ready to be shipped or delivered, today the product introduction is usually the last step in bringing products to market.

The timing of the product launch is critical to its success. Seasonal products should be introduced prior to the start of the season when they are to be used. Products should be introduced when members of the target market are most likely to consider promotional messages. Popular vacation or holiday periods, for example, are not a good time to launch most new products. To the extent possible, the launch should be scheduled on a date when it is less likely to be overshadowed by other news stories or events. This increases the likelihood that the media will respond to press releases and give mention of the product. It is also more likely that prospective customers will pay attention to the product message. In addition to choosing a date when the advertising and promotion will get the most mileage, launch preparation and events should be scheduled so that everyone involved in the sale and distribution of the product is ready. Merchandisers need time to arrange for shelf space and store displays; customer inquiry hotlines and the salesforce need to be prepared to answer questions (about features, functions, price, and more); distributors need adequate stock of the product; and major customers should receive priority notification and delivery. Indeed, timing plays a major role in determining how effective the launch is in garnering the attention and interest of the target market.

Advertising and promotion drive the purpose of the product launch; that is, to make the target market aware of the new product and of the reasons that they should purchase it. The media (i.e., radio, print, television, and Internet) is the most effective means of reaching widespread markets. Advertisements, press releases, press briefings, persuasive conversations, and other techniques will start the process of getting the product message out to the target market. The combination of techniques selected will depend on the means of reaching the market as well as the available budget. A little ingenuity and finesse will get the message out without an exorbitant budget. Many marketers announce new products at industry trade shows and conferences where the press attends in large numbers and can be assembled fairly easily. A creative marketer can also put a spin on the product message linking it to a current event or trend, thereby increasing the opportunities for the media to use it. Others will contact a media person or analyst with whom they have an established relationship to give them the first shot at the story. The relationship and role that the media plays in the product launch can influence their receptiveness in the future. The manner in which the marketer communicates with the media will define their role in the product launch.

The message conveyed during the launch will establish the manner in which the target market views the product. One of the most powerful ways to validate a message is to accompany it with a testimonial from someone who has nothing to gain. Customer testimonials always carry weight. For new products this means one of the customers who used it during the beta test phase. While satisfied customers might be quite willing to offer testimonials, they should only be used prudently. In addition to advertisements, article press releases, and briefings, other forms of promotion include product collateral and product demonstrations.

Collateral helps to accentuate the message by providing a tangible reminder of the features, functions, and benefits of using the product. It is used during the launch to educate the press, partners, salespeople and, most importantly, prospective customers. Product demonstrations, or demos, also help spread the message. Demos can be particularly useful for IT products and services. They are an excellent means of proving that the product does indeed perform the functions that are advertised. Demonstrations presented during launches must function as described. They are most valuable when they show the product as part of a working, real-world solution that is easily understood and valued. Product demos that are partial or fully functional versions of the product are given to the media or prospective customers for a period of time. This allows them to gain a feel for the product; to develop a level of comfort with the value that the product actually delivers. The message delivered during the product launch should be consistent, clear, and persuasive, whether the media, partners, or prospective customers receive it. The medium used—ads, briefings, demos, or articles—to convey the message should tell the world that this new product will deliver on its stated goal. It is an integral part of bringing the product to market.

Promotion

If you want to win market share, you first have to capture mind share.

A successful promotion campaign delivers compelling messages to members of the target market that prepares them to purchase the product. The timing, content, and method of communications define the overall campaign. Promotion is encouraging the acceptance of something. Giveaways, discounts, sales pitches, and advertisements are all forms of promotion. While promotion includes advertising, advertising does not include all forms of promotion. Although many people consider promotion to be synonymous with marketing, we have learned that it is impossible to achieve marketing success with promotion alone. Nevertheless, promotion is an integral part of the marketing process. Too often technology-based companies spend too many resources trying to get the market to do what they want rather than trying to do what the market wants. Promotion should focus on explaining how an existing need or desire is fulfilled. The promotion must close the gap—to convincingly explain *why* the prospect should buy.

Some successful promotion campaigns recognize trends that exist and capitalize upon those trends to create a wave of emotion for the product. To accomplish this, one must understand the target market—their buying criteria, psychographics, and demographics. The developer of the campaign learns what the target market does to collect purchase information. This helps to determine the preferred communications methods, and prioritize them. The promotion campaign might include any combination of mailings, e-mailings, advertisements, trade shows, and other forms of promotion. The mix of these techniques will determine the efficiency of the promotional campaign. The effectiveness of the message delivery combined with the efficiency of the mix will determine the success of the promotional campaign.

Developing the Marketing Communications (Marcom) Plan

The Message

The essence of communications is the *idea* that is conveyed to the person receiving it. The idea, implanted by a message, might express an outcome from using the product or, it may simply prepare the recipient to become more willing to receive future messages. An idea and a message are combined with a call to action to form a *promo communiqué*.

An idea or message is usually communicated through words, pictures, or sounds. Newspaper advertisements and product collateral use words and pictures to deliver messages. Television commercials and radio spots add the element of sound. When the opportunity presents itself the two other senses, the ability to smell and touch, might be invoked to convey a message.

Mailers can be scented, for example, to give a fresh, outdoor aroma. News alerts might be accompanied with a beep or ring to announce their arrival. It is possible to induce a feeling with words, sounds, and pictures but there is not often the opportunity to directly affect the sense of touch and smell using traditional promotional tools. The creative marketer will augment the power of a message by learning to touch every sense in order to convey the concept to prospective customers.

A promotional idea is the reason the prospective customer should purchase, or consider purchasing, the product. The purpose of the message is to implant that idea in their mind. For example, one promotional idea behind portable wireless devices is to stay competitive by being kept informed. The message, therefore, is to maintain immediate access to information. The message is most effective when it expresses what the customer will achieve as a result of using the product. The depiction of the idea in this example might be a salesperson closing a deal because she learned, while in front of the customer, that current inventories in nearby warehouses will allow an order to be delivered when they need it. The idea is that she closed the deal; the message is that the portable wireless device allowed her to do it. For more information, visit 5Ps.com/Feature -Benefit-Response

This can be expressed in terms of features and benefits too. One of the features and functions of a portable wireless device is to provide immediate access to information. The benefit is to remain competitive by staying informed. The outcome is closing the sale. The customer can be asked to confirm the benefit by asking, "Is this something that would help your sales efforts?" A response of "yes" corroborates value and helps move the prospective customer closer to purchasing.

To develop a message that works, the marketer must first understand the idea that will appeal to the target market or a benefit that is desired by the target market.

This requires knowing the psychographics of the target market. What interests them? How do they earn a living? What are their habits? For a business, what are their goals and objectives? Which requirements have been defined? Once the needs, desires, interests, or requirements of the target market are understood, the marketer needs to clarify how their product fits. That means understanding the value proposition of the product or service as it pertains to the target market.

Knowing the prospective customer's major buying criteria, also known as their *sweet spot*, and meeting those criteria very succinctly, is a fast path to a done deal. The successful salesperson will only deliver the amount of information necessary to close the deal. Once they have asked the customer what they need to make a decision to buy, and the customer responds, the salesperson can proceed in meeting those criteria or finding another customer that they can satisfy. After presenting the customer with just what they needed to make a decision, the salesperson asks for the order. If the criteria were complete and accurate and the salesperson met those criteria, he or she will get the order. If not, new criteria or objections will be revealed. The marketer gathers the information needed to define the target market's buying criteria through research. The principles of identifying the idea and benefit, then matching them to the product's appropriate features and functions, are applied to develop the promotional message. Once the content of the message has been developed, it must be constructed for delivery to the target market.

Table 3.4 *Promo communiqué structure*

PROMO COMMUNIQUÉ STRUCTURE
GRABBER Close More Business Starting Today
MESSAGE You can… when armed with the information you need, when you need it. Find product availability, price changes or breaking news stories that impact your clients—immediately—all in a device that fits right in the palm of your hand.
CALL TO ACTION Get the XYZ portable wireless device at the introductory price of $50. Call 800-555-1212.

Promotional communications lead with a grabber (see Table 3.4). It is *the most compelling reason* that the listener should pay attention to the message. The grabber appeals to the interests or requirements of the target market. The next part of the promo communiqué is the body of the message itself. The promotional message should be straightforward and succinct. It expresses how specific features and functions of the product meet the identified wants, needs, or requirements of the target market. The final section of the promo communiqué invokes the response also known as the call to action. Together, the grabber, body, and call to action comprise the message, which is the core of the promotional communication.

A message can support more than one idea and an idea can be supported by more than one message. The manner in which they are combined depends on how they complement each other and the nature of the target market that the message is directed toward.

In the following example, Idea 1—Message 1 (Table 3.5a) is directed toward the product salesperson on the go. Idea 2—Message 1 (Table 3.5b) might be also directed toward that salesperson; however, this message appeals to their need to impress their boss. The final example, Idea 1—Message 2 (Table 3.5c), uses the same idea or grabber as in Table 3.5a.

This message is promoting a different set of functions of the product and is targeted at brokers, however. The marketer can use promo communiqués in Table 3.5a and Table 3.5b for target markets that purchase for salespeople. The results of each promo communiqué can be measured

Table 3.5 Adapting messages to the target audience

(a)

IDEA 1—MESSAGE 1
GRABBER Close More Business Starting Today
MESSAGE You can... when armed with the information you need, when you need it. Find product availability, price changes or breaking news stories that impact your clients—immediately—all in a device that fits right in the palm of your hand.

(b)

IDEA 2—MESSAGE 1
GRABBER Impress Your Boss Today
MESSAGE You can... when armed with the information you need, when you need it. Find product availability, price changes or breaking news stories that impact your clients—immediately—all in a device that fits right in the palm of your hand.

(c)

IDEA 1—MESSAGE 2
GRABBER Close More Business Starting Today
MESSAGE Send orders to purchase or sell stock, options or bonds. Change the strike level of an order. Recalculate your clients' portfolio. Do this and more while you're with your client—all as you approach the 19th hole.

to determine its effectiveness. The promo communiqué in Table 3.5c is directed toward brokers.

The initial promo communiqué may be the entire message that the marketer wants to express, or it may just be the first of several communiqués. Likewise a message might contain two or three points that can be delivered at once or at different times. The choice depends on the method of communication that is being used at the time as well as the overall promotional mix.

Delivering communiqués in parts will depend on the amount of attention that can be garnered, the amount of time available, and the promotional medium used. There are many factors that contribute to the amount of attention that a promo communiqué can attract. Momentous announcements, eye-catching animation, and entertaining music are only a few of the tools that capture one's attention.

Once attention has been captured, one or more messages will be delivered according to how much can be retained by the amount of time allowed. The number of messages should be limited to what the typical person can absorb and retain—usually three to five topics. When messages are delivered in short periods of time, such as television or Internet ads, radio spots, and some demonstrations, they might be delivered in a sequential fashion over a period of time so that they tell a story, or entrench an idea in the minds of the target market.

On the other hand, prospective customers may view some forms of promo communiqués repeatedly over extended periods of time. Print ads, collateral, and exhibit displays fall into this category. When the prospective customer or members of the target market have the interest and opportunity to peruse information about a product, the promo communiqué can include more messages or a full product description. The selection of promo communiqués and the manner in which they will be delivered is known as the promotional mix. The optimum mix depends on the types of media that members of the target market are likely to receive, the timeframe over which the product manager needs to establish the product in the market, and the amount of resources available to produce and deliver the communiqués in the mix. The optimum mix will, obviously, deliver the maximum market penetration with the resources invested.

The investment in promotion is determined by the product business plan and may range from 15% to 30% or more of revenue, depending on the stage of its life cycle that the product is in.

The message is at the core of the promotional mix. It determines how each promo communiqué will help prospective customers to determine why to buy the product. It is the message that starts the purchase decision. When the message fits the needs, desires, or objectives of the target market, the promotional campaign has been given a solid cornerstone.

The Image

The image is a visual depiction of a concept that one will remember when they think of a product or company. It can represent the amalgamation of all of the company's products or services.

It can signify the outcome received from using the company's products or services. In many cases, the image represents one or more facets of a company's character. The definition and selection of a company or product image requires careful thought, for it will define it to the world and remain with it for years to come. An image is a desired statement about a product or company that is portrayed through a logo.

The logo is a visual and graphical representation of a company or product for all to see. A logo will immediately or eventually embody the product or company's image. The image can be captured in the visual look of the logo or it can be associated with the logo over time through a series of advertisements and other promo communiqués. Some logos have been given life through animation. Logos may be also given definition with sound. Logos can also be given life through words, or a byline, that accompanies it. The Discover*IT* logo, for example, is usually portrayed with the byline "simplifying the complexities of technology." The picture, name, and byline of the Discover*IT* logo capture the essence of all of the products and services they offer that help people to understand and use IT. Other logos describe an amalgamation of products and services that serve a common purpose. Many marketers have learned to use words, pictures, and sounds to create logos that help to develop and reinforce a product or company's image. For a comparison of logos with different definitions see Table 3.6.

Table 3.6 Image comparison

NAME RECOGNITION	OUTCOME OR AMALGAMATION	REPRESENTS
YAHOO!	Discover *IT*™	5 p

Logo Is a Communiqué

A logo is part of and, thus, a type of promotional communication. As in any type of communication, a logo should be simple, succinct, and easy to retain. Graphically this means simple lines, shapes, and minimal colors. It should be easy to produce graphically and adaptable to animation. A simple logo can be included fairly easily in all types of promo communiqués from print to multimedia. A logo should appear in every place possible and appropriate to represent the company or product. This might include business cards, product collateral, stationery, company vehicles, advertisements, promotional giveaways, and the product itself. A simple logo will help ensure inclusion and consistency in these and other places.

Exercising Control

In order to maintain control and consistency over a logo, it should be made available only to approved parties in a camera-ready document or graphics file. These items should be accompanied by an official picture of the logo to ensure that it is not distorted when reproduced. It should also include any instructions that explain when and how the logo should be used. Logos, like names, may be assigned a trademark or service mark to restrict their use to the owner of that mark. This increases the control that a company may exert over its logo.

A company or product image is its statement to the world. Customers, suppliers, employees, resellers, business partners, regulators, shareholders, and others will be influenced by the image. Despite the best intention of impartiality, a well-promoted image will have a conscious or subconscious effect on anyone exposed to the promotion. The logo helps to define the image of a company or product.

External Factors Affect Logo

Of course, the manner in which a company operates, treats its employees, and treats others will help shape its image. The degree to which a product will fulfill the expectations of its customers will help shape its image. Needless to say, the logo is not the defining point of a company or product. It is, however, the starting point. It can also be a turning point. The logo and its portrayal can be a cornerstone in product introduction. Many marketers have used logos in creative and strategically placed advertising and promotion to stop a tide of bad publicity and recapture a positive image. After all, it is the image—embodied by the logo—that will stick with a product or company for many years. It is quite valuable, therefore, to establish a strong, positive image at the onset.

Presentations

Tell 'em what you're gonna tell 'em, tell 'em and tell 'em again.

Any presentation for or about a company or its product is a promotion opportunity. This is true of a presentation given by a company representative, or one given by a third party providing information about the company or product. Ideally the marketer will have some degree of control over the person delivering a presentation about their product or service. Unfortunately this is not often the case. The marketer should, therefore, gain influence over the message delivered through the content and flow of presentation material provided.

The amount of influence that a marketer has over a presentation is first determined by its positioning. The first step is to know your audience. A presentation might be developed for prospective customers, existing customers, analysts, investors, business partners, the media, stakeholders, or any combination of these parties. By understanding who the audience is, the presentation can be developed to address their questions and concerns. The next step is to define the focus of the presentation. Determine the objective to be achieved and the idea that is to be conveyed. Next, develop the presentation so that it tells a story. When people attend presentations they have decided to devote a certain amount of time to pay attention, often at least 20 min, to what the speaker has to say. In appreciation for that time and to hold their attention, the presentation should be interesting. When one tells a story they convey information in a flow that is natural to absorb and retain. The audience, focus, and delivery of a presentation set the stage for how effective it is in establishing the idea that is intended by the marketer.

The content of a presentation will comprise information about the topic as it pertains to the audience. A presentation should be informative, interesting, and entertaining. It should include information of value about the topic of focus and demonstrate how it relates to the product. This can be accomplished in several ways. Statistical information is often included early in presentations to gain attention. Statistics can set the stage with trends and projections that support growth of the product or service. Case studies offer examples of how people comparable to those in the audience are dealing with situations that have or could be resolved with the product. Whether statistics, a case study, or another technique is used to set the stage for the topic that is to be conveyed, it should include information that is of interest to the audience. This is the beginning of the story.

As it unfolds, the product or service is introduced. The product should *complement* the message. It is the *answer* to the issue that has been developed in the story. This allows the interest to mount and the audience to focus on the solution—the product. Relevant information about the product should be presented succinctly and in a format that the audience can easily understand. The information about the product should be comprehensive but not overwhelming. With the exception of technical product briefings, detailed information is often supplied with handouts or by answering questions. At the end of a sales briefing the attendees should be prepared to purchase or, at the very least, be prepared to take steps to prepare to purchase the product and conduct its implementation. If the audience is not comprised of prospective customers, the attendees should be prepared to endorse the product and present it to others. A well-developed presentation makes it easy for a good speaker to accomplish these objectives.

The visual display of the presentation should be aesthetically pleasing. Regardless of the medium used, the colors, fonts, and graphical images should be clean, clear, complementary, and crisp. The product or company logo should appear unobtrusively on one of the corners of the presentation materials. The logo can be accompanied by the company or product byline or in some cases, the presentation byline. To the extent possible, the look and feel of the presentation should be consistent with that of the company or product image. Contact information can be provided at the beginning and the end of the presentation. The opening page should have the name of the presentation and the website or phone number, in relatively small font. The closing page should have complete contact information include the mailing address, phone number, and e-mail address or website address. In addition to contact information, the presentation should have pictures virtually everywhere. If possible, animation should be used. If words are necessary they should be limited to titles and points that are less than one line long (usually presented in bullet formation). The attendee should not have to read words to receive information from a presentation that is delivered by a speaker. As a matter of fact, the presentation materials alone should lack full meaning without a speaker. A presentation that can be reviewed and received without a speaker is a demonstration (see next section). It is the speaker who brings meaning and life to presentation materials.

An exceptional speaker is proficient in techniques that capture an audience's attention, engages them throughout the presentation, and leaves them with a lasting message. One of the old adages of speaking is: tell them what you're going to tell them, tell them, and then tell them again. A speaker who knows how to get rapt attention from the audience will use an opening that establishes their position and get the audience's attention. The purpose of the presentation is embodied in the symbolism of the opening or it is linked with an appropriate segue. The speaker fluently moves from the opening to the purpose in a manner that keeps the audience entrenched in what they have to say. The speaker reveals the presentation materials (slides, media clips, or other items) as he or she presents the purpose of the presentation. An eloquent and polished speaker not only sets the stage for an attentive audience, he or she employs skills that enhance the delivery throughout the presentation. A presentation with exceptional content is made ordinary by a poor speaker. Whenever possible, choose a speaker with better than average skills to deliver the presentation.

The delivery of a presentation is often completed by providing handouts to the attendees. The handouts should include copies of materials that are appropriate to distribute accompanied by notes that explain the presentation. Handouts offer another promotional opportunity. The cover page should highlight information about the company and product. It should include complete contact information as well as the name of the presentation. Product collateral such as specification sheets or a white paper may be included at the end of the handout package. The handouts are the final part of the presentation that solidifies its promotional contribution.

A presentation is a strategic part of developing marketing communication. The message and image provide the concept and scope of the communications. The presentation provides a comprehensive communication that endorses the value of the product. The selection of venues and audiences for delivering presentations is part of the promotion plan. Of course, equipping different parties with presentations extends the choice of venues and audience beyond the control of the product manager. The quality of the presentation content and handouts will help influence its placement. Clearly, the development of marketing communications is given value by the place and frequency of its delivery.

Delivering the Communication

In a mutually friendly conversation, the person delivering the message is responsible for communicating clearly. It is also the responsibility of the recipient to listen attentively. In a promotional communication, however, it is the responsibility of the marketer to capture the attention of the person to whom they are communicating and hold their attention long enough to convey the idea they want to put forth. To achieve this, the marketer must also know where they can reach members of the target market. To deliver effective communication, the marketer should focus on *reach* and *capture*.

Collateral

The purpose of collateral is to promote the product and inform the customer. Collateral includes product literature, company overview sheets, price sheets, case studies, white papers, and other literature relevant to the sale of the product or service.

Promotional literature includes a description of the product and benefits that are readily understood. This information should be pointed and succinct, and presented in a form that is easy for the reader to comprehend and remember. A snapshot of technical specifications is also included to facilitate the reader's evaluation and a decision. A date is usually not included to avoid undue obsolescence of the literature and also to encourage prospective customers to contact the company if there are questions. For similar reasons, pricing is typically presented separately. Mature products or products for which price is a primary evaluator will generally, however, include prices on product literature. Literature and other forms of collateral are used as a tool to move the prospective customer forward in the purchase process by providing information about the product in a positive yet informative light.

Collateral can be delivered in many forms. Paper brochures, digital media, and websites are among the most popular forms of delivering collateral. Regardless of the form in which collateral is delivered, the look and feel should be consistent. That is, the colors, logos, and other defining words and images should be the same. Finally, contact information including company name, mailing address, phone and fax numbers, e-mail address, and website is a standard part of product and company collateral.

Documents that are distributed to prospective customers should be kept up to date. Well-designed and developed collateral is a positive complement to sales efforts. Substandard collateral, on the other hand, can inhibit sales efforts or, at best, reduce the quality and value perception in the mind of the prospective customer. As is the case with all elements of marketing, it is advised to always put your best foot forward. Collateral represents the product and the company when there is no one else available to do so.

Demonstrations (Demos)

I'm from Missouri—show me.

Showing a product while telling the prospect what it can do, *the show and tell sell*, has been successfully used by marketers for thousands of years. Trade has always been one of the driving factors in the development of civilization and society. It is the foundation that supported the establishment and growth of civilizations and societies. Marketing enables trade. Marketing provides the connection between needs or desires and a solution to those needs and desires. Marketing makes trade happen. Trade is the exchange of goods or services. Trade goes back thousands of years. Since 3000 B.C., long distance trade has connected people.[5] History shows that the Roman Empire (period), Maya people (about 1000 B.C.[6]), Mesoamerican culture (A.D. 250–800/900[7]), and other civilizations were built upon and flourished through trade.[8] Transportation routes, communications, currency creation, financial systems, and other components of modern day civilization were built in response to the need to support trade. Truly, *marketing is what makes the world go 'round.* Demos are surely what drove ancient marketing and remain a compelling sales tool today.

Seeing a product work goes a long way in the decision process. This is particularly true of IT-based products and services, Many IT-based products offer functionality that is either incomprehensible or unbelievable to the customer. In some cases, customers understand what can be *done*; however, they have not developed a level of comfort that allows them to conclude the sale. Demonstrations, also known as demos, bring reality to IT-based products, particularly those that employ new technologies.

Demonstrations, or demos, can be divided into three categories based upon the amount of time that the prospective customer spends with the product—the *performance*, the *perusal,* and the *trial.*

The performance, often referred to as a dog and pony show, is delivered by an individual with good presentation skills and product knowledge. In major companies, this is characteristically someone in sales or product marketing. *Performance demos* are typically delivered at conferences, seminars, briefings, and on sales calls. When a prospective customer is given access to the product or service for a short period of time, it is referred to as a *perusal demo.* Prospects can spend time with products at trade shows, evaluation centers or, they may be provided with a loaner product to use for a short period of time. Depending on the deal that was put in place (often based on the type of product), the loaner period could last from a few days to a couple of weeks. When a customer evaluates a product for 30 days or more, it is considered a *trial.* Performance and perusal demos are traditionally provided free of cost; however, many trials are paid for by the customer. A limited quantity of product may be offered at a substantially reduced price for trial.

A performance demo is an integral part of a sales presentation. Whether the occasion is a sales call, trade show, or seminar, a performance demo is an opportunity to help the prospect decide to purchase the product or service. As with other forms of sales and promotion, the performance demo should tell a story and also be part of a story itself. It should accentuate the message being delivered by proving that the product can deliver the identified benefits and value. A successful performance demo is one of the defining moments of a marketing or sales presentation (see Presentations in this chapter, p. 180).

The nature of the perusal demo or trial may change with the type of product being provided. Hardware manufacturers will provide a group of products, known as a demo pool, that are used exclusively for customer demos.

Hardware demos are full feature and functional products that are provided for a limited amount of time. Some companies may lease demo equipment for extended periods or sell them at a deep discount. Network carriers offer demos by providing limited access to their networks. Access is typically limited to a certain period of time, although the demo can also be limited by the functions or features made available. Network demos also usually include the access device (such as phone, computer, access card, and other devices) that the prospective customer will use. Finally, software companies typically provide one single user version or a limited function copy of their product. Accounting software, for example, may only allow a limited number of vendors to be input or only support time periods that have passed. Time, capacity, and other functions may be disabled so that prospective customers may appropriately test the software without having full functionality. The features and functions of software products may also be viewed on their websites.

Demos are provided in a manner to put the product's best foot forward. The person using the product or service must receive a level of support that ensures they will have a positive experience. The support necessary for demos and trials is a cost of marketing. In many cases, if support is not included the time and effort to provide a demo is wasted.

There are several advantages and disadvantages to providing demos. Demos can help prove the value of a product or service by allowing the prospective customer to see the reality of the product performance. Many demonstrations of IT products are captivating. It is a good way to get the prospect's attention. The demo can also serve as a conversation piece to get the customer talking about what they might achieve by using the product.

That conversation creates a situation that makes it easier for the salesperson to sell. Perusal demos and trials allow customers to become comfortable with the look and feel of a product or service. They increase the likelihood that the prospective customer will purchase the product. One of the major risks of live demonstrations is that the product may not work. If the product does function as promised, it may not achieve the sought after result. When a product demonstration fails to meet the expectations of the prospective customer, it creates a huge hurdle for the salesperson to overcome. A demonstration should be delivered by someone who is very proficient in using the product. This allows them to respond to on the spot inquiries to show features and functions. In addition to requiring a skillful presenter, a demonstration can be expensive to set up. Since resources are required to install, support, or deliver a demo to prospective customers, the marketer should ensure that demos are provided to those who are most likely to purchase the product. Demos are a proven means of moving customers to purchase. When used effectively, they deliver a strong return on the promotional investment.

There are several issues that must be taken into consideration when deciding upon or preparing for a demo. First and foremost, a demo, particularly delivered at no price to the prospective customer, presents added costs and delay to the sales cycle. A live demonstration also poses an additional cost and risk. Demos, therefore, should only be delivered when absolutely necessary to close sales that offer a sufficient return. Second, demos should be prepared to ensure that it functions properly. To achieve this, particularly with a pre-release product, a *controlled* or *contained* version of the product is created. This may be accomplished by limiting or disabling certain features or functions. For software products, or software used to demonstrate hardware or network products, a *self-running* demo may be used.

The marketer preparing the demo must also consider the resources that are required to deliver it. Depending on the type of demo being prepared, these include, but are not limited to, network accessibility, power available, projection equipment, and the product itself. The risks of delivering demos include the piracy of software, network congestion that inhibits its operation, and improper or inadequate support. Many considerations are diffused when the customer pays for the demo. When a customer pays for a perusal demo or trial, they typically are more committed to its success. A paid demo is a win–win situation. The marketer will take these and other issues into consideration to ensure that all demos prepare the way for booked sales.

Demonstrations, or the show and tell sell, have proven to be a successful form of promotion for many years. To prepare the way for future sales, the marketer will assess the audience, the venue, prospective customers, technical environment, and more. To learn the five rules to live by when preparing and delivering a demo, visit www.The5Ps.com/LEM/DemoRules.html. When managed correctly, demonstrations provide a strong boost to the sales effort. They are an effective and established promotional tool for IT products.

Advertising

When people hear the word marketing, they usually think of promotion, sales, or advertising. Advertising is one of the more popular, and least understood, media of promoting products and services. The purpose of advertising is to send messages to prospects that convince them to buy a product or, at least, consider purchasing it. A series of ads that are developed and placed to move a group of people toward purchasing is called a media plan. To build a media plan, the marketer must define the content and the placement of ads. This entails developing the message, producing the copy, quantifying the number of people reached who fit the customer profile (or assessing the target market reached), determining how often ads will be placed (frequency), and measuring the results achieved. An excellent way, therefore, to understand the role and value of each advertising medium is to review it in terms of message, copy, reach, frequency, and response (see Table 3.7).

Table 3.7 Advertising components

ADVERTISING—SECTION OUTLINE
1 Message
1.1 Content
2 Copy
2.1 Look
3 Reach
3.1 Placement of ads—where
3.2 Placement—how often
4 Frequency
5 Response
5.1 Measuring results

In addition to knowing how many people in the target market are likely to see, hear, or interact with the ad, the marketer should know how well the message will be received. This means knowing the demographics as well as the psychographics of the audience. Certain demographic factors such as age, income, education, sex, occupation, and more may give insight into a person's ability and desire to buy. Psychographics, on the other hand, may help us to understand the decision process of an individual or group of people. Does a low price mean a bargain or poor quality? Is this person an impulse buyer or does this purchase warrant more investigation and thought? Psychographics defines the mental process that most members of the target market will go through before making a purchase decision.

Once the marketer knows what they want to say to the target audience (message), how they want to say it (copy), the most effective way to communicate with them (reach), and how often to communicate to be heard (frequency), the selection of medium can be made.

The choice of with whom to team up should be driven by giving power to the message and synergies between the entities before price. In addition to choosing advertising partners, the marketer must also decide what to say in ads and where they should be placed. The collection of advertising decisions is made more powerful by optimizing the marketing mix.

As in the Marketing Mix section in Chapter 2, the marketer should carefully determine the selection and mix of advertising that will send the most powerful, reinforcing message to most of the members of the target market. The choice, timing, and delivery of ads can maximize the effectiveness of the marketing dollar. That's how to optimize the mix.

Television

Television (TV), radio, print, mailings, the Internet, and word-of-mouth are the most popular advertising media. TV has a broad reach, offers the power of audio visual messaging, includes some targeting tools, and can be quite expensive. National, regional, and local timeslots are available to advertisers to help them control reaching their target market as well as costs. Prices for 30-second, 5-second, and 1-minute ads can vary substantially, depending on the size of the audience. A local cable channel may have rates that small businesses can afford while ads placed during the Super Bowl can only be afforded by advertisers with deep pockets.

Radio

Radio has been around since the 1920s, and it continues to be a widely used and effective means of advertising and promotion. The demographics and psychographics of many radio show audiences are well known. Ad spots are usually 60-second, 30-second, or 10-second (i.e., billboards). Costs are lower than TV and the reach is typically regional or local. Satellite radio offers national reach for advertisers. Radio also offers promotional opportunities through interview, commentaries, or mentions. Radio hosts, or disc jockeys (DJs), can increase the sales of music and other products by embellishing benefits during commentaries, and before or after ads.

Print

Print is one of the oldest advertising media and is still used effectively to reach targeted customers. Newspapers, magazine, and other print media provide information about their subscribers and readership to help advertisers determine the most effective means to reach their target audiences. Publications may also offer special issues or inserts to advertisers who want to craft more extensive messages or advertising.

A press release can be a nice way to spark a new idea or accentuate an "in-market" message. Introducing a new initiative while instilling an idea that emphasizes a compelling product benefit, for example, can spark a new idea. A recently introduced, or in-market product can get an added push from a press release announcing a new channel that inherently high-lights a unique function of the product.

When integrating press releases into the marketing mix, the marketer should remain mindful that there are certain days of the week and times of the day that are most effective for releasing press announcements to the media and public.

Internet

The emergence of the Internet has created an enigma that transcends multiple components and phases of the marketing process including pro-motion, advertising, sales, and product or service delivery. While the role that the Internet plays is addressed in the appropriate sections of this book, the disparate marketing functions that the Internet supports are addressed in this section.

As the functionality of the Internet and its number of users exploded at the turn of the century, so did the opportunities for marketers to use this medium to reach prospective customers in their target markets. The Internet offers a new vehicle for promoting and selling products and ser-vices. More effective promotion and higher sales from the expanded func-tionality available are primarily limited by the imagination and creativity of the marketer.

Multimedia help bring the reason for buying to life, like the captivat-ing power of TV. The ability to track and qualify prospective buyers, and to qualify their level of interest, puts the power of computing into the hands of the marketer. The multimedia version of the Discover*IT* logo, for example, shows an animated learning trip ending in the excitement of gaining new knowledge, accentuated by a blinking exclamation point. While the static logo—Discover*IT*—represents the same meaning, the animated logo gives it life.

The role of the Internet in marketing can be put into context by over-laying its functions on the marketing cycle. First presented in Chapter 1, this perpetual cycle begins with the identification of an idea and continues with customer confirmation and feedback that contributes to the identi-fication of the next idea. To review the basic steps of the marketing cycle, visit www.The5Ps.com/LEM/MarketingCycle.html. For an explanation and overview chart of how Internet marketing components align with the marketing cycle, visit www.The5Ps.com/LEM/InternetMarketing.html

Opt-in databases, cookies, and other Internet tools and functions provide the marketer with the ability to track and learn more about prospective customers. While many of these tools do not allow the marketer to definitively identify an individual or specific person, the tools do provide the marketer with demographic and psychographic information that empowers promotion and the sales cycle. An overview of the components of Internet marketing is provided in the table at www.The5Ps.com/LEM/InternetMarketing.html

Click-through rates (CTRs), for example, is a measure of how many times the site visitor clicks or searches for information. Each click offers the opportunity for a new message, or ad impression, to be delivered to the visitor. The true value of the CTR is dependent upon the content, design, and structure of the site as well as who is doing the clicking. Ideally, the site would be designed and structured so as to take the visitor through the buying decision, and allow them to purchase, without losing their interest. The ability to do this with the least number of clicks is best. Landing pages are commonly used as the first and only—or the last page—that the visitor sees. These pages are designed so that the visitor sees everything they need to make a decision to purchase, on one screen or while scrolling down the page. At the decision point, the visitor has the option to enter their credit card or another method of payment, and purchase the product or service. One such landing page is www.PgMPCoach.com

There are many more considerations for engaging in Internet marketing. Ensuring secure purchase transactions, avoiding being labeled a spammer, and managing unexpected inquiries or purchase volumes are just a few of the hurdles marketers must plan for to be successful. Indeed, the power of the Internet for marketers and others will continue to flourish as the number of users grows and technology scrambles to capitalize upon this medium and channel.

Mailings (Postal Mail and e-mail)

Sending promotional mailers has been a popular means of soliciting customers for many years. According to the Smithsonian's National Postal Museum, the American Anti-Slavery Society (AAS) took their campaign to a new level with what could be called the first use of a direct mail campaign 1835. "The brief 1835 direct mail anti-slavery campaign was relatively short-lived, and unsuccessful in the short run. But it found success in the long run, by spurring the slavery question into wider national debate."[9] Today, product announcements, special offers, and promotional discounts are a few of the marketing tools that have been sent via mailers. Promotional mailers are typically sent via postal mail, also referred to as snailmail, or via e-mail.

There are several considerations that are unique to each type of promotional mailer; however, the fundamentals that drive a successful mail campaign remain the same. These are the list (target audience), copy (what you say), timing (when), repetition (how often), and response (what do they think?).

The list is the key to mailings. The quality of the list is the first determinant of how likely each mailer will yield positive results. The number and type of fields that characterize contacts on the list will determine how closely the marketer can match their selection to the target market. The accuracy of contact information determines whether the promotional mailer will be received by the prospect. There are a seemingly unlimited number of sources from which to secure mailing lists with vast differences in the quality of data offered. Magazine and other subscription lists are popular with many because their addresses are validated by regular mailings. In addition, the interests of their recipients can be partially defined by the type of publication received. Naturally, the accuracy of the address depends on the method of delivery of the publication. Publications sent out via postal mail tend to have more accurate postal addresses while newsletters sent via e-mail have more accurate e-mail addresses. There are business and consumer databases that have been compiled and maintained for many years. Many databases contain defining information about each contact that can be quite valuable to the marketer trying to narrowly define selection criteria that fit the target market. Revenue, profit, number of employees, standard industrial classification code (SIC), and North American Industry code (NAIC) are only a few of the fields of information available in many business databases. Age, income, sex, and education are a few of the fields available in selected consumer databases. A list of databases available for promotions sent via e-mail or the U.S. mail can be found at www.The5Ps.com/LEM/PromoDatabases.html

Trade Shows

Face-to-face is the most effective means of communicating. Nothing replaces the ability to see, feel, interact with, and observe body motions and other unspoken gestures and feelings conveyed during a live exchange between two or more people. Relationships are solidified and sales are closed most effectively through face-to-face meetings. Trade shows are a highly efficient means of creating a high volume of face-to-face encounters in a concentrated period of time. The astute marketer begins preparing for the trade show 6 months to 2 years before the event, if not earlier.

An important step is convincing prospective buyers to attend the trade event. When the focus is a major event that attracts large numbers of buyers, the goal is ensuring that your targeted buyers have scheduled sufficient time with your managers, executives, and salespeople to close the sale or at least substantially move along the sales cycle. The marketer may use a combination of meetings, briefings, exhibits, demos, presentations, press releases, media appearances, giveaways, and other sales and promotional techniques to gather leads and contribute to the sales effort at trade shows. Each of these marketing techniques is discussed further in this chapter.

The strategies and processes that allow each of these marketing techniques to be successful can be explained in its own chapter or book. As in all marketing efforts, they should embrace a common, reinforced message, be timed so that message is well received by the targeted customers, and include the ability to receive and retain responses from the targeted customers.

Trade shows became an important component of technology marketing with the launch of the Computer Dealer Expo (COMDEX) in 1978 in Chicago, Illinois. As a salesperson selling computer timesharing in Chicago, I vividly remember COMDEX. It gave us the opportunity to explain complex, unknown, technology to our prospects at one time, in one place with the resources assembled that were not often available. If I began preparing my prospects to attend COMDEX at least 6 months in advance of the event, I was likely to meet quota at, or soon after, the trade show. Later in my career, I would become an advisor to COMDEX, an industry expert for their media spots, and even delivered a keynote in one of their coveted sports. The first time that a sitting U.S. President visited a trade show, was at my Discover*IT* Wireless Computing Showcase, delivered at Spring COMDEX in Chicago.

I've also served as advisor to and delivered speeches at the Consumer Electronics Show (CES), PC Expo, the CTIA[10]—The Wireless Association Show, the National Association of Broadcasters (NAB) Show, and other events. Though the size (attendees and exhibitors), number, and influence of trade shows continue to change over time, their role and efficiency as a promotional tool for marketers continues. Information about trade events can be found at www.The5Ps.com/LEM/TradeEvents.html

In the real world, marketers do not have enough time or money to participate in all trade shows that might generate leads and revenue. So how do you choose the right events? First, the marketer should choose the event that offers the group of prospective customers with the greatest collective buying power. Second, choose the events that offer the most cost effective means of delivering your message with the strongest reinforcement options; for example, exhibits, conference presentations, media spots, and on-site publications timed to deliver and reinforce your message to your prospective customers. Lastly, you need the capacity to participate and deliver. The selection of tools should be consistent with the overall marketing plan, and processes should be in place that facilitate the delivery and follow-up after all events.

Public Relations

Press releases are a stable of public relations and are discussed briefly with print as a form of advertising. Public relations is much more than writing and delivering well-placed and timed press releases. This discipline includes setting up and conducting interviews, press announcements, briefings, meetings with industry analysts, and all other forms of communications that present the client to the public in the desired manner. The public relations professional creates opportunities, postures the client's message, and makes every effort to help create and entrench the image that supports the client's goal and objectives.

Press releases often precede and follow-up public relations activities. They can be used to accentuate and emphasize messages throughout the marketing cycle to help tell the story. Press releases document the taking points of media spot press conferences, briefings, TV appearances, and other promotional activities. Many marketers prefer to issue press releases on Tuesday, Wednesday, or Thursday, for they feel the most attention is received on those days. While four companies seem to dominate companies offering the delivery of press releases, there are many options available to direct, compose, and distribute press releases. For a list of sources to assist with press releases and other public relations services, visit www .The5Ps.com/LEM/PublicRelations.html

Engaging Advertising and Promotion

Once your target market has been identified and defined, and the product or service you would like to sell to the people in that market has been thoroughly described, the next step is to determine how to communicate what you have to offer. The marketer should give pensive time and consideration to what name and perception to create. Some choose to describe what the product "is"; others describe the results to be achieved from owning or using the product. People have other reasons for choosing product names that may not relate to what would be purchased or why it would be purchased. A name selected for any other reason is likely to require a greater promotional effort to convey the reason the prospective customer should purchase the product.

The process of preparing to promote a new product includes:

- Selecting a name
- Creating a logo
- Securing the trademark
- Acquiring the domain
- Decide whether to brand

My first commercial logo was created in 1980. After fine-tuning my marketing plan and defining my brand, I applied for the trademark and launched the DiscoverIT brand. I made the mistake of not confirming the domain first and was held hostage by an individual demanding an exorbitant price. The Internet Corporation for Assigned Names and Numbers

(ICANN; formerly Internic)[11] did not act on my application to transfer the domain, so it remained hostage until he sold it to another company. Over the years, I successfully defended my trademark from several companies who tried to infringe upon it. The money spent protecting my mark from others who realized its commercial value may have been better spent in building the business; it's a classic chicken and egg dilemma. Lesson learned: build the customer base with your *purpose, value,* and *principles* first. Then build or buy the brand once you've reached critical mass. The key is to determine when you will reach critical mass so that resources will be deployed at the best time.

My next brand was created before the first printing of this book. I had developed The 5 Ps after entering the corporate environment. As I learned to apply theories from my MBA program, I began to blend marketing, finance, and operations principles in a manner required to deliver results. After a decade in global corporations and 10 more years as an entrepreneur, my 5 Ps framework was sound. Having created the Discover*IT* Showcase and launching it at the leading events of the time, I was often asked how I did it. In response to these questions, I wrote the first article about The 5 Ps. It was embraced and widely distributed, and published again 2 years later. Fifteen years later, when the economy slowed down, I completed this book. I negotiated acquisition of the domain, The5Ps. com, applied for the trademark, launched an interim site, acquired the toll-free number, and submitted my manuscript for publication. I also submitted a project to two crowdfunding sites to raise capital and jumpstart the sale of this book. The projects offered first run copies signed by the author, custom success articles for the buyer, conducting 5 P assessments, and article reprints. My goal is not to establish "The 5 Ps" as a world class brand. Rather, my goal is to help provide a foundation for a line of products focused on business and technology. You can find the results of this effort by visiting www.The5Ps.com/LEM/AdvPromo.html

Choosing the product name, creating the logo, and protecting these strategic items are the first steps of the promotion plan. Building a comprehensive promotion plan with a budget sufficient to implement the plan until the product reaches critical mass, is an integral part of the marketing plan. The astute marketer will identify and count every resource necessary to achieve success before they build and launch the product or service.

Product Life Cycle Management

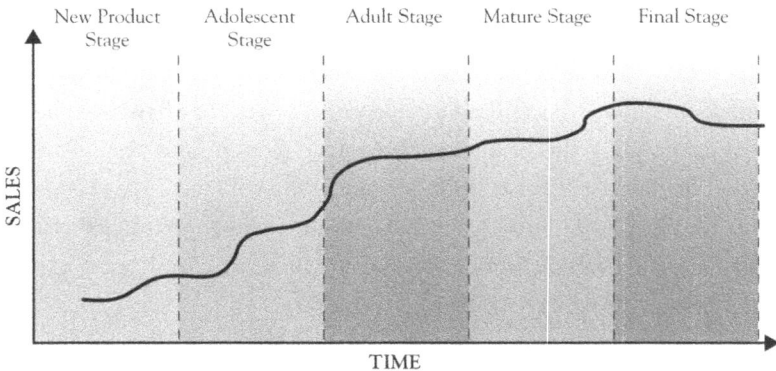

Figure 3.3 Product life cycle curve

Early theories of product life cycle management were fairly conservative, risk free, and predictable. A product was introduced, carefully nurtured, and every effort was made to give it a long, profitable life. When sales units or revenue from such activity was graphed over a period of time, the curve looked like an "S" turned on its side. The product life cycle was depicted by a sure and steady S-shaped sales curve.

The late 1980s ushered in a change in this fundamental principle. New IT products began to be introduced with increased speed. Next generation products were launched while the products they introduced were still in a profit-producing phase, even the growth phase, of their life cycle (see When Cannibalization is Profitable, Chapter 2). While the Marketing Mix Matrix (Chapter 2, figure at www.The5Ps.com/LEM/MktgMixMatrix.html) highlights the application of the 5 Ps of marketing given the product's stage in its life cycle and the dispersion of the market, this section shall provide a general description of each phase in the life cycle (see Figure 3.3).

New Product Stage

Emerging Technologies

New products are handled very carefully during the early phase of their life cycle. All development and preparation that takes place prior to introduction of the product sets the stage for its success or failure. The approach taken during the new product stage might vary based on whether the product is based on a new technology or an existing technology. A new product based on an existing technology that is commonly understood doesn't require the amount of customer education as a product based on a new technology. A new PC, for example, with a faster processor, more memory, and new features will be readily understood by virtually everyone who is planning to purchase an upgraded, second, or first time PC.

A new gizmo, on the other hand, that allows human thought to be converted into ASCII text (this product has not been produced at the time this book was written) has to be explained to prospective customers. The promotional message for products based on new technologies must explain what the product does, how it works, how it should be used, and possibly other ramifications of its use. The need to educate prospective customers on a new technology changes the promotion, distribution, pricing, and other elements of the product plan.

The promotional message has multiple challenges for a product that incorporates new and emerging technologies. This is particularly true for a product in the early phase of its life cycle. Whenever appropriate, the message must educate and sell prospects on the new technology. For example, when the new technology is a key product differentiator, the message should capture the value of that difference and deliver it to prospective customers.

When the new technology requires a new level of understanding to use and maintain the product properly, the message should initiate an understanding of its use and value. Promotion is also often more focused on the high potential target markets during the product's early stage of life. To further qualify target markets, the product manager might use the *shotgun approach*, sending a message to multiple target markets, so that they can determine which provides the highest initial response. This allows the product manager to focus promotional resources on the target markets which are ready to receive the product and make its early stage successful.

The price of a product that incorporates a new or emerging technology is often set as high as the "early adopter" market will bear. This allows the product manager to focus on those customers who will invest the time necessary to understand the product and derive the maximum value possible. Since it often requires more time and promotion expenditure to convince a larger number of customers to purchase products based on new technologies, the highest price that the market will bear will also usually maximize revenue.

Many product managers choose to use selective distribution sources for new products so that they can maintain control over whom the product is sold to and how it is sold. Direct sales channels, such as the company's salesforce or Internet site, offer the product manager the opportunity to exercise considerable control. Preferred resellers are also often included in controlled distribution situations. In the early stages of a product's life cycle, there are several changes that might be implemented to adapt to market needs. Product "fixes" might be implemented in the field to solve problems or enhance functions that were not known before the launch. Prices might be lowered or restructured to adapt to the target market's willingness and ability to pay.

Promotional messages might be changed to provide a more compelling reason for prospective customers to buy. When products are distributed through a limited number of sources over which the product manager can exert considerable control, these changes are much easier to implement.

During the early phase of the life cycle for a product that incorporates new and emerging technologies, support is critical. Support can be used as a tool to close the gap in promotion and packaging for a new product. The new customer has developed a set of expectations of what the product will help them to accomplish and what they must contribute to realize the expected results.

Support will help the customer to understand how to achieve their expected results, or to help them accept what the product *actually can* deliver. This helps to smooth the edges of the new product's launch as the product manager works on delivering fixes to improve packaging and refining the promotional message. Indeed, exquisite support is a major contributor to the success of a new product.

Applying Existing Technologies

Products that employ existing technologies have a different set of circumstances to consider in the early stage of their life. Considerations are often akin to those of products in the CPG industry and other more mature industries. The product's basic features and functions may be widely understood by the target market. This core level of knowledge could soften, or strengthen, the need for education in the development of the promotional message, product packaging, training, and other forms of support.

Repackaging products that employ existing technologies might be all that is necessary to sell that product to a new market. The Internet began to take on a new life when access was made possible using user-friendly software with GUIs, or browsers. The popularity of pagers among young Americans began to explode as these devices began to sport creative and colorful casing. Of course, lower prices and expanded distribution helped fuel this growth. Even the early days of portable computers were marked with products that primarily employed technology that was in existence at the time. The first portable computers were over 20 pounds and touted virtually no battery life; however, they included casing with handles in a form factor that was conducive to carrying. Salespeople and others who realized high value from having their computer with them formed the early market for these luggable computers. Indeed, repackaging a product that employs existing technology to reposition it to a new market is a clever and inexpensive means to launch a new product.

The creative marketer might employ a unique combination of technologies to differentiate the product. As electronic technologies mature, they tend to become smaller and conform to popular standards. A unique combination might simply be a hybrid product that is the convergence of multiple technologies. For example, in the latter half of the 20th century, this happened with stereo equipment. Many manufacturers combined turntables, receivers, CD players, cassette players, and recorders and synthesizers into a single product. The same phenomenon occurred in the early 21st century as cellular telephones, personal digital assistants, and broadcast video technologies were combined into portable devices. A unique combination could also be an amalgamation of existing technologies that may fit a new, unforeseen need.

For example, Internet e-commerce systems used structured query language (SQL), security techniques, backend transaction processing systems, and other existing technologies to create automated payment functions. Automated telephone attendants used voice response, multi-plexing, adjunct processors, multiplexing, and other switching technolo-gies that were already in existence. In some cases, these new products gave new life to technologies that were "looking for a home." The product that is created from a unique combination of technologies is not new because of the technologies; it is new because of *what the technologies now allow the customer to accomplish.* The Internet e-commerce products allowed customers to pay for a product or service without having to go to a store, meet with a salesperson, or even speak to an order processor by telephone. The automated telephone attendants allowed the customer to gather information, change their account, or even make a payment with-out having to wait to speak to a representative. When existing technolo-gies are used to create a new product, it is usually not necessary to prove that it can perform as promised; the focus may be placed on the ultimate result that it can deliver.

Promoting tried and true technologies can be used to gain customer confidence in a product that employs existing technologies. The new cus-tomer does not have to be convinced or take a leap of faith to believe that the technologies are real. They have seen these technologies in the features and functions of products that already exist. The *new and improved* or *we do it better* message is generally quite effective. The new product leverages the suc-cess of old products that have already proven the viability of the technology.

Products that apply existing technologies can also use pricing bundles and other changes in pricing structure during the early phase of their life. This can be an effective means for a new product to share in the exist-ing, perceived value of an established product. For examples of products that employ new or emerging technologies, visit www.The5Ps.com/LEM/EmergingTech.html

The prospective customer may immediately recognize the new value proposition, if the message ties the deliverable from employing exist-ing technology, tothe value being received by those who currently use the existing product. Earlier we discussed smartphones (i.e., cellular telephones, personal digital assistants, and broadcast video in one device) as an example of using a combination of technologies to differentiate a product. Many smartphone manufacturers and wireless network carriers seek to differentiate their offerings by combining these devices and the network service in a bundled pricing deal. New products that employ existing technologies can also receive a real boost in their early phase by being bundled with nontechnological products or services. For example, travel services might include a low-end personal digital assistant for their subscribers. Banks and brokerage firms might offer a computer with software to access their services to their trust and other selective customers. Aggressive promotional campaigns for such bundles can be a real shot in the arm for the new product that employs technology that the travel services, bank, and brokerage customers readily understand and can use. Since the products being bundled are paid for over a period of time, the cost of the bundled device can be spread out so that it becomes a negligible portion of the overall purchase.

The early phase of a product that employs existing technologies is also marked by a new selection of distribution channels. Since distribution channels are based upon the ability to reach the target market, a new product that employs existing technology is likely to need a different choice of distribution. This is assuming that the new product is using the technologies in a different manner than the old product that employed the same technologies. While members of the new target market may well use the same distribution channels as those used by the old product, it is also conceivable that the new target market uses new channels.

To use an earlier example, pagers were originally sold through specialty electronics stores and paging outlets. As the consumer market for pagers grew, particularly the youth segment, distribution grew to include consumer electronics stores, department stores, convenience stores, and others. Indeed, new distribution channels might be well suited for a new product as well as a larger and more knowledgeable market.

Adolescent Stage

As technology-based products and services mature, a number of strategies may be implemented to manage growth and improve profitability. For many products, product performance stability is reached during this stage; a surge of competition occurs during this stage; breakeven is not reached until this stage. To be sure, the adolescent stage is critical during the product life cycle.

The product's features and functions are being polished during the adolescent stage. The product itself is improved as fixes are implemented and key enhancements are implemented. This is, of course, easier to achieve with products that are designed in a modular fashion. Software functions are added, network services may be added, hardware upgrades are implemented, and new peripheral devices emerge. These all contribute to improvements in core product or service functionality. Packaging, on the other hand, may not receive the degree of changes that the product receives. Software–user interfaces may receive relatively minor changes such as those to accommodate new functions. Likewise, network–software interfaces might change. Major changes in packaging are generally not feasible or cost effective during this stage.

A dramatic change in the user interface for software or networks will change the basic *look and feel* of those products and services. This not only can be cost prohibitive, but it also changes the fundamental product offering. Likewise, changing the casing of hardware products requires bringing in design, production, shipping, and other members of the product delivery team. The time and expense of changing packaging will, in most cases, change the product's business plan and overall life cycle profitability. Remember, change must be delivered so that your customer will accept it or they may migrate to another product. An important mission, therefore, during the adolescent stage is to refine the product's features and functions without causing an appreciable negative impact on the product's life cycle profitability.

Promotion during the adolescent stage remains aggressive to achieve strong growth in product sales. A successful new product stage will deliver an initial pattern of growth for the product entering the adolescent stage. The total revenue potential from all initial target markets has been confirmed, the media plan and overall promotion plan have been validated, and promotional resources are applied full steam to a proven course of action. In some cases, the selection of target markets may change during the new product stage. Some target markets may be disqualified and new markets with large potential may be identified and added to the target mix. When the mix of target markets changes, the media and promotion plans will change. The product manager will closely monitor all promotional activity during the adolescent stage to maintain the growth necessary during this stage to fend off competitors and achieve critical mass.

The increase in growth is often partially accommodated through an increase in sales and distribution channels. As product sales increase, more salespeople are successful selling it, more resellers seek to offer it, and more stores want to carry it.

As new sales sources are added, the product manager must take steps to protect channel partners who demonstrate allegiance or strategic positioning through pricing, support, and other sales support. The challenge of the product manager is to provide more opportunity for prospective customers to purchase the product while managing delivering sufficient product, providing sufficient support, and minimizing channel conflict. Effectively managing sales and distribution channels is essential to handling growth during the adolescent stage. This is necessary to establish a sales pattern and installed base to carry the product through the next stage of its life cycle.

The objective of pricing strategies during the adolescent stage is to support aggressive growth while maintaining profitability. Rather than engage in price wars or unnecessarily lower the value of the product, to compete effectively on the price front many product managers will run special promotions that carry discounts for customers or distributors and resellers who offer bundles or other special offers that include the product. Product prices during the adolescent stage generally remain steady or are decreased only enough to realize targeted growth. To avoid weakening product price during this stage, astute product managers will use product enhancements, expanded channels, or more effective promotion to compete effectively and increase sales.

Adolescence sets the stage for achieving maximum profitability during the adult phase of the product life cycle. Aggressive growth is sought so that the product may build a substantial installed base and favorable status with the target market. People love a winner. The product manager must fend off competition, maintain profitability, increase product marketability, and provide sufficient opportunity for customers to purchase the product. This positions the product for the mature stage that is often a strong contributor to lifetime profitability.

Adult Stage

The primary objective of many IT products during the adult phase of their life cycle is to maximize profitability and protect their market position. Product enhancements are often delivered through free or paid upgrades, subscription price increases, or ancillary products. Superb support is essential to maintain customer loyalty. Pricing, channel, and promotional strategies are designed to sell as much as possible while protecting the installed base.

Ensuring Upgrades

A major strategic decision during the adult phase of the product life cycle is what features and functions to include in product upgrades. This includes what other products with which to maintain compatibility. The functions might include software drivers, software, and hardware components that enable product interoperability, or data transfer routines. In addition to maintaining compatibility, product upgrades can include feature and function enhancements. The pertinent decision for the product manager is which products to maintain compatibility with, as well as which features and functions to include in upgrades versus which ones to include in the next generation product. It is logical to maintain compatibility with products that are popular, complementary to the existing product, and those that can be made compatible within the resources designated in the product plan (see Maintaining Upward Compatibility, Chapter 2). As for the decision which enhancements to offer, the product manager should consider how many years, or months, remain in the product's life.

Additionally, the product's market position and the projected launch date for the next generation product will help determine which enhancements to release. Many enhancements are reserved for the next generation product or support plan customers.

Another challenging decision during the adult phase of the product life cycle is *when* and *how strongly* to push customers to migrate to new products. The market environment coupled with the customer's readiness to change will drive their propensity to migrate (see Migration, Selling New Products and Services, Chapter 2). The cost of migrating customers must be balanced against the cash flow requirements of the product plan. When market conditions drive down the price of maintenance and support, the product manager must ensure that the costs of support are covered by the related revenue and purchases associated with the product migration. While maintenance and support offer an additional revenue stream associated with the product, as customers begin to migrate to the next generation product the revenue from this source decreases. The product manager must balance support resources made available to customers with the revenue received for delivering support services. When the balance threatens product profitability, the product manager must consider moving customers to the next phase of the product life cycle. The product manager does not want to face a situation where they cannot provide adequate support regardless of how much the customer is willing to pay.

One way that product profitability is maximized during the adult phase, is by keeping the price firm or offering decreases that are only large enough to meet the needs of the market. While some customers are migrating to the next generation products (if they are available), other new customers may still purchase the current generation products during this phase.

There are sometimes fewer new customers, however, than existing customers during the new product and adolescent stage. One reason for this is that the market skimming channel partners and competitors disappear. One reason for this is because margins often get smaller and the cost of entry is higher after the adolescent stage.

The objective of promotion during the adult phase of the life cycle is to maintain market awareness and their desire to purchase available products. Campaigns during this phase also encourage the purchase of maintenance and support services. Promotion of next generation products can also serve to maintain product profitability targets by balancing support revenue with the cost of delivering maintenance and support.

Mature Stage

As products move through the adolescent and adult phases of their life, their market position and level of profitability will generally define the mature phase of the cycle. The primary objective during this phase is to aggressively move customers to the next generation product while maintaining profitability. If a next generation product is not planned, the product manager must determine how long profitability can be maintained and act accordingly. Changes in market conditions can sometimes create a new wave of interest in a product during its mature phase. Such a revival will bring an infusion of profits without extreme effort on the part of the product manager. The real challenge of the product manager, however, is to maximize profits while maintaining the integrity of the company.

Maximizing Profits

A changing mix of revenues and expense usually marks the mature phase of the product life cycle. To maintain profitability, the product manager must continually monitor and maintain a balance between those factors that affect revenue and expense. Revenue from the sale of product and related support services is rapidly declining during this phase. Additionally, revenue from licensing, bundling, and other deals is also likely to decline. While expenses may also decline, they typically do not do so at the same rate and timing as the decrease in revenue. Support resources, for example, will likely benefit from the accumulation of answers and fixes gathered over the life of the product. The production of replacement product, spare parts, and ancillary products will not enjoy the same efficiencies at levels achieved during the adolescent and adult product stages. Production cost per unit is, thus, likely to increase. This causes a vacillation in profits that is difficult to control without compromising the quality of product or service. A reduction in the cost or quantity of raw materials or components in the manufacture of hardware, for example, will almost invariably reduce its quality. The failure to deliver software fixes, for example, can be perceived as an inability to maintain the product's performance.

To avoid or minimize these perceptions, efforts to move the remaining customers to the next generation product must be successful. If another product is not planned, or available, different strategies will be engaged. If a replacement product is not planned, a typical strategy is to maximize the profit to be earned for the remainder of this life cycle stage or sell. It is difficult to sell a product at the end of its life cycle. New products with improved technologies are usually already on the market. Moreover, a significant amount of the customer base has already moved to the next generation or a competing product. Therefore, there is neither technology, a critical mass of customers nor an acceptable level of profit to offer a potential buyer.

An exception might be a product that carries or a service that offers a recurring revenue stream. A subscription-based network service, for example, may offer several periods of future revenue whose present value is quite compelling for a prospective buyer. This is the exception to the norm in a world of fast paced technological development. Since it is difficult to impossible to sell a product at the end of its life cycle, maximizing profits is the likely answer when the company cannot offer a next generation product.

When the company has a next generation product that is ready to be delivered, the product manager places emphasis on encouraging customers to purchase that product. The incentive to purchase can be through advertising and promotion, upgrades that offer a reduced price, or easy migration or other creative offers. Another popular incentive that partially offsets the fall in revenue is raising support prices. The revenue from purchasing the next generation product is attributed to that product, not the product that is being replaced. An increase in the price of support, therefore, usually cannot compensate for the decline in revenue from customers who no longer purchase support. After all, there is only so much that customers are willing to pay for support. The primary reason for an increase in support prices during the mature phase of the life cycle is the movement of customers to the next generation product.

This brings us back to the primary means of maintaining profitability during the mature stage: *The product manager must continually monitor and maintain a balance between those factors that affect revenue and expense.* Remember, revenue from product sales and support decreases. Inventories are close to or fully depleted during this phase. Revenue from bundling and other product related deals also decreases. The economies of scale associated with activities that comprise expenses are reduced. That is, it becomes more expensive to provide what is necessary to produce, deliver, and support the product.

When support efficiencies are maximized, however, support resources can decline. A portion of the support staff is reallocated to the next generation or other new products. It becomes more difficult to determine the level of parts and replacement inventory to maintain. The decline and virtual elimination of promotion costs helps the process of managing profitability, a little easier. To be sure, maintaining profitability during the mature stage can be one of the most challenging responsibilities for a product manager.

When to Withdraw Support (Cost and Forced Migration)

Throughout the mature stage of the life cycle, the product manager is trying to migrate the remaining customers to the next generation product or simply maintain profitability as long as possible. Invariably there will be customers who choose to continue using the product. Some portion of these customers may also continue to use support that is available. At some point during the mature stage, providing support is no longer cost justified. When there is no longer a financial or strategic advantage to providing support, it should be withdrawn.

The decision to withdraw support, and the process of carrying it out, is driven by customers. It is customers, after all, who provide revenue. To minimize the negative impact from withdrawing support, the product manager must understand the installed base. Who is currently using the product or service? Why haven't they migrated to the next generation product? What is necessary to move customers to the next product? When customers refuse to migrate, what is the magnitude of the loss if you force them out?

Withdrawing support is more than merely discontinuing technical support hotlines. It is also the elimination of spare parts inventories, repair services, software upgrades, and other forms of assistance. Once the product manager has thought through the process of delivering support, a withdrawal plan can be created. In addition to redeploying staff and removing inventories, everyone associated with delivering support should be notified, including all partners.

The timing and process of withdrawing support is important to maintain profitability, migrate customers to the next generation product successfully, and close out the product without damaging the company's reputation. The product manager must determine the cost of maintaining support for the older product. When the cost of delivering support exceeds revenue, or the risk of losing customers who will not migrate is assumable, support should be withdrawn.

When the product or service can no longer garner enough customers to deliver an acceptable return, it is in the mature stage of its life cycle. A product also enters the mature phase when it is strategically advantageous to replace it with a next generation product. By this stage, promotion is virtually nonexistent. It is focused on the next generation product. Pricing generally stays the same with discounts offered for upgrade to the next generation product. Every effort is made to migrate customers while maintaining profitability, or maximizing profitability until the product is taken off the market.

Final Stage

> *You got to know when to hold 'em, know when to fold 'em.*
> *"The Gambler," song written by Don Schlitz and recorded by Kenny Rogers*

At some point, all good things must come to an end. When a product is retired, more is required than just stopping sales activity. The product manager should take steps to withdraw it from the market completely. This is particularly important if a next generation product is planned or if the company plans to remain in business. Customers and partners should be notified that the product would no longer be sold or supported. Production lines that are exclusive to the product should be shut down and others should be adjusted, if necessary, to reduce any costs associated with the manufacture of the product. All administrative processes that support the product should be stopped.

The decision on how much time and other resources should be spent to withdraw the product depends on the impact on the market and the company of retiring the product without covering all the bases. If a prospective customer has not been made aware of the next generation product and seeks to purchase a retired product, it is likely that they will turn to a competitor. Moreover, in some instances it may cause that prospect, and others, to question the viability of the company or its other products. Likewise, a business partner needs to be able to advise their customers and prospects on available solutions. They also need advance notice so that they can eliminate excess inventories. The product manager must determine how to withdraw the product efficiently and responsibly.

Product Life Cycle—In Conclusion

Effectively managing the product throughout its life cycle is essential to its success. The stages in the life cycle come at varying times for different IT products. The increased pace of technological advancement drastically reduced the life span of many products in the IT industry. In addition to shorter life cycles, self-cannibalization, co-opetition, convergence, changing standards, and the demand for interoperability are a few of the challenges facing the product manager of an IT product. The need to address technological demands presents a strong temptation to give them a false sense of top priority. Nevertheless, market share and profitability are still the major measuring sticks for products and services. Overengineering and late market withdrawals are just two of the symptoms that can affect an IT product that is not managed effectively throughout its life cycle.

Mastering Management of Sales Channels

Distribution is a key controlling element of many industries. The success of companies operating in publishing, consumer goods, and communications (the media) is dependent upon distribution. Before the Internet, authors primarily relied upon major publishing companies that had accounts with at least one of the two book distributors that dominated the market. Only a publisher with sufficient volume could commit to the quantities of annual book sales necessary to maintain an account. The Internet offered a new distribution channel that leveled the playing field. Now Amazon.com and BarnesandNoble.com offer viable distribution programs for authors.

When I lived in France during the 1970s, bread shops (boulangeries), pastry shops (pâtisserie), butcher shops (bouchèrie), tobacco shops (tabacs), and other small shops were found in neighborhoods throughout Paris as well as smaller cities and towns throughout France. As the larger stores (supermarchés) began to emerge, the options for getting goods to market changed. Smaller vendors and shop owners feared for their survival in the wake of megastores and powerful distribution networks. Today, many smaller businesses in France, the United States, and other countries that could not produce the volume or secure an account with distributors have closed their doors.

Product, packaging, pricing, and promotion don't matter without place. The marketer and producer have to get their product to market if they are to generate revenue and complete the marketing cycle. I discussed earlier how transportation routes evolved around trade routes,[12] and vice versa. Today, distribution is much more developed. Some channels are used strictly for delivering products or service, while others are means for selling those products and services. There are many channels through which products and services can be sold or delivered. For an overview of sales and distribution channels, see the table at www.The5Ps .com/LEM/ChannelOverview.html

There are several things that marketers can do to help their business partners sell products and support their customers. I have provided sales and technical training to employees of business partners. Not only did we create excitement for our products and services amongst our partner's staff, sales increased dramatically as a result of their efforts.

Many marketers offer second or third tier hotline support to partners who provide hotline support to customers. To help protect partners from shouldering the cost of obsolescence, marketers can accept returns or upgrades. To help drive the message, placement, and frequency of ads, marketers can launch a cooperative advertising program for their business partners.

In short, business partners are customers too. Marketers should structure deals that include the types and amount of support necessary to ensure success for all: the firms they represent, their partners, and customers. This helps them influence customers who comprise their installed base. Happy customers who have used the marketer's products and services are likely to continue using those products and services in the future. The result is ongoing or future revenue from these customers. To be sure, providing outstanding customer service is a powerful tool that helps marketers to generate revenue and profits.

The Importance of Customer Service

Every single person who has a reason for the company to succeed should be an enthusiastic supporter of customer service. That means every employee, every stakeholder, *everyone*. Customer service is responsible for the assembly and pursuit of everything necessary to make the customer happy with owning and using your product or service. Maintenance is a one-time repair or an expected, ongoing sustenance of a product or service. Support offers the opportunity for a more extended personal interaction. Support is every technique, process, person, or function assigned to facilitate customer service. Support may include training, hotlines, manuals, technicians, and more.

The brilliance of customer service is to exhibit Herculean patience while employing tools or creating solutions for even the most unreasonable and obnoxious customers. A refund or credit and heartfelt apology, delivered with believable sincerity, can be a solution for an irate customer.

It is virtually always less expensive to keep an existing customer than to win a new customer. Every time that the marketer can interact with or receive information from a customer, is an opportunity to protect existing revenue or earn future revenue. The customer might purchase support, buy a new product, or tell others about their positive experience using your product or service. Some of the supplemental products and services available to improve the user experience are highlighted in Table 3.8.

Table 3.8 Customer service*

CUSTOMER SERVICE		
Service Tools	Definition & How to Use it	Marketing Options
Maintenance	Everything necessary to keep the product or service working for the customer. Repairing or upgrading equipment. Monitoring networks. Some may consider software upgrades maintenance.	• Assist 3rd party sales and delivery partners to offer maintenance • Build brand with momentum after repair is accepted by customer
Support:		
▶ Training	Self-paced or instructor-led courses that direct customers on how to use products and services.	• Collect customer and buyer contact info • Document needs and desires • Deliver self-paced in many forms (online, CD/DVD, book, etc.) and use customer interaction options available
▶ Hotlines	A phone number, often toll-free, that reaches groups of people who can answer questions, resolve problems or direct customers to a remedy. The people should be well trained, have immediate access to most answers, and access to second or third tier of experts to help.	• Categorize and track sources of problems • Identify trends and feed to product development
▶ Manuals	Well organized pamphlets or books with instructions and answers for the customer. Should contain contact and other critical information. Coupons and special offers may be included.	• Use unique phone numbers or emails to identify source of contact • Include upgrade or referral offers
▶ Technicians	People trained and skilled on the application and use of specific products and services.	• Canvass to learn what customers want • Leverage knowledge to improve product performance

Note: *Presentation version at www.The5Ps.com/LEM/Table_3-8.html

Customer service is a natural opportunity for increasing sales. Promotional upgrade and conversion offers can be made to existing customers through manuals, training, hotline representatives, on-site technicians, Frequently Asked Question (FAQ) databases, or quick study guides. More importantly, customer service personnel can learn and gather what customers require to buy a new or replacement product. This information should be routinely collected and fed into the product management cycle. Customer service vehicles can be used to encourage customers to find new customers. Referral fees, 2-for-1 coupons, and other incentives can be delivered, *with poise*, during many customer service interactions. It is important that the integrity of customer service is maintained by delivering promotions as an *option* rather than an *objective* of the customer service interaction.

Managing Partnerships

I coined the term "co-opetition" in the early 1990s after it had become apparent that competitive companies had to work together to deliver comprehensive, end-to-end solutions to customers. The rapidly declining cost of computing coupled with the deregulation of the telecommunications industry created a burgeoning IT market with an increasing number and wide variety of players. This was a far cry from the industry of the 1960 through the 1980 period which primarily consisted of IBM and the BUNCH (Burroughs, Unisys, NCR, Control Data, and Honeywell).

New technologies, changing economic conditions, and an expanding customer base are just a few of the factors that have driven the expansion as well as the consolidation of segments of the IT industry over the years. The vertical and horizontal expansion resulting from mergers and acquisitions, however, has not obviated the need for co-opetition. Competitive firms often must team up to deliver the software, hardware, networks, service, and support that customers demand from total systems solutions. Such partnerships require more depth and flexibility to all facets of the marketing plan. High integrity while ensuring the long-term viability and success of essential products and services should be the goal of the marketer engaged in co-opetitive partnerships.

When business goals change or the win–win advantage of partnerships ends, the marketer should make efforts to bring a mutually beneficial and formal end to the partnership. Merely cancelling contracts or withdrawing support can do irreparable harm to the brand name and company's reputation. For more information, visit www.The5Ps.com/LEM/WinWin.html

The Raison D'être: Making It Worthwhile

Results Measurement

The marketing mix is the combination, and the order, in which the 5 Ps and their accompanying tools are used to generate revenue. It is a strategic means of optimizing results. The real success of a marketing effort is measured by the results that are achieved. The ultimate result is the amount of profit earned throughout its life cycle including all revenues and expenses at the time of exit. Interim measures are: (a) the progress of the market effort (soft measures) and, (b) the intermediate results achieved (hard measures).

Soft measures include market share, competitive rank, exposure to the target audience, clicks on a website or web-based communication, click-thrus on web communiqués, and other ways of determining the exposure of the product or movement of prospective customers toward a purchase. Research firms collect information and perform studies to assess the valor of exposure and progress measurements. These measures are only as valuable, however, as their ability to direct marketers on improving their effectiveness of moving prospects toward closing and, ultimately, closing sales.

Hard measures are the ultimate measure of success. They include sales units, sales revenue, number of customers, and profit. By tracking these measures on a weekly, monthly, or quarterly basis, marketers can observe trends and track them against marketing efforts. For example, the graph in Figure 3.4 shows monthly sales units over a 2-year period. Notice that sales increase in June, 3 months after an advertising campaign starts, and again in October, 1 month after the website is enhanced with e-commerce functions and search engine optimization (SEO). The launch of a discount promo in July, on the other hand, yields no increase in sales.

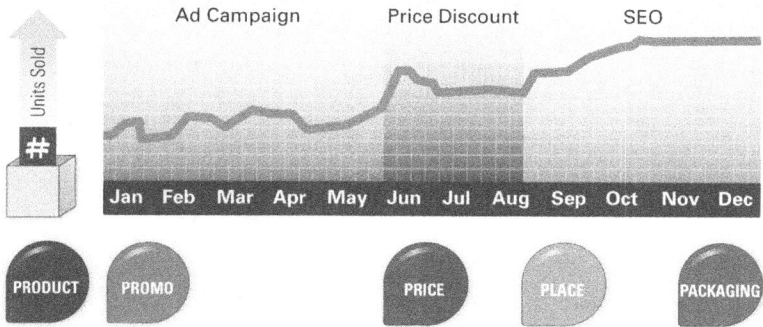

Figure 3.4 Mix impact over time

The marketer will analyze and review each of the 5 Ps (product, price, place, promotion, and packaging) as well as external and environmental factors to determine what might have caused the increase in May through June and the decline in June through July. Surely the ad campaign and price discount contributed to the increase in units told; however, we do not know what caused the decline in June through July. Understanding the reason for the decline will help the marketer select the best timing for future promotions.

While it can be difficult to tie and track promotions (includes ads) and other specific elements of the 5 Ps to revenue, it is not impossible. Defining and tracking financial results is essential to measuring, ranking, and assessing the viability and future funding requirements of the marketing program. One important measure is the number and value of sales generated from each marketing element. For example, the number of units sold after a specific promotion campaign would be measured by the conversion rate. If the average units sold per month is 1,000 and after a promotion campaign that increases to 1,300, the conversion rate for the promotion is 300/1,000 or 30.0%.

The astute and seasoned marketer will refrain from attaching undue excitement and measures to red herring phenomena or measures that have not *earned the right* to carry marketing weight. The CTR, for example, is a measure of how many times a human or electronic visitor has navigated from one place in a website to another. Each click is not necessarily a measure of interest or intent to purchase. The marketer must consider many factors to determine how effectively the website and related tools contribute to identifying, qualifying, and moving customers to buy. After all, CTR does not matter if there is no measurable increase in sales attributable to it.

To select the optimal mix of tools, the marketer must know the cost of winning a new customer. Some describe this as acquisition cost. Customers are not acquired; they are won. The marketer must earn the right to be awarded their business. A direct salesforce is often the most expensive way to win a customer. It is often also the most effective, particularly for high priced, complex products and services. Telemarketing and Internet marketing are often less expensive, yet highly effective for identifying quality leads or closing sales of modestly priced, noncomplex products. The marketer will optimize the mix of Ps by knowing the people in the target market and responding to their needs, interest, and desires.

Once all of the relevant measures are gathered, prioritized, and applied to the calculations that measure progress, the marketer has a bellwether and reporting mechanisms to help them apply the 5 Ps and adjust the marketing mix. The ultimate measure of marketing success will always be the amount of profit earned by a product or service during its lifetime. All marketers should develop a process for tracking and measuring profit at any point and also cumulatively for the point in the life cycle. For more information on putting it into action including how to optimize the mix, when to change the mix, which "P"s to change, and orchestrating the 5 Ps, visit www.The5Ps.com/LEM/Optimize.html

Epilogue

Trade was the impetus for the advancement of languages, transportation routes, currency, and other foundations of modern day civilization. Marketing is the foundation of trade. Marketing is much more than sales and promotion. It directs every step of the business cycle from the identification and creation of a product or service that meets a need or want, through the production and delivery to earn a sustainable profit. Marketing fuels business. The 5 Ps framework, presented in Chapter 1, has been applied to the business of finance, professional services, government, and other industries. This book presents The 5 Ps framework as it applies conventional marketing theory to the business of technology.

But I do not stop there. After presenting a modified theory as it is reflected in the real world, this book goes on to present strategies, tools, and techniques to apply The 5 Ps to deliver measurable results. The marketing manager must be creative, adaptable, savvy, and remain focused on the mission. Methods to achieve these things are outlined herein. This book is a comprehensive blueprint of *how to turn technology into value*

Notes

Chapter 1

1. McCarthy (1971), p. 44.
2. The GOSPA explanation herein is the intellectual property of ACT Inc.; ACT grants Business Express Press permission to use here.
3. Control Data acquired The Service Bureau Corporation (SBC) from IBM in 1973 as a result of a lawsuit against IBM. SBC, a subsidiary formed in 1957 consisted of service bureaus operating since 1932, was known to be the training ground for IBM senior executives.
4. Please keep in mind that an *objective* for an executive may be the *goal* for a manager who reports to him or her. GOSPA is not absolute for any position. It is relative to the person or manager for whom it has been developed.
5. Tellis, Gerard, and Golder (1993), p. 158.
6. Shenkar (2010).
7. Williams (1995a).
8. Source: to obtain sight or knowledge of for the first time. http://www.merriam-webster.com/dictionary/discovering
9. Source: discovery, finding, or productive imagination. http://www.merriam-webster.com/dictionary/invention
10. Source: studious inquiry or examination; *especially*: investigation or experimentation aimed at the discovery and interpretation of facts, revision of accepted theories or laws in the light of new facts, or practical application of such new or revised theories or laws. http://www.merriam-webster.com/dictionary/research
11. Source: the introduction of something new; in technology, an improvement to something already existing. Distinguishing an element of novelty in an invention remains a concern of patent law. The Renaissance was a period of unusual innovation: Leonardo da Vinci produced ingenious designs for submarines, airplanes, and helicopters and drawings of elaborate trains of gears and of the patterns of flow in liquids. Technology provided science with instruments that greatly enhanced its powers, such as Galileo's telescope. New sciences have also contributed to technology, as in the theoretical preparation for the invention of the steam engine. In the 20th century, innovations in semiconductor technology increased the performance and decreased the cost of electronic materials and devices by a factor of a million, an achievement unparalleled in the history of any technology. http://www.merriam-webster.com/dictionary/innovation

Chapter 2

1. Williams (2000).
2. Williams (1995b).
3. FedEx service marks used by permission.
4. DiscoverIT^{TM} used by permission from ACT Inc.

Chapter 3

1. TUMAC used by permission from ACT Inc.
2. Lifestyles vary with many factors including cultural and economic differences of consumers.
3. Many venture capitalists, especially in a poor economy, will not fund product development. If there is compelling evidence that profits will follow from the introduction of the product, the venture capitalist *might* provide funding. Compelling evidence could include customers with outstanding orders, customers who have paid nonrecoverable engineering (NRE) fees, or companies selling comparable products with little or no competition.
4. IBM had to sell The Service Bureau Company to Control Data in 1973, as a result of another lawsuit over the fear, uncertainty, and doubt (FUD) created by IBM's pre-announcement of a non-existent System/360 Model 92.
5. Whipps (2008).
6. Minster (n.d.).
7. Maestri (n.d.).
8. For more information on the history of trade, visit The5Ps.com\Trade
9. Pope, Historian, and Curator. (2010).
10. CTIA was formerly known as the Cellular Telecommunications Industry Association.
11. The Network Information Center (NIC), also known as InterNIC (http://www.internic.net), was the Internet governing body primarily responsible for domain name allocations from 1993 until 1998. After 1988, the responsibility was assumed by the Internet Corporation for Assigned Names and Numbers (ICANN; http://www.icann.org) .
12. Gregory (2009).

References

Gregory, S. C. (2009). *Ancient trade and civilization.* Retrieved July 9, 2009, from http://www.aurlaea.com/article-177-ancient_trade_and_civilization.html

Maestri, N. (n.d.). *Merchants of Mesoamerica Ancient Traders of Mesoamerica.* Retrieved from http://archaeology.about.com/od/mesoamerica/a/mesoamerican_traders.htm

McCarthy, E. J. (1960). *Basic marketing: A managerial approach* (4th ed.). Richard D. Irwin, Inc.

Minister, C. (n.d.). *Ancient Maya Economy and Trade.* Retrieved from About.com Guide: http://latinamericanhistory.about.com/od/Maya/p/Ancient-Maya-Economy-And-Trade.htm

Pope, N., Historian., & Curator. (2010). *America's First Direct Mail Campaign.* Retrieved July 29, 2010, from Smithsonian National Postal Museum Blog: http://postalmuseumblog.si.edu/2010/07/americas-first-direct-mail-campaign.html

Shenkar, O. (2010). *Copycats: How Smart Companies Use Imitation to Gain a Strategic Edge.* Boston, MA: Harvard Business School Publishing Corporation

Tellis, G. J., & Golder, P. N. (1993). Pioneer advantage: Marketing logic or marketing legend? *Journal of Marketing Research 30*(2), 158.

Whipps, H. (2008). *How Ancient Trade Changed the World.* Retrieved February 17, 2008, from ET: http://www.livescience.com/4823-ancient-trade-changed-world.html

Williams, V. (1995a). *The Five P's of Marketing Emerging Technologies.* Retrieved November 1995, from NEWAVES: http://www.veronicawilliams.com/downloads/Article_TheFivePs_VW.pdf

Williams, V. (1995b). *Wireless Computing Primer.* ISBN-10: 1558515534.

Index

OTHER TITLES IN OUR MARKETING STRATEGY COLLECTION

Naresh Malhotra, Georgia Tech, Editor

- *Developing Winning Brand Strategies* by Lars Finskud
- *Conscious Branding Funk* by David Levis and Anne Marie
- *Marketing Strategy in Play Questioning to Create Difference* by Mark Hill
- *Decision Equity: The Ultimate Metric to Connect Marketing Actions to Profits* by Piyush Kumar and Kunal Gupta
- *Building a Marketing Plan: A Complete Guide* by Ho YinWong, Roshnee Ramsaran-Fowdar and Kylie Radel
- *Top Market Strategy Applying the 80/20 Rule* by Elizabeth Kruger
- *Pricing Segmentation and Analytics* by Tudor Bodea and Mark Ferguson
- *Strategic Marketing Planning for the Small to Medium Sized Business Writing a Marketing Plan* by David Anderson
- *Expanding Customer Service as a Profit Center Striving for Excellence and Competitive Advantage* by Rob Reider
- *Applying Scientific Reasoning to the Field of Marketing Make Better Decisions* by Terry Grapentine
- *Marketing Strategy for Small- to Medium-Sized Manufacturers: A Practical Guide for Generating Growth, Profit, and Sales* by Charles France
- *Dynamic Customer Strategy: Today's CRM* by John F. Tanner, Jr.
- *Customers Inside, Customers Outside: Designing and Succeeding With Enterprise Customer-Centricity Concepts, Practices, and Applications* by Michael W. Lowenstein

Announcing the Business Expert Press Digital Library

Concise E-books Business Students Need for Classroom and Research

This book can also be purchased in an e-book collection by your library as
- a one-time purchase,
- that is owned forever,
- allows for simultaneous readers,
- has no restrictions on printing, and
- can be downloaded as PDFs from within the library community.

Our digital library collections are a great solution to beat the rising cost of textbooks. e-books can be loaded into their course management systems or onto student's e-book readers.

The **Business Expert Press** digital libraries are very affordable, with no obligation to buy in future years. For more information, please visit **www.businessexpertpress.com/librarians**. To set up a trial in the United States, please email **sales@businessexpertpress.com**.